MALLARMÉ

L'Après-midi d'un Faune

WALLACE FOWLIE

MALLARMÉ

WITH FOURTEEN LINE DRAWINGS BY
HENRI MATISSE

Phoenix Books

THE UNIVERSITY OF CHICAGO PRESS

THE UNIVERSITY OF CHICAGO PRESS, CHICAGO & LONDON
The University of Toronto Press, Toronto 5, Canada

To Hazel and Marjorie

ACKNOWLEDGEMENTS

Some of the following pages have appeared in

MODERN PHILOLOGY, YALE POETRY REVIEW, ZERO, THE TIGER'S EYE,
THE OUTCAST CHAPBOOKS, POETRY (Chicago)

The drawings by Henri Matisse are reproduced by courtesy of the Art Institute
of Chicago, and of Editions d'art Albert Skira, Geneva.

CONTENTS

PART III: *BEYOND THE WORK*

MALLARMÉ

Girl's Head

INTRODUCTION

THE MAN

AN ESSENTIAL quality characterizes the biography of each poet. If that of Baudelaire appears moral, and Rimbaud's psychological, Mallarmé's is markedly aesthetic. His intoxication was cerebral and his passion was for words. The facts of his life might well appear drab and monotonous, but Mallarmé's friendship with artists and poets, his constant preoccupation with poetic theory and the work he meditated, which became synonymous with his own destiny, colour the biography of this poet and convert it into an ardent adventure of the mind.

No particular drama emerges from the first twenty years of his life, between his birth in Paris in 1842 and the publication of his early poetry in 1862. He was a shy affectionate boy who was raised by his grandmother. Never strong in health, mild and courteous in temperament, silent rather than talkative, he passed through various schools, wrote verse very early, and became a *bachelier-ès-lettres* in 1860 at the lycée of Sens. The following year he met at Sens a young teacher, Emmanuel des Essarts, and began with him a warm friendship based largely on a mutual love for poetry. Mallarmé discovered Baudelaire this same year of 1861. Two copies of *Les Fleurs du Mal* were confiscated by his family, but the third copy seems to have remained concealed from his father and step-mother and to have exercised on the young man the first strong literary influence.

Mallarmé was gently insistent upon not following the advice of his family on the choice of career. A second important friendship, with Henri Cazalis, two years older than Mallarmé and destined to become the poet Jean Lahor, turned his mind more and more to literature. Also, he had fallen in love with a young school teacher of German extraction, Marie Gerhard, who accompanied him to London in 1863. Mallarmé explained later in his autobiographical letter written to Verlaine, that he had wanted to learn English in order to read Poe. The trip to London helped to determine his career because there, after one brief return to France in March when he came of age, he learned English well enough to receive a teaching certificate. There also, in the Catholic chapel at Kensington, he married Marie Gerhard.

Mallarmé's first appointment, in the fall of 1863, was as teacher of English in the lycée of Tournon, on the Rhone River. This was the beginning of a thirty years' teaching career, eight of which were spent in the provinces, and twenty-two in three different lycées in Paris. The provincial exile was more painful than the Paris period. At no time does Mallarmé seem to have enjoyed the work of teaching. It was merely his livelihood. His poetic work and meditations were constantly being interrupted by the monotonous duties of the school teacher: classroom recitations and the seemingly never depleted stack of papers to be corrected.

The eight years in the provinces were spent in three different cities. At Tournon, first, life was, on the whole, miserable for Mallarmé. Attacks of rheumatism were brought on by the cold winters, and a tendency to insomnia, which was never cured, developed perhaps from the constant exhaustion due to teaching. His salary was insufficient, especially after the birth of a daughter, Geneviève, on November 19, 1864. At the lycée, Mallarmé met with stubborn ill-mannered pupils, who resisted his lessons and made fun of him. After the publication of his poem, *L'Azur*, the pupils had scrawled over the blackboard the final line: *Je suis hanté. L'Azur! l'Azur! l'Azur! l'Azur!* Mallarmé was a weak disciplinarian. The classroom inspector and the headmaster inevitably graded him severely at the end of each year. Not only were the pupils bored, but the parents began protesting and his colleagues grew suspicious of the man's eccentricities. *On ne veut plus de moi à Tournon,* was Mallarmé's own sad comment.

But for the poet's life, the three years at Tournon were extremely rich and productive. Here were formed his slow meticulous writing habits. Here Poe replaced Baudelaire as dominant literary influence, and here the composition of *Hérodiade* was begun in 1864. His correspondence of those years, and particularly the letters addressed to Henri Cazalis, reveal that Mallarmé had already discovered the major assumptions of his aesthetics, that of depicting not the object itself but the effect produced by the object (*peindre non la chose mais l'effet qu'elle produit*). Work on *Hérodiade* alternated with work on *L'Après-Midi d'un Faune*. Both of these early versions were destined for dramatic reading. Mallarmé was thinking of the theatre and in the summer of 1865, in Paris, was introduced to the actor, Coquelin. But even the first version of *Hérodiade* and *L'Après-Midi* were judged as too difficult for dramatic presentation, and by the end of 1865, the poet had ceased thinking of *Hérodiade* as a tragedy.

From Tournon, Mallarmé moved, in October 1866, to Besançon, birthplace of Victor Hugo, where he taught one year at the lycée. In this more eastern city, the climate was even more rigorous than at Tournon. The lodgings Mallarmé found there were poor and incommodious, and the weariness from teaching continued relentlessly. His consolations were the meditations and plans he made during this year for his work, and the letters from the outside world, from friends and writers. To Henri Cazalis, he wrote: *La Poésie me tient lieu de l'amour* (14 May 1867). He received from Paul Verlaine a copy of *Poèmes Saturniens*. The death of Baudelaire, on August 31, 1867, shocked and saddened him. Baudelaire had been his first master, the poet of analysis and perfection, whose example both of artist and man had guided Mallarmé for six years.

He greatly feared having to begin a second year at Besançon and tried in various ways to receive an appointment elsewhere. At the last minute, to his great joy and relief, he was sent to the lycée at Avignon, in the warmer and far more poetic land of Provence. Here he arrived on the 11th of October 1867, and soon made friends with the Provençal poets, *les félibres*, and especially Aubanel.

The poetry written at Tournon had been easily accessible and quite in keeping with current Parnassian models. But after the year of meditation at Besançon, the new poetry, composed at Avignon, marks a definite change in poetic style. Mallarmé had found by this time his own mode and his own originality. We know from a letter written to Lefébure, on the 3rd of May 1868, that he was working on the sonnet, *Ses purs ongles*, which is perhaps the first of his really difficult poems. In the letter, he discusses the rhyme in *-ix*, and wonders if he dare use the invented word, *ptyx*. At this time he is reworking the two long poems, begun in Tournon, *Hérodiade* and *Le Faune*, and writing the dramatic work, *Igitur*, which remained unpublished during his lifetime.

Despite Mallarmé's preference for Avignon over Tournon and Besançon, and despite the valued friendships of Catulle Mendès and Villiers de l'Isle-Adam which developed during this period, he underwent a long depression beginning in 1869. He complained openly very seldom, but finances were troubling him as well as his onerous duties of teacher, his illness and general fatigue. However, he was more successful as teacher in Avignon. His pupils preferred him to other teachers and some of his colleagues seem to have esteemed him. But nevertheless, a kind of crisis was reached in May 1871, when suddenly he left for Paris, convinced that a change was needed. He arrived in the capital, almost penniless and uncertain of the immediate direction his life was to take.

During the course of the summer, in July, a second child was born, this time a son, who was named Anatole. By the end of the summer, Mallarmé accepted a teaching post at the lycée Fontanes, soon to be called Condorcet, and the small family took up residence in Paris, first, in an apartment at 29, rue de Moscou. The established poets' welcomed Mallarmé's arrival in Paris. Leconte de Lisle, Hérédia, Verlaine, Mendès, Banville all showed him signs of recognition and esteem. On the first of June 1872, Mallarmé met Rimbaud at a dinner where the adolescent poet, in the midst of older men, misbehaved in true *voyou* fashion. After the death of Gautier, on October 23, 1872, Mallarmé began the preparation of his homage to Gautier, his *Toast Funèbre*, which confirmed the growing belief that he was a difficult author.

In 1874, the Mallarmés moved to the rue de Rome, first at number 87, and then 89, and in the summer went to Valvins for the first time. The lines of what the poet's life was to be for the next twenty-four years were fairly clear and established. First, the basic and yet very unreal and obscure career of teacher which Mallarmé continued in Paris until his retirement in 1895. Secondly, the vacation periods in summer, mostly spent at Valvins, where he recuperated each year from his dual role of pedagogue and literary master. Thirdly, this vocation of leader which grew steadily during the Tuesday evening gatherings at Mallarmé's apartment on the rue de Rome.

For thirteen years Mallarmé taught at the lycée Condorcet (1871-1884), where on the whole he had a mediocre reputation. He was attacked by the headmaster for his absurd literary publications, and considered by the pupils an ineffective teacher. One year, 1884-5, was spent at Janson de Sailly, and then Mallarmé made his final change, to the College Rollin, in 1885. There, resigned, he continued for seven more years the labour of school teacher whose correcting was never over. Mallarmé was almost fifty-two years old when, in 1893, he applied for his retirement and pension, which were granted by the end of the summer. Only five years at the end of his life were free from what he had always considered the academic strain and enslavement.

Valvins, the summer retreat for the poet during so many years, is a village on the Seine, near Fontainebleau. Mallarmé and his wife and daughter occupied a small peasant's house, situated at just a few kilometers from the river. There he enjoyed the relaxing diversion of a tiny sail boat, his *yole*, which he humorously called his 'yacht' and because of which Manet used to address him as *mon capitaine*. Valvins provided Mallarmé with the yearly interval of freedom when he could dream, walk, sail his boat, talk with the country folk, and receive his friends who called at Valvins more and more frequently as the years passed, and have with them more leisurely and intimate conversations than his Paris life allowed.

The apartment of the Mallarmés on the rue de Rome, which was destined to become during the last twenty years of the century the site of the most persuasive and far-reaching literary disquisitions, was composed of a vestibule leading into the main room, serving both as dining room and living room where the gatherings were held, a small adjoining room where Mallarmé slept and worked, the bedroom of Mme Mallarmé and Geneviève, a bathroom and a kitchen. There was always some pet to be admired by the visitors, such as the pair of green parakeets, maliciously referred to as 'the academicians', or Lilith, the black cat who during a twelve year régime rubbed herself against the legs of the leading writers and artists of the day.

The meetings were initiated during the winter of 1880, when Gustave Kahn, irritated that Mallarmé was not being recognized, began calling on him in the evening. Others soon joined him. Tuesday became the day of the week when Mallarmé was at home, and as the number of the callers increased, the legend of the Tuesday evenings (*les mardis*) grew and the faithful were known as *les mardistes*. It was not until 1884 that Mallarmé's fame reached a degree which can be called considerable. Two books appeared that year which were widely circulated and which called attention to the poems of the obscure school teacher. *Les Poètes Maudits* of Verlaine and *A Rebours* of Huysmans. To the faithful followers of Mallarmé: Stuart Merrill, Verlaine, Moréas, Villiers de l'Isle-Adam, were added a whole new group of defenders who, by 1885, became assiduous at the Tuesday evenings: Rodenbach, Saint-Pol-Roux, Charles Morice, René Ghil, Hérold, Fontainas, Henri de Régnier, Vielé-

Griffin, Albert Mockel, Arthur Symons, Whistler. A few years later, in 1891, a group of very young writers entered the ranks of admirers and first crossed the threshold of the celebrated apartment: Pierre Louys, André Gide, Paul Valéry, Camille Mauclair.

By this time, the *mardis* had established their definitive form. Mallarmé spoke in almost a monologue. A religious hush fell over the disciples who felt insulted if one of their members, a new-comer, perhaps, dared to speak or question. The master usually stood throughout the evening, from nine to twelve, by a small stove. The early *mardistes* saw on the walls of the room Manet's portrait of Mallarmé and a sketch of Hamlet and the ghost, as well as a pastel of Odilon Redon. In the later years were added a sea painting of Berthe Morisot, a nymph of Whistler, an orange-coloured woodcut of Gauguin, and a Rodin piece representing a faun and a nymph. These were gifts of the artists to the man whose presence among them became symbolic and precious as the years passed.

Mallarmé was somewhat smaller than average size. His neatly trimmed beard and large straight nose contradicted the satyr-like expression which came from his very wide pointed ears. He wore over his shoulders a Scottish plaid shawl and smoked constantly either cigarettes or his favourite pipe whose bowl was of clay and whose stem was of goose bone. On the table a large bowl of tobacco could be dipped into by anyone who wished to smoke. About ten in the evening, Mme Mallarmé and Geneviève would bring in a tray of grogs, and then quietly disappear. Many of the habitués were wealthy and worried about smoking the tobacco and drinking the rum of the poet who was never free from financial worry.

The *mardis* represented a kind of literary pilgrimage. Mallarmé was listened to as if he were an oracle. Many of his disciples have described the evenings, but there is no record of Mallarmé's conversations or monologues. On the one hand, his speech is described as being very lucid, and on the other hand, as being similar in style to his prose essays collected in the volume, *Divagations*. This would seem to be contradictory because of the infinite subtlety of style and idea in the essays. His wisdom, as it appears to us now, is a kind of doctrine; but when it was first dispensed by means of his words and the example of his life, it bore no marks of a fixed literary creed because of the mildness of the master himself, because of his gentle interest in literature, because of the searching and somewhat obtuse quality of his thought.

There is a kind of mildness which succeeds in exerting a deeper influence than belligerency can. This was Mallarmé's mildness which, because it was inflexible, was also penetrating. His urbanity made him appear detached from whatever subject was under discussion, as the clouds of smoke from his pipe almost concealed him. But because he didn't discourse in acknowledged critical terms and because he seemed isolated in excessive detours of politeness, his listeners made a greater effort to understand and incorporate his thought.

Without willing it therefore in any usual way, Mallarmé became the master of symbolism. If symbolism, as a movement in literature, can be considered a school, with all the coherent and doctrinal tenets on which a 'school' relies, Mallarmé is its master and principal exponent. Even before Victor Hugo's death (1885) and during the most successful years of Leconte de Lisle and Hérédia, Mallarmé, with the gentleness of a philosophical sage but also with the persistence of a saint, gave evidence to his revolt against the oratorical lushness of romanticism and the cold picturesque realism of Parnassian poetry. The power of poetry, he taught, is not in its moving rhetoric nor in its precise images, but rather in its suggestiveness.

Whistler's portrait of Mallarmé catches the elusive and almost feminine qualities of the poet's features. The composition of the painting seems to indicate that Mallarmé's appearance stood for something that was not immediately visible. His delicate traits stood for a sensibility which is difficult to express directly in art and which can only be suggested. In the same way the poetic work of the master, and the poetic work of his best disciples, was first considered obscure because it failed to speak directly and logically as did the poetry of the Romantics and Parnassians.

The master of symbolism was first dubbed the master of obscurity, and he became the scapegoat for all that was eccentric and exaggerated in art. But today Mallarmé is no longer referred to as a *fumiste*. His poems still appear suggestive of themes larger than those contained in themselves, but they appear to us more and more as the poems of essences; that is, as the poems of condensed and perhaps distorted experience. However bare their communication, the poems, as complete unities in themselves, are more precise and tangible than the meditations of Lamartine and the sobbings of Alfred de Musset. The master of symbolism, who whimsically accepted all attacks and vituperations, has never ceased to teach the meaning of poetry through his work, because what he considered

17

the most real part of his life and wisdom was slowly and laboriously distilled into his poems. His life became a book. The analysis of this book has been the exercise and joy of subsequent symbolists and of those poets who have felt in sympathy with symbolism.

Most so-called schools of poetry have their origin in some new or renewed use of language. The instrument of poetry, after all, is the word. What word is conjured with and how it is manipulated are the two means of measurement we have for any poetic sensibility and intensity. The degrees which poetry may represent between simple expression, easily accessible to the poet's period and other periods, and complex or precious expression, much less accessible to the poet's period but increasingly clear to subsequent periods, are innumerable. Yet somewhere between the limits of simplicity and preciosity can the position of each poet be fixed. Mallarmé was so close to the utmost limit of the second pole that he can justifiably be considered a master of preciosity.

His courtship with language, his over-indulgence with the sound of words and with the sensuous value of images, his avoidance of the usual in language and the cliché, his violence with syntax and grammar are all subsidiary characteristics to his major trait: the verbal ornateness of his imagination. This we call preciosity. It involves both elaborate expression and elaborate sentiment. It may involve the mysterious process of a simple sentiment generating a complex expression to such a degree that the expression subsumes the sentiment and ends by existing alone in a glory of words. It may also involve the equally mysterious process of discovering through the use of verbal expression some innate but previously hidden sentiment. It is impossible to say with a master of preciosity, like Mallarmé, whether his florid imagination is generated from his sentiment or is generated by the power of words.

This master of preciosity, in his early love poems (*Placet Futile*) and in parts of his later love poems (*Prose pour des Esseintes*) recalls quite naturally the French emulators of Plato and Petrarch of the 16th century and the court poets of the 17th century. Like them, he can sue for his lady's favour with the homage of his art which seems to be created with the double intent of amorous wooing and poetic enjoyment. Like them, he composes the poem of an event, *la pièce de circonstance,* as the French call it. In fact, all poems, Mallarmé discovered, are only poems of circumstances and incidents. A poem must, by necessity, impinge upon something. Hence, the impure origin of every poem. The poet is defeated before he begins. He must deceive himself with preciosity, with the exterior and final beauty which conceals a troubled creation.

If Mallarmé recalls the practice and belief of Renaissance poets and can be considered their modern master in preciosity, he bears also a close relationship to the art of the Middle Ages in his fundamental idealism and in his cult for analogy. The 'demon' of analogy, he calls it. As each poem necessarily has to be about something and therefore a poem of circumstance, so does the development of every theme seem to depend upon analogy. The threat of impurity becomes graver with the progress of the poem as the initial beauty is forgotten and surpassed in the newly discovered beauty of some analogous image. The mediaeval artist used the entire exterior world as a kind of lesson book for Eternal Beauty, as a kind of initiation to an invisible mystery which our human mind cannot comprehend by itself. For him there was an immediate purpose in art: the portrayal of real objects and real beings; and an ultimate purpose in art: the transcendency of all objective material beauty and the final realization, if not contemplation, of the Fixed Source of beauty. The lesson of Mallarmé is not different from this. The familiar objects of the house, flowers, swans, mirrors, tombs are objects in which he finds both an innate beauty and a metaphysical use. He survives as a poet through his practice with analogy.

Mallarmé perhaps appears to us as the most authentic symbolist because of his appropriation of analogy in poetical writing. By definition no poem can be completely pure, thought Mallarmé. This is true and in accordance with Mallarmé's aesthetics, as it is also with Plato's. The object named will always remain impure when considered in relation to the idea of the object. However, the fatal impurity of art is greatly lessened in Mallarmé's work because of his use of analogy when the inital symbol is compared to other symbols and the poem grows along a web of perceptions and images all of which are removed from any specifically named object. Every name is a symbol and generates other symbols. There is no need and no desire on the part of the reader to go behind the immediate series of symbols in a Mallarmé poem. They attain an autonomous life and meaning of their own, and hence a purity similar to that of *La Vita Nuova*, for example, or of any art whose beauty seems to come solely from its own symbols and to remain independent of the experience which preceded its form in art.

The entire poetical work of Mallarmé, easily contained in a single small volume, appears, the longer it is examined, to be the diminished fragments of a greater work. The actual poems consigned to his book reveal both their own intense beauty and the lesson on poetry which Mallarmé's unwritten work suggests. Since his death, Mallarmé has grown into himself, which is the stature of a master-cleric, seated invisibly behind the known fragments of his work from where he is teaching a vaster doctrine than this printed communication unfolds. Like the mediaeval theologian, Mallarmé knew that no matter what purity his work could achieve, it was of little importance when considered in relation to the whole truth of his belief. At best, he could only teach negatively—as the philosophers of the Middle Ages were most adept in describing what God was not.

The very first word of his sonnet, *Salut,* which is a greeting to his readers and disciples, is the word, *rien,* which seems to bear both its Latin etymological meaning of 'a thing' and its modern French connotation of 'nothing'. The work is both positive and negative, both present and absent, but the passion of Mallarmé is that of a cleric: to paint the end,

> *Imiter le Chinois au cœur limpide et fin*
> *De qui l'extase pure est de peindre la fin*
>
> (Las de l'amer repos)

The cleric isolates himself with the familiar objects of his world, contemplates them and instructs himself on the meaning they reveal about greater realities than themselves. The poet Mallarmé, like the cleric, with the same detachment, with the same love for beauty, with the same astonishment at human intervention in things of the world, fixes his perceptions concerning the objects surrounding him in words which appear to him more enduring than the objects they designate. As the teaching of the cleric, the one who knows, is propagated through his disciples and thus immortalized, so are the poet's words similar to flowers which never fade, flowers of some eternal garden, which can always be looked at with the same kind of immediacy. Their beauty is both reminiscent of the origins to which they owe their creation but which have now disappeared, and shining with the brilliance of their own colouring which will not change in time.

The master-cleric easily became the master-poet in a very special sense. In his brief work, many of Mallarmé's pages deal directly with the meaning and the function of the artist. *Toast Funèbre* to

Gautier; the 'tombs' of Poe, Baudelaire, Verlaine; the 'hommages' to Wagner and Puvis de Chavannes, are all poems of self-exploration and analyses of the poet as a living man and the poet as an immortal artist. In a sense, these poems, particularly those on Poe and Baudelaire, are the culmination of a belief about the poet which had been growing in the modern conscience ever since the Renaissance. Or rather, it is a belief about the poet's 'word'. The sanctity of the poet is his word. It is a word infallible that cannot be changed. It is the word that has been abandoned by the poet and made autonomous.

The final role, therefore, of Mallarmé was that of the absent master because he abandoned his word, in the same way that literary writing becomes worthy of the name, 'poem', when it is emptied of life and of all that changes. The poem must become irresistible as life can never be. The law of the love of beauty which is ultimately the law of poetry is one which delivers and frees. As death delivers man, so does poetry, in its profoundest function, deliver the poet. After the holy hour of lamps, after *l'heure sainte des quinquets*, Mallarmé leaves his room and assumes the role of the absent master. As the poet enters death, so his work enters life.

A prolonged and intricate series of roles, the vocation of Mallarmé: teacher of English, master of symbolism, master of preciosity, master of analogy, master-cleric, master-poet, and finally the absent master. Seven degrees which end in extinction. Seven steps which culminate in nothingness. But this very nothingness is a new vigour and a new life which are consecrated by the poet's disappearance.

The critic, Albert Thibaudet, admirably described the position held by Mallarmé, when he pointed out that the beginning of the 19th century was dominated by Chateaubriand who taught the poetry of religion, and that the end of the century was dominated by Mallarmé who taught the religion of poetry.

But Mallarmé's biography is in reality that of his work. The serenity of his character and his almost coquetish politeness were means of protecting himself. As his fame grew and the number of his friends increased, the practical problem of his life must have become that of salvaging time for his writing. The sparseness of his work can hardly be wondered at when one considers his ever-present teaching career and the time lavished on friends, the innumerable letters and visits demanded by disciples. Mallarmé must have been embarrassed by the output and fecundity of his disciples, who published infinitely more than their master. On his desk there was always a pile of new inscribed volumes, each one of which would have to be read and acknowledged in a letter of high praise and only faint and delicate criticism.

The years in passing were marked at intervals by the publication of some long worked-over poem, each one of which became a literary event. In 1877, it was the sonnet on Poe, composed in order to commemorate the anniversary of Poe's death which was being celebrated in Baltimore. Then ensued a few fairly obscure years in the life of Mallarmé, during which his son, Anatole, died on October 7, 1879, at the age of eight. The last months of the tragic illness had been alleviated by the kindness and generosity of the writer and dandy, Robert de Montesquiou, destined to be mercilessly portrayed by Proust in his character, le baron Charlus. A few years after the death of his son, in 1883, Mallarmé lost one of his most intimate friends, the painter, Edouard Manet.

In 1885, the publication of *Prose pour des Esseintes,* in *La Revue Indépendante,* incited a wave of attack. The symbolism of the poem is difficult to decipher, and it was ridiculed as being a monstrosity and a defiance of all the rules of reason and art. Likewise, in 1886, the sonnet to Wagner (who had died the same year as Manet), appearing in *La Revue Wagnérienne,* was considered a linguistic scandal. But the accusations levelled at Mallarmé became even more vociferous when, on June 13, 1886, appeared in *La Vogue,* his sonnet, *M'introduire dans ton histoire.* The sonnet seemed so incomprehensible that its final phrase, *vespéral de mes chars,* became a kind of battle cry of Mallarmé's opponents. They used it in derision to describe loosely whatever was commendable. Instead of saying, *c'est très bien!* they would say, *c'est très vespéral de mes chars!* This was mockery, but it was fame, too.

Not until 1887, did Mallarmé authorize a collection of his poems. But this early expensive edition hardly counted since it provided only forty-seven copies. Five years later, in 1892, when Mallarmé was fifty years old, an edition of selected works, published by Perrin, under the title, *Vers et Prose,* was the first volume of Mallarmé made available to the public. At this time, the geographical divisioning of Paris corresponded to a literary divisioning. The left bank school of poetry was headed by Verlaine, and the right bank by Mallarmé.

Not only did the poet celebrate in verse the artistic greatness and importance of a Baudelaire or of a Wagner, but also the luxuriant hair of his close friend, Méry Laurent. For years she was his neighbour on the rue de Rome. There is no literal proof that Méry was Mallarmé's mistress, but she was at all times a kind and commodious friend, and she seemed to prefer Mallarmé to all the other men who sued for her favour. She began a career as professional dancer, but her real success came after the dancing rather than during it. She was model and friend of Manet, at whose studio Mallarmé first met her about 1881. Through the generosity of an American dentist, Dr Evans, Méry attained to the status of a *demi-mondaine*. Mallarmé's love for her was at all times peaceful. He was not a man to be over-wrought by passion or jealousy. He called her his *paon* (peacock), and she was for a time at least a reigning muse. The setting was classical: the boudoir-salon apartment of a very pretty woman where exquisitely devised dinners were served. There is no record of any quarrel between Méry and Mallarmé, or of any temporary estrangement. It is quite evident that neither she nor he felt any profound or consuming love for the other. Méry was fascinated by Mallarmé's elegant speech and wit, and by his goodness. He was attracted by Méry's love for artists, by her beautiful hair and her body which had been reproduced in so many of Manet's paintings.

From 1882 on, Mallarmé's most intimate friends seem to have been Huysmans, Villiers de l'Isle-Adam, and, to some extent, Léon Bloy. In 1888 he made two new friends in Whistler and Henri de Régnier. Villiers' illness and death in 1889 (Mallarmé was a witness at his marriage *in extremis*, performed in order to legitimatize a son of Villiers) were a source of grief. In 1890 a young man from Montpellier, Paul Valéry, entered the ranks of admirers by a letter written on the 20th of October. The following year, 1891, Valéry paid his first visit to the rue de Rome, and André Gide presented to Mallarmé his first work, *Les Cahiers d'André Walter*. Early in 1892, on the 15th of February, Mallarmé presided over the banquet of poets held under the auspices of the periodical, *La Plume*, and recited to the gathering his sonnet, *Salut*, a subtle and delicate 'greeting' in which he designates himself, but with becoming modesty, as the master of the new poets. He received an ovation on the reading of his sonnet, and proceeded to proclaim Verlaine president of the society.

Mallarmé's friendship with Verlaine had begun in 1866 when Verlaine, then 22 years old, sent to Mallarmé, who was two years his senior, a copy of his first book, *Poèmes Saturniens*. A rich correspondence was carried on between the two poets, to the extent of about fifty letters of Verlaine to Mallarmé, and about twenty answers of Mallarmé. During many years, because of the extreme divergence of their lives and temperaments, they didn't see one another. Their friendship began again, however, after the appearance of Verlaine's *Sagesse*, in 1881. Two years later, Mallarmé consented to write to Verlaine his long autobiographical letter which was the basis of Verlaine's article on Mallarmé in *Les Poètes Maudits* of 1884. Mallarmé called on Verlaine in his room during one of his last illnesses. It was not a reconciliation, because there had been no melodramatic estrangement, but it was a symbolic rejoining of old ties, a reaffirmation of esteem and affection. The Bohemian Verlaine, during the visit, forgot the timidity he had felt at the idea of Mallarmé coming to his room and Mallarmé, who never judged or condemned his fellow men, was deeply touched by the scene of poverty and illness, by the vision of a great poet outlawed.

Verlaine died in January 1896. Among those present at his funeral were Cazalis (Jean Lahor), de Sivry, Vanier, Coppée, Barrès, Montesquiou, Lepelletier. Gabriel Fauré was at the organ in the church of St. Etienne-du-Mont. And Mallarmé also was present. His *adieu*, spoken at the grave, is one of the best examples of his prose, which, like his verse, was so often composed for such an occasion as the death of a friend and artist.

Mallarmé succeeded to Verlaine, as prince of poets, in Paris. He met Proust two or three times, but never influenced him so decisively as he did Claudel, Valéry and Gide. In fact, Proust, who perhaps met Mallarmé through his friendship with Méry Laurent and Reynaldo Hahn, published in an issue of *La Revue Blanche* (June-July 1896) an article entitled, *Contre l'obscurité*, which might be interpreted as marking some slight hostility toward Mallarmé's theories. In 1897, *La Revue Blanche* published the sonnet on Verlaine, which like so many other poems, aroused a wave of protest. This time the attack was so strong and specific that the disciples drew up an apology of defence which was signed by Gide, Valéry, Verhaeren, Schwob, Paul Fort.

Mallarmé's death occurred at Valvins, at the end of summer, 1898. On the 8th of September an attack of suffocation overcame him. It was a familiar manifestation of a life-long malady, a kind of chronic laryngitis which had bothered him for almost thirty years. Before his death, which came the following day, he requested his daughter Geneviève to burn all his papers, to publish nothing posthumously. Until the very end, Mallarmé remained the perfectionist in his art, willing to reveal to the world only those few fragments which had to some degree measured up to his rigorous ideals.

Because of the literal inaccessibility of those ideals, Mallarmé must have considered the artist's fate ridiculous and paradoxical. The image of Mallarmé as school teacher during his least successful years, at Tournon, for example, serves almost as a symbol for the ironic fate of this kind of artist. *Le père Mallarmé, on ne fiche rien dans sa classe,* was the usual verdict of his young pupils. Throughout the disorder and frequent uproar of the classroom, the teacher would keep his head bowed over his book and at intervals would call upon a different pupil to recite. But it seems that the pupils, concentrated on their own activities, didn't pay much attention to this master who was lost in his own thoughts.

Mallarmé was a man characterized by his separateness from life. An extreme and highly stylized portrait of Mallarmé is to be found in the character of des Esseintes, hero of Huysmans' novel, *A Rebours*. The fervent adventure of the artist's mind, pursued throughout a banal existence, was a cerebral intoxication and possessed none of the disruptive passions of the ordinary man. His life was consecrated to a search for what he might have termed the 'pure' communication, and not for the immediate kind of communication which most men would regard as their goal.

The familiar portraits we have in mind of this poet: Mallarmé seated at his teacher's desk in the classroom and completely cut off from the uncomprehending pupils; Mallarmé in his salon standing beside the stove and talking to his friends, but at a spiritually great distance from them who were indistinct in their veil of smoke; Mallarmé in his boat on the Seine at Valvins; Mallarmé with Méry or with his wife and daughter; Mallarmé at the banquet of poets reciting to them his new sonnet; Mallarmé at the Lamoureux concerts during which it is said he used to draw out bits of paper and jot down words which were never seen later and which were perhaps the initial form of some line or some poem; Mallarmé at the bedside of Villiers or of Verlaine: these are all the exterior portraits of a man's life. They have been faithfully traced by friends and biographers, and recently, in 1941-2, in the admirable and elegant *Vie de Mallarmé* by Henri Mondor. But their literal importance diminishes, and they are beginning to glow with the colour of legend, as the strangeness of the poems becomes familiar. Time works for the great artist a fatal substitution: a change which Mallarmé meditated and a triumph which he planned. The poems grow in clarity as the figure of the man loses its physical and once-loved personal traits. As the life of the work becomes more real and more strong, so the disappearance of a poet becomes more justified. It was possible once to jeer at Mallarmé and ridicule his verse, but that chapter belonged to his life. It was only when the poet was irrevocably separated from his work, that it was able to begin its new cycle of significance, when those who had not written the poems, but for whom they had been written, were the only ones called upon to defend them.

PART I

THEMES OF THE WORK

Les Fenêtres

CHAPTER I

VALUE OF THE SYMBOL

A STUDY of the symbols of a poet leads to the centre of his achievement as well as to the heart of his existence.

Mallarmé's life as poet was exceptionally unified. He discovered himself as poet as early as twenty, and his poetic consciousness remained intact throughout his life. No hesitation at the beginning of an inevitable career; no subsequent vacillation throughout its course. His consciousness of a poet had only to progress within itself and grow on its own assurance.

Each day, for such an artist as Mallarmé, as well as for all artists who live in a constant awareness of their vocation, goes on the process of sifting experience, of clarifying it, of giving to all the chance accidents which befall them a permanent aspect: a symbol. Mallarmé's law of living was the law of his work. The rigour of his words and their fundamental reduction to the symbol cannot be separated from the way in which he as an artist lived and apprehended the universe. We say 'symbol' rather than 'metaphor' because of its deeper significance, because of its closer relationship with the experience of life, because of its more challenging mystery. A metaphor is a way of describing an experience or an object, but a symbol is a way of recreating or recasting or even deepening a significant experience.

Poetry is therefore the strange labour of converting impression into expression. The symbol is its secret and exalted goal for ever representing, because it is a symbol and not real, an equivocal distillation.

To the complexity of his memory, the poet opposes the bareness of a symbol. In his real existence, time, for the poet, is incorporated into complexity and change, but the symbol, in his achievement of artist, is the passage out of duration into the consciousness of creation. The symbol is a formula representing the oneness of life and concealing its multiplicity.

Before the formulation of the symbol, something real transpired at the beginning of each poet's career, even of such a poet as Mallarmé who, in its revelation, was far more discreet and taciturn than most.

It is something private and literal concerning experience which Nerval refers to in *El Desdichado*, which Baudelaire evokes in *Bénédiction* and Mallarmé perhaps in his early poem, *Le Guignon*. The experience of that something is what we usually call sentiment, in all its multiple and changing aspects. The artist—and this is what distinguishes him from other men—knows that there is something superior to sentiment, something that will separate him from the anguish and dominion of sentiment. It is the expression of sentiment (not its experience): a verbal system, in the case of the poet, which is capable of giving unity to multiplicity, of giving meaning to sentiment. A poem is a surprise and a mystery, even for the poet himself who composes it, and that is because it testifies to a sentiment even if it doesn't succeed in explaining or proving the sentiment.

In a sentence of Baudelaire describing Poe's belief about poetry, he formulates an aesthetic creed which has dominated a century of poetic endeavour. He said that Poe was the kind of poet for whom the goal of poetry is identical to its own principle, that it has within it nothing but itself.[1] This marks the first and necessary steps in the understanding of the symbol which the work of Mallarmé will help clarify more than that of any other single poet.

But no matter how pure and dominant the symbol grows, the paradoxical gulf between the personal experience and limitation of a poet and the limitlessness of his symbol never completely disappears. The second, which we are defining as the goal of the poem, cannot exist without the first. This first part of the paradox, although limited, personal, literal and trivial, is the vaguer of the two. What a poet was, despite his usual brief reporting of it at the beginning of his career (*Le Guignon*), is far more difficult to ascertain than what he created subsequently as a worker of symbols. Mallarmé was dazzled by this truth of a poet, by this faith in the greater accuracy and 'realness' of the poet's word.

His greatest strength was his belief in his own strength, which for us is perhaps best defined as a creative sentiment. It is almost a kind of innocency, a gift from the gods, recalling Plato's portrait of the poet as one inspired and filled with a holy madness. And yet Mallarmé never believed in writing under some divine dictation. He would not have subscribed to the surrealist process of automatic writing. His was another process, the practice of an extraordinary consciousness whereby the object became real, once its 'idea' was conceived. He never followed the development of an original inspiration or rhetoric which would have ended in a Hugoesque form of lyricism. The work, even before its completion, for Mallarmé, had to be centred in some objective symbol. Between the impression and its expression, between the sentiment and its symbol, Mallarmé practised his strength and economy of an artisan.

To discover beauty within a human experience demands an act of the will. Every young poet is more or less conscious of this. In adolescence, poetry is vaguely the poetic and the beautiful. But human experiences accumulate and one's consciousness of them deepens, until, for a time at least, the experiences themselves occupy and confound the poet's consciousness. It is after that period when the real poet emerges, if he is to emerge at all. It is fairly easy to see that the mature man obtains some degree of peace and stability by a reintegration of experience. A philosopher constructs his system almost as he would a dyke in order to withstand the inrush of perception and consciousness. And the poet, likewise, seeks a strength within his experience, but independent of his experience. He constructs a symbol as another man builds a dam or a bridge, to ward off danger or to join two lands.

(a) SYMBOL OF THE BLUE SKY

In his earliest poetic period, when Mallarmé was still strongly influenced by Baudelaire, he was concerned, in such a poem as Les Fenêtres,[2] with the type of symbol he was eventually to make markedly his own.

The poem falls easily into two sections, each of twenty lines. The theme of the 'windows' is already in the first part, but the expression is so Baudelairian that one thinks almost of a literary pastiche. The setting is a hospital and the character is an old man dying. In order to escape the white room and the ultimate experience which he knows awaits him because of his weakness and the administering of the final rites, he drags himself to the window, in order to see the setting of the sun. The intense light transforms everything for him. The horizon is suddenly filled with golden galley ships floating down a purple river. Even the perfumes are evoked, and the passage ends practically with a line of Baudelaire:

> Dans un grand nonchaloir chargé de souvenir![3]

Baudelaire is not completely absent from the second section of the poem, where the poet explains the image (as explicitly as Baudelaire does in L'Albatros) by saying that he is the dying man striving to separate himself from all banal happiness and living. He has fled toward the windows in order to look out at something that is not life.

> *Je fuis et je m'accroche à toutes les croisées*
> *D'où l'on tourne l'épaule à la vie, . . .* [4]

Through the glass of the windows, he sees the infinity of morning light. The moment is a ritual of purification at the end of which, as in an efficacious ritual, something happens. He is reflected and sees himself an angel, as if the transparent glass became translucent. He dies to the world behind him and is reborn as pure spirit in another realm consecrated to Beauty. What has operated the change? The poet answers (here the voices of Mallarmé and Baudelaire are indistinguishable) that the transformation is due either to artifice or to the supernatural.

> *et, béni,*
> *Dans leur verre, lavé d'éternelles rosées,*
> *Que dore le matin chaste de l'Infini*

> *Je me mire et me vois ange! et je meurs, et j'aime*
> *—Que la vitre soit l'art, soit la mysticité—*
> *A renaître, portant mon rêve en diadème,*
> *Au ciel antérieur où fleurit la Beauté!* [5]

But the two stanzas of illusion and evasion are over quickly. The ominous phrase, *Ici-bas est maître,*[6] reminds the poet of the world's constriction. Stupidity is malodorous. He looks out at the blue sky but, now, at the same time feels the oppression of the world. The poem ends, not with a solution of the drama, but with a question raised because of the vision and because of the poet's helplessness at realizing it. He asks how he can break through the glass of the window and escape. He has two wings but they are featherless and if he does escape, he will therefore be running the risk of falling through the space of all eternity.

> *Est-il moyen, ô Moi qui connais l'amertume,*
> *D'enfoncer le cristal par le monstre insulté*
> *Et de m'enfuir, avec mes deux ailes sans plume*
> *—Au risque de tomber pendant l'éternité?*[7]

The very disproportion between the poet's desire (*mes deux ailes*) and its realization (*sans plume*), between his imagination (*l'azur*) and the world's reality (*amertume*), provides him with his final ironic lucidity.

A poet's life is a repetition of the myth of Icarus, composed first of vision or the flight of the imagination, and secondly of the loss of the vision or the fall from the adventure of the spirit into the reality of the world.

Les Fenêtres is essentially a poem on the adventure of the metaphor. It illustrates what a metaphor fatally becomes in the experience of a poem. The 'windows' in the first five stanzas represent the facile meaning of a metaphor, and in the last five stanzas they represent the fuller meaning of a symbol. The poet clings to them first because of their own beauty, and then experiences through them a desire to pass beyond. A symbol is apprehended first in its own beauty and then in the liberation which it creates.

The night theme in the poetry of Mallarmé has an aspect, of secondary importance, by which night is conceived of as possessing the power of a prison. It is a haunting and focused force directed on the mind of the artist. Whether it be the ceiling of a room, or the close sky, or a fog, the symbol of night which at other times translates the experience of expansiveness, here becomes that of compression and imprisonment. This symbol was originally Baudelaire's, as in *Spleen: Quand le ciel bas et lourd*, but was inherited by Mallarmé.

The poem, *L'Azur*, first published in *Le Parnasse Contemporain*, in the issue of May 12, 1866, belongs to the series of poems composed at Tournon, between 1863 and 1866, and contains, despite its title, a dramatic treatment of this particular role of night. It owes much to Baudelaire, but it is not purely Baudelairian. It is rather an example of Mallarmé's use and appropriation of a Baudelairian theme, the reappearance of a familiar symbol which now translates a somewhat different experience.

The third prose poem in *Le Spleen de Paris*, which Baudelaire calls *Le Confiteor de l'Artiste*, contains some analogies with Mallarmé's *L'Azur*. In it Baudelaire speaks of the vagueness of autumnal days when the feelings of the poet are piercing and intense. *Solitude, silence, incomparable chasteté de l'azur!* The sky has the infiniteness and the depth of his reverie. The intensity of this kind of contemplation ends by creating a positive form of suffering. It would seem that the very thought of infinity, when prolonged as by contemplation of the sky, causes in man a feeling of consternation and anguish. For Baudelaire, in his prose poem, a study of the beautiful may turn into a duel between the artist and the object of beauty during which the artist himself may succumb.

This is, to some degree, the legend and the background of *L'Azur*. The years at Tournon, when Mallarmé worked on this poem and others, such as *Hérodiade* and *L'Après-Midi d'un Faune* (in their first versions), *Don du Poëme, Sainte, Pitre Châtié*, were among the most lonely and painful of his career. Yet he was formulating during that period his poetic theory. *L'Azur* is one of Mallarmé's earliest expressions of his doctrine on poetics and on the role of the poet. And it stands throughout his career as a fairly adequate statement of belief. Its own form is dramatic, or rather, melodramatic. This approach Mallarmé loses or willfully alters in other poems. He has described the poem in some detail in a letter to Henri Cazalis and states there his conviction that the poem contains a real drama.[8]

On no other poem has Mallarmé provided a more extensive commentary than on *L'Azur*. His letter to Cazalis is almost a manifesto and far more expansive than the kind of letter he will write at later periods of his life. It even bears some resemblance with Poe's *On Poetic Composition*, based on an explication of *The Raven*. Before the actual exercise of writing began, Mallarmé explains that he had to overcome his feeling of impotency (*terrasser ma navrante impuissance*). Then began the struggle between the purity of the poem's idea and the false rhetorical phrases which formed in his mind and which, if they had been expressed, would have deformed and alienated the subject. Mallarmé had to commit violence on his mind to remain within the original subject matter of his poem (*rester implacablement dans mon sujet*) and to banish all the lyric effusions which would have degraded the work. He states that each word of the poem required hours of search. His guiding belief, of acknowledged Poe origin (*idées léguées par mon grand maître Poe*), was that every element of the poem must contribute to a general effect. Every word must prepare and lead to the dénouement. No dissonance, no flowery embellishment is allowed to interrupt the pure effect of the symbol.

I say 'symbol', because one senses in *L'Azur*, even more than in *Les Fenêtres*, that the meaning of the blue sky has taken on for Mallarmé an intense inescapable preoccupation. From the opening line, which characterizes the sky in its quality of serenity, eternality and irony, to the closing line which states the hypnosis of the word itself and its meaning, we follow a unified struggle against obsession.

Like the unseizable, the incomprehensible beauty of flowers, the blue of the sky is a mockery for the poet who feels incapable of reproducing any such purity and impotent in the awareness of his own genius. Each day the blue sky is visible and each day the purity of the work to be achieved torments the artist. The opening of the poem is general, but with the second stanza the subject becomes the poet Mallarmé who tries to break the spell of the sky by fleeing it. To the poet, in his feeling of guilt at not being able to comprehend and recreate the purity of the blue, the sky appears reproachful. What kind of night, he asks, can he cast over the endless and ubiquitous scorn?

> *Et quelle nuit hagarde*
> *Jeter, lambeaux, jeter sur ce mépris navrant?* [9]

The vocative word, *night*, united with its adjective, *wild* or *savage*, is blasphemous in this particular context. It turns the drama into something unnatural and perverse, because with its evocation the poet turns against the ideal.

In three different ways, in the three succeeding stanzas, he tries to create a kind of blackness in order to efface the presence of the sky. He calls first upon the fog to rise up and build a vast silent ceiling.

> *Brouillards, montez! . . .*
> *Et bâtissez un grand plafond silencieux!*

Then he addresses Ennui as if he were a mason able to block up with mud from the swamp the holes in the fog made by birds. Finally, as if the fog might not be sufficient, he demands that the chimneys continue to send out smoke and extinguish in its moving prison of soot the sun as it sinks into the horizon.

Momentarily he succeeds in his plan. The sky is blotted out. *Le ciel est mort.* He is able to forget the Ideal, since it is no longer visible, and sink into the boredom of matter and darkness. His brain, like an empty jar of rouge, and therefore no longer able to colour an idea, wants only to stagnate in oblivion and obscurity.

> *Car j'y veux, puisque enfin ma cervelle, vidée*
> *Comme le pot de fard gisant au pied d'un mur,*
> *N'a plus l'art d'attifer la sanglotante idée,*
> *Lugubrement bâiller vers un trépas obscur . . .* [10]

But the power of the sky returns in full force. This time the colour is converted into sound and the poet hears the blue metal voice of bells ringing the angelus. It pierces the fog and reaches the poet who can no longer escape. He is now haunted and obsessed. The word

Azur rings continuously like a bell. The poet cannot cease being a poet. He must live with his suffering and with the agony of his ideal.

In *Les Fenêtres,* the windows signify the means of flight from the world, from the realm of matter: a hospital room and all that occasions disgust and illness. The climax of the experience is that moment when the window becomes a mirror and the poet sees himself as an angel: *Je me mire et me vois ange!* In *L'Azur,* the blue of the sky signifies the irony of the Ideal, its distance from the world, its inescapableness and its ubiquity. Two climaxes mark the experience in this second poem: the momentary blackening out of the sky: *Le ciel est mort,* and the final triumph of the blue which transfixes the poet and brings on a state of hallucination. The phrase, *Je suis hanté,* corresponds to that of the other poem, *et me vois ange.* In both of them, the poet sees himself as something different from his ordinary self. He becomes temporarily in his angelic and hallucinated selves a type of Narcissus. Later, the Venitian mirror (*la glace de Venise*) of Mallarmé's room, is taken to be a kind of window or an entrance into another world. In it he sees not the literal self whom others saw when they looked at him, but a being who doesn't resemble him. The symbols of the window and the sky of *Les Fenêtres* and *L'Azur* easily become the symbol of the mirror in *Hérodiade* and *Ses purs ongles.* At least, they are closely related and form the fundamental symbol in Mallarmé's repertory. We begin with it because itself is a beginning. To see oneself translates the need to feel oneself unique and totally different from all others. The poet needs to feel that, even more than he feels the need of knowing who he is. What we might call his mirror-uniqueness is created by him. In a certain sense it doesn't belong to him. It is the personality of the man seeing himself an angel in a window-pane or haunted by the blue sky. Later it will be the personality of *Hérodiade.* The gift of the poet is not only that of regenerating the word and making a new language out of it, but also of creating a new soul for himself. Every poet allows himself to some degree to be imprisoned by the myth of Narcissus. Behind every poetic masterpiece in which we are able to read the story of a unique soul, is another spirit, collapsed and consumed by all the illusions of the world. The poet is Narcissus. The poem is an effigy. The adolescent of the myth saw on the water the traits of pure and tantalizing and unrecognizable beauty. The young poet of Tournon learned to construct in his first poems an invisible theatre for the performances of an unknown and original being. Art is fiction. And fiction is that endless liberty for man to create for himself a new conscience. To create a poem is a way of protecting a being which the poet really isn't. But that unreal being, created in the poem, and whom we are calling Narcissus, renders uninteresting and even inefficacious the real man. As the symbol grows in intensity in the work of Mallarmé: the window, the blue sky, the mirror—the man who underwent the initial experience of horror, hallucination and escape, disappears into the fictional self performing the experience of the symbol.

(b) SYMBOL OF HAIR

Of all the obvious symbols in Mallarmé's poetry, that of a woman's hair has been the most discussed and analysed. Not only does it appear frequently throughout the poems, from the earliest of 1862 to the sonnet of 1885,[11] but it bears some fairly constant particularities.

Except by the critic, Pierre Beausire, not much attention has been paid to the early sonnet, *Tristesse d'Eté*, written in Tournon, in 1864. It contains most of the characteristics of the symbol. The hair which attracts Mallarmé is blond (*l'or de tes cheveux*) and the summer sun has enhanced its lightness and fire. The poet describes it as something he sees on the sand. The image is essentially visual. The woman is asleep, but from the first line we learn that before falling asleep, she had struggled (*ô lutteuse endormie*). The struggle must have been an amorous one because there are still tears on her cheeks out of which the sun has composed a love potion (*Il mêle avec les pleurs un breuvage amoureux*). The reason for the sadness and the struggle is revealed in the second quatrain where the poet remembers the woman having said, under the inspiration of the flaming spectacle of the sun, 'We will never be one body under the desert and the palms.'

> '*Nous ne serons jamais une seule momie*
> *Sous l'antique désert et les palmiers heureux!*'

The poet has accepted the inevitable separation, and precisely because of what the woman's hair has come to symbolize for him. It is a warm river where he can drown the soul that is haunting them and therein reach the void which the woman doesn't know.

> *Mais ta chevelure est une rivière tiède,*
> *Où noyer sans frissons l'âme qui nous obsède*
> *Et trouver ce Néant que tu ne connais pas!*

In this contemplation of the sleeping woman, the poet wonders if his heart, which has been wounded, will be able to reach the insensibility of the sky and of stones (*L'insensibilité de l'azur et des pierres*). That is the state of feeling, or lack of feeling, he wants to attain, and the vision of the hair on the sand will help him. What would seem to be at the beginning the theme of eroticism turns immediately into something else, into something of a more philosophical nature. Mallarmé's eroticism is not easy to define. His kisses had been fearful (*ô mes baisers peureux*). A timidity is always mingled with his sensuality, to such a degree that it assumes equal importance. Whatever had been a struggle between the man and woman is over, and the sun flaming on the two bodies, the one lost in the oblivion of sleep, and the other striving to attain to a void by conscious contemplation of the woman's hair, consumes the entire scene in some willed conflagration. The hair is the memory of the woman's beauty and love, as well as the means to forgetting them.

In a much later sonnet, of 1885, where Mallarmé's art has reached its full power of condensation and intensity, the symbol of hair is used centrally with all its accompanying themes and characteristics. The familiar nouns: *chimère, miroir, chevelure, diamant,* and the verbs, *expirer* and *étouffer,* are all in this single sonnet, which begins with the line, *Quelle soie aux baumes de temps.* The silk, referred to in the first quatrain, on which a Chimera seems to be collapsing, becomes clearly in the second quatrain a flag. The day is one of celebration and flags line the avenue.[12] The woman is combing or arranging her hair and it reaches beyond the mirror she faces. The poet is saying to her that no silken flag has the beauty of her hair.

> *Quelle soie aux baumes de temps*
> *Où la Chimère s'exténue*
> *Vaut la torse et native nue*
> *Que, hors de ton miroir, tu tends!*

Because of the day outside, the holes in the flags, recalling military struggle and victories, are reversed. But inside the room, the poet has the hair of his mistress which he can contemplate and worship.

> *Les trous de drapeaux méditants*
> *S'exaltent dans notre avenue:*
> *Moi, j'ai ta chevelure nue*
> *Pour enfouir mes yeux contents.*

La Chevelure Vol

In this act of worship, the poet is transformed into a princely lover who renounces the glories of the world, military and governmental, in order to kiss the hair and conceal in it all his worldly desires as one would conceal a diamond to enhance the beauty of a woman's hair.

> *Non! La bouche ne sera sûre*
> *De rien goûter à sa morsure,*
> *S'il ne fait, ton princier amant,*
>
> *Dans la considérable touffe*
> *Expirer, comme un diamant,*
> *Le cri des Gloires qu'il étouffe.*[13]

The sonnet is unquestionably a love poem, but it is passionless, as is *Tristesse d'Eté* and the other poems of Mallarmé where the woman's hair is the symbol of love. The voluptuousness which Baudelaire sought in the black tresses of Jeanne Duval is quite absent from the serenity which Mallarmé finds in the blond hair of his mistress. In the way she handles her hair, Mallarmé's mistress exhibits a boldness and assurance of love which never seems to be shared by the poet. He, timid and overcome, seems able only to hide his face in the tresses. He sees the golden beauty of the hair, but immediately closes his eyes in it as if he wanted to transform an impulse to love into a forgetting of love or a sleep of love.

*

The exact date is unknown of the important sonnet, *La chevelure vol d'une flamme*, which contains the most prolonged example of the hair symbol. It was first published as part of the prose poem, *La Déclaration Foraine*, which appeared in the August 12, 1887 issue of *L'art et la Mode*, and which was later included in the collected volume, *Divagations*.

In the prose poem, Mallarmé and a friend, who is quite obviously Mme Méry Laurent, are driving through the countryside. They pass by some rural fair or celebration and stop to visit it. Mallarmé had wanted to escape just such a crowd, but he and Méry are struck by one of the tents or stands which is empty (*une baraque, apparemment vide*). The sun is setting and the two visitors are saddened by the starkness and emptiness of this one tent. Méry orders Mallarmé to beat the drum (*un suranné tambour*) and call in some of the spectators. He plays the part of barker, asks a sou for admission and promises its return if the show is unsatisfactory. When the crowd is assembled, he turns about to see what his accomplice is going to do. She simply sits on a table and takes a pose. No dancing and no singing is added to the pure exhibition. The poet senses the curiosity of the public and feels that he must have recourse to the absolute power of a metaphor. He takes a last glance at Méry, at her hair, her hat and dress, and then recites the sonnet, *La chevelure vol*. At its conclusion, he tries to alleviate the astonishment of the crowd by explaining that the woman, whose charm was exhibited to them, needed no special costume and no theatrical prop. Mystified, they agree with these words, still spoken from the barker's viewpoint, and slowly move away into the bigger crowd outside. Méry and Mallarmé, in their turn, after their strange co-operative effort at 'performing' before a part of the holiday crowd, find their way back to the carriage and drive off through the night.

The sonnet is remarkably suited for such a use and such a scene. The figure of the woman is subsumed into the beauty of her hair which dominates the poem. The poet as hero is almost non-existent. He recites the lines about her and to her while occupying an insubordinate position.

The first quatrain gives the exterior visual picture of the hair.

> La chevelure vol d'une flamme à l'extrême
> Occident de désirs pour la tout déployer
> Se pose (je dirais mourir un diadème)
> Vers le front couronné son ancien foyer [14]

From the beginning to the end of the sonnet the hair is seen as a flame. Initially it is a flame in flight, which, as it is unwound, seems to coil from one side of the head toward the other and take the form of a crown. The limits would be the east and the west: the beginning or the dawn (*son ancien foyer*) and the fulfilment of desire (*à l'extrême | Occident de désirs*). At the moment of fulfilment there comes the premonition of death. When the diadem of hair glows with its highest light, one senses that its radiation is going to decrease immediately.

After the first stanza of flame and light, we learn in the second that no lamp or artificial lighting illumines the scene.

> Mais sans or soupirer que cette vive nue
> L'ignition du feu toujours intérieur
> Originellement la seule continue
> Dans le joyau de l'œil véridique ou rieur [15]

The light from the hair which seems alive[16] in the darkness (*sans or*) merely continues or represents the inner fire of desire. This fire had been first reflected in the eyes. The love scene needs no artificial light with the flame of desire first caught in the eyes of the beloved and then perpetuated in her hair.

The sonnet is in Shakespearean form and continues with a third quatrain and a couplet containing a brief but significant comment on the poet as lover, he who had seen the diadem dying and who had sighed.

> *Une nudité de héros tendre diffame*
> *Celle qui ne mouvant astre ni feux au doigt*
> *Rien qu'à simplifier avec gloire la femme*
> *Accomplit par son chef fulgurante l'exploit*
>
> *De semer de rubis le doute qu'elle écorche*
> *Ainsi qu'une joyeuse et tutélaire torche.*[17]

The hero portrayed in his nakedness and tenderness is a familiar figure in Mallarmé's poetry. His portrait is sketched or half-sketched in *Le Pitre Châtié, M'introduire dans ton histoire* and *L'Après-Midi d'un Faune*. He appears diminutive and timid by comparison with the woman. He is stifled or drowned in the woman's hair (*Quelle soie* and *Tristesse d'Eté*), which needs no jewels to augment its beauty. The head is that of a goddess assured of her dazzling beauty. Whatever doubt has grown up between the man and the woman in the form of night is scraped, as if it were a block of some hard substance, by the fire rubies cast off from the hair, now conceived of as a torch joyfully flaming and protective.

The meaning of the last six lines is difficult to analyse. Much depends upon the interpretation given to the verb *diffame,* which is perhaps best understood in the context of the prose poem, *La Déclaration Foraine*. There, in the setting of the country fair, only one role is played in the improvised scene, that of the woman who exhibits herself before the crowd. The poet who recites his poem beside her is only a voice and the words he says must have been incomprehensible to the spectators. There is no artificial illumination in the tent and the model wears no jewelry. But to expose her and to speak words about her, even if the words are those of a difficult sonnet, is to debase her. The anecdote of the fair is in one sense the writing of the sonnet, the exposing of Méry Laurent (or of some other woman) to the experience of all the readers, the curious and the serious ones, those who will understand something and those who will understand nothing.

The man of the sonnet, as well as the false barker of the fair, is no lover. He is the poet, concerned with what remains from an experience. The woman is a flame: her hair is an example of synecdoche because it represents her entire being, the source of voluptuousness in which man is able to lose himself and forget himself. Only at the end of the sonnet is the 'doubt' announced. But it is the gravest and obscurest of doubts, undefined in the poem itself and cast in an image that is barely perceptible. It may well be the great doubt, of existence, the fear that comes to every man of holding on to life, of protecting oneself from the despair of life. Only woman, by means of her abundant hair, when she is seen by man, may cover the doubt with rubies as if her hair were a torch shedding sparks over whatever obstacle it encounters. That is the 'exploit' accomplished by the head of hair, the temporary vision of the poet causing oblivion and release.

Of all the poems depending largely on the symbolism of hair, the sonnet, *Victorieusement fui le suicide beau,* is the most difficult and the most rewarding. In it, the symbol is the most significantly explored because it is cast in a more elaborate action and setting. All the themes associated with the symbol are repeated in the sonnet: the radiation and lightness of the hair, the coming of night and its opposition to the living flame of the hair, the aftermath of physical love and its metaphysical consequences, and finally, the timidity of the hero. This last theme, always the most important, is revealed in a new and striking and perhaps definitive light, as if it combined *Hérodiade* and *Le Pitre Châtié,* Méry and the terrified hero of *M'introduire dans ton histoire.*

The definitive version of the sonnet, when compared with the early version[18] provides a study of the development of the symbol in the poet's art. From a direct love poem one moves into a prolonged conceit containing far more than the original poetic idea and scene.

First quatrain

early version:

> *Toujours plus souriant au désastre plus beau,*
> *Soupirs de sang, or meurtrier, pâmoison, fête!*
> *Une millième fois avec ardeur s'apprête*
> *Mon solitaire amour à vaincre le tombeau.*[19]

definitive version:

> *Victorieusement fui le suicide beau*
> *Tison de gloire, sang par écume, or, tempête!*
> *O rire si là-bas une pourpre s'apprête*
> *A ne tendre royal que mon absent tombeau.*[20]

The first version portrays the fictional life of the poet: the 'disaster' with its oxymoron of blood and celebration, of murder and fainting, eternally repeated. Each time his solitary ardour prepares to conquer the tomb. The experience of love, which is just over, leaves in the poet a feeling of emptiness and loneliness. He thinks of the disaster that was magnificent, composed of blood and triumph, and the curious smile (cf. *M'introduire*) crosses his face.

The definitive version brings a radical change, especially to the first line, of which only the final monosyllable remains. The 'disaster' is rendered more specific by the image of 'suicide', around which the entire stanza is going to be composed. The concept of victory, originally introduced in the fourth line by the verb *vaincre*, is transposed to the opening word, *Victorieusement*, a long adverb and a very bold part of speech with which to begin a sonnet. It creates the atmosphere which never diminishes or changes throughout the fourteen lines. The subject is a victory but which has fled and which is therefore some kind of suicide whose beauty is described in the four parts of the second line, a seemingly endless alexandrine. This line also has been completely reworked. Its opening phrase, *tison de gloire,* introduces the image of fire which by definition flares up and then ends in a kind of suicide, an extinction of itself. The second phrase, *sang par écume,* far more pictorial than the original and vague *Soupirs de sang,* retranslates the suicide and its vanishing. The last two, *or, tempête,* repeat the victory in a martial sense and a suicide in nature. One thinks of the sky with the final word, *tempête,* and suddenly all the preceding words are seen in the image of a sunset committing on itself the sin of destruction. *O rire,* the beginning of the third line and all that remains from the far looser phrase of the first version, *Toujours plus souriant,* is a pause for the poet, after the long double line. He laughs at the vision of glory spread out on the sky and watches the second vision which follows. *Là-bas* is the 'horizon' which occurs in a manuscript version,[21] that may well be prior to what we are calling the first version, where the third line is: *Une millième fois sur l'horizon s'apprête.* The *pourpre* not only describes the first colour of night following the sun suicide, but it recapitulates the possible military victory and glory and it announces the *royal* tomb with which the fourth line is concerned. The purple band of early night spreads across the horizon forming a tomb which is empty because the body of the sun has descended through it. But the tomb is the poet's. He calls it *mon absent tombeau*. It is his, but it remains at a great distance from him. Absent, he watches his own suicide and funeral ceremony.

Second quatrain

early version:

> *Quoi! de tout ce coucher, pas même un cher lambeau*
> *Ne reste, il est minuit, dans la main du poëte*
> *Excepté qu'un trésor trop folâtre de tête*
> *Y verse sa lueur diffuse sans flambeau!*.[22]

definitive version:

> *Quoi! de tout cet éclat pas même le lambeau*
> *S'attarde, il est minuit, à l'ombre qui nous fête*
> *Excepté qu'un trésor présomptueux de tête*
> *Verse son caressé nonchaloir sans flambeau.*[23]

Many more resemblances mark the two versions of this quatrain. The outstanding change is that from *coucher* to *éclat*. A 'sunset' was therefore the original idea of the first stanza, and deliberately Mallarmé removed the precise word of proof and substituted the more general word, *éclat*. With this substitution, the word, *suicide*, expands and dilates with many possible meanings or applications. The mystery of the symbol grows as the mysteriousness of the experience deepens. The second change is that brought to the phrase, *dans la main du poëte*, which in itself is literal and obvious. It is omitted in the final version, but implied in the adjective, *caressé*, applied to the indifferent languor of the girl's head. By this very subtle change, the figure of the poet is obscured and the head of the woman attracts as well as radiates all the light of the scene. The head, originally called a 'too playful treasure' (*un trésor trop folâtre de tête*), becomes a 'presumptuous treasure' (*un trésor présomptueux*). The term of simple description designating childishness is replaced by a term far more significant for the entire symbol. The head is 'presumptuous' because it rivals the power and the richness of the sun or of whatever great brilliance flooded the scene of the initial stanza. Both the setting and the action of this second quatrain remain unchanged. It is concerned with the coming of night, with the immobility of two beings, and with the flaming colour of some intimate experience which remains in the woman's hair. In the reworking of the four lines a new but important psychological trait in the woman is brought out: the presumption of her flaming hair and the languor of her pose as she allows her hair to be caressed by the poet.

Tercets

early version:

> La tienne, si toujours frivole! c'est la tienne,
> Seul gage qui des soirs évanouis retienne
> Un peu de désolé combat en t'en coiffant
>
> Avec grâce, quand sur les coussins tu la poses
> Comme un casque guerrier d'impératrice enfant
> Dont pour te figurer, il tomberait des roses.[24]

definitive version:

> La tienne si toujours le délice! la tienne
> Qui seule qui du ciel évanoui retienne
> Un peu de puéril triomphe en t'en coiffant
>
> Avec clarté quand sur les coussins tu la poses
> Comme un casque guerrier d'impératrice enfant
> Dont pour te figurer il tomberait des roses.[25]

The last three lines are identical, with the exception of the second word. *Grâce* becomes *clarté*, which emphasizes the head as an object of light. Dr Bonniot, in his article (see Note No. 18), has pointed out that the last two lines, the same in the two versions, exist in one of the drafts of the *Ouverture* for *Hérodiade*. The changes of the first tercet are significant to some degree. *Frivole*, which repeats *folâtre* and announces *enfant*, is altered to *délice*. In the final version only two words, *puéril* and *enfant*, remain to designate the youthfulness of the heroine, but they are strong and sufficient words. The opening of the second line, *Seul gage*, is prosaic. It is converted very simply into *Oui seule*, which introduces a delicately balanced line almost completely composed of a repetition of the sound *i*. The initial *oui* is heard again at the end of the line in the word, *évanoui*. In the third line, the early phrase, *désolé combat*, is changed into *puéril triomphe*, by which the woman appears as triumphant child in the new relationship imposed by the sun suicide and the reign of midnight.

The tone of the tercets is cajoling and caressing: *La tienne si toujours le délice!* and gradually deepens into greater fervour as the symbol of the head of hair grows into its extreme warrior form of a helmet. The light of the hair has for the poet been captured from the colour of the sunset. That triumph of capture is visible when the girl arranges her hair. She is diminished into a young girl in the new setting of night when the familiar universe vanishes. As her head falls back on the pillow, she appears more than ever as a child and the sheen of her blond hair causes it to resemble a metal helmet. She is *warrior,* because of the metal colour of her hair; *child,* because of her contrast with the immensity of night and because of her playful indolence after the passion of love; *empress,* because she has triumphed in her experience and reigns over the night by the sun brilliance lingering in her hair. Suddenly, in a flash of surrealistic fancy, the girl's head which he had just now caressed, becomes for the poet so realistically a helmet, detached from her body, that he imagines roses falling out from it, roses which in their colour and texture would represent the girl whom he had loved and who had disappeared momentarily even as the sun had disappeared. The sonnet begins and ends with a suicide: a first suicide of passion climaxed and resolved, and a second suicide where the body of the beloved disappears into a void and leaves only its figuration in metal and roses.

The designation of 'child empress' in this sonnet leads one back to Mallarmé's most constant preoccupation, that of the princess Hérodiade. The resemblances of theme and vocabulary are numerous between *Victorieusement fui* and *Ouverture*. The poet in the sonnet and the nurse in the *Ouverture* describe the woman and the princess as a child. The sky is characterized in both poems by the word, *pourpre,* and the scenes are reminiscent of some warlike moment (*siècle belliqueux* in *Ouverture,* and *casque guerrier* in the sonnet). 'Roses' are evoked in both, and the child appears isolated from the world (*l'enfant exilée en son cœur précieux*) even in the presence of the poet-lover. The hair of Hérodiade is described as being asleep (*Le parfum des cheveux endormis*). At the end of the poem she is compared to a swan hiding its eyes under its wing. The languor of the girl in the sonnet is so great that only her hair seems visible and it is so immobile that it comes to resemble a polished helmet carelessly placed on a pillow.

The hair is closely associated for Mallarmé with a moment of stillness coming after a strong experience of power and colour. It reflects what the immediate past was. In its contemplation the poet remembers a victory and foresees a tomb. It marks a very complicated psychological and physical change taking place in both the man and the woman. The possessor of the hair becomes almost disincarnate. She loses her femaleness and becomes a triumphant child. (In one poem the hair is compared to a silk flag.) She becomes symbolically what the man is becoming: a hero after being a lover, the one who beholds and experiences a dying of himself and who at the same time feels growing in himself a new warlike candour. The sun sinks into its own glory, the night spreads over the sky in the form of a purple tomb, and a glimmer from some metal ornament rises up from the flamboyant abyss into which love and death had vanished.

Love, death and war seemed such obvious themes in *Victorieusement fui*, that Teodor de Wyzewa, as early as 1886, in *La Vogue*, published an exegesis stating that Antony and Cleopatra were the two characters in the poem! The dominant word of the sonnet is that of *suicide*. Mallarmé, in changing the word *coucher* to *éclat*, tried to avoid giving to his symbol of suicide the single meaning of sunset. Yet the image, after its full resonant description in the second line, *Tison de gloire, sang par écume, or, tempête*, continues to recur: in the illuminated head that needs no torch at midnight (line 8), in the mention of the 'vanished sky' (*ciel évanoui*) of line 10, and in the final word of the sonnet, *roses*, which is the deliberate reduction of the long expansive second line, the symbol of the symbol.

It is far from unusual to draw an analogy between the physical experience of love and suicidal death. The opening of the sonnet resembles a triumphant climax, followed immediately by a stretching out of space (*si là-bas*) and a descent of darkness (*une pourpre s'apprête*). From the outside world of the symbol, the scene shifts to a closed-in-space. From the red splendour of a sunset we turn our gaze to the faint outline of a golden head of hair resting on a cushion as if it were a capsized helmet. Everything literally sinks into the abyss of a tomb: the sun sinks below the horizon, the bodies of the man and the woman dissolve into the blackness of night, the power of love is spent and reduced into a child's fatigue, the hair of the girl is converted into a metal casque.

The 'suicide', explained first by the sun and then by love, may also be interpreted as being the creation of the sonnet, the suicide of the poem. As the literal metaphor describes a suicide of light and love, so the poem is inevitably an entombment of experience, representing a shrinking and a metamorphosis of what was once real. The jar of rouge (*le pot de fard*) in *L'Azur* and the helmet (*un casque guerrier*) of *Victorieusement fui,* was once the means or the object of beauty, but in the elaboration of the symbol they become empty and shell-like. The reader has to imagine what once filled them, as in the blackness of night one has to imagine the sunset. The poem at best is skeletal, an empty object: a conch-shell, a window, a mirror, a jar of rouge, a helmet, a tomb. To return to the source of the experience, the reader's imagination would have to fill in the void. But the shell of the poem has its own purity. Its outline gives sufficient relief and emphasis to make of it a poetic transcription. Its peculiar power is precisely its emptiness, its suggestiveness.

What was the real experience is for ever absent from such a sonnet as *Victorieusement fui*. But far more than the totally mysterious suicide it refers to, we follow the circle of hair because it is the one link between the metaphor of the sonnet and the experience that has vanished. If the sky of the opening would seem to symbolize the total presence and beauty of woman, the metal helmet at the end, out of which roses have to be imagined as falling, symbolizes that memory and bond with which love terminates its course. The experience becomes the poem even as in the poem the head of hair turns into a metal lustre. The blood of a suicide no longer exists save in its distant analogy with the red petals of imagined roses.

(c) SYMBOL OF THE VOID

The three sonnets, published together in *La Revue Indépendante* of January 1887, form a kind of suite or trio because of a common theme and a common use of the octosyllabic line.

In the first sonnet, *Tout Orgueil fume-t-il du soir*, all kinds of pride which rise up in the heart of the poet at evening are described as being a torch which has been abruptly extinguished in such a way that its aftermath of smoke, which would continue it, cannot replace the flame. The poet realizes that the immortal smoke will not replace the extinct flame of pride. The important word, *Orgueil*, of this quatrain resembles the word, *suicide*, of the sonnet, *Victorieusement fui*. It appears in the first line, as abstracted and as bare as *suicide* in the other poem, and then it is immediately in the second line transcribed by a metaphor. The same process continues in *Victorieusement fui* where the second line describes metaphorically the *suicide*.

Girl's Head

Curiously the third movement in the quatrain is the same in the two poems. In the 'suicide' sonnet, the sky, after its moment of brilliance, becomes a dark purple, an expansive tomb for a king. In the 'pride' sonnet, the torch, after some oscillation extinguished it, cannot be put back into place or raised to its former degree of light.

> *Tout Orgueil fume-t-il du soir,*
> *Torche dans un branle étouffée*
> *Sans que l'immortelle bouffée*
> *Ne puisse à l'abandon surseoir!* [26]

The room is empty, but the poet imagines the family heir returning to it. It would be cold if the man came into it from the corridor. The single note of description leads one to see rich trophies which have fallen from the wall. The theme of emptiness is accentuated by this imagining of an inhabitant, by the coldness of the room and by the metal trophies that have fallen from their position on the walls.

> *La chambre ancienne de l'hoir*
> *De maint riche mais chu trophée*
> *Ne serait pas même chauffée*
> *S'il survenait par le couloir.* [27]

The memories of the man, were he to inhabit the room, would be anguished. Now begins the elaboration of the 'Pride' announced at at the beginning. *Affres* is a stronger word than *Orgueil,* and in the same way it opens up into an image, this time of claws (*serres*), such as a bird's, 'necessary' in seizing the tomb, characterized by the word 'disavowal' (*désaveu*). The world has disavowed or forgotten the man (artist?). The meaning gradually emerges from the accumulation of the words: *Orgueil, immortelle, passé, sépulcre de désaveu.* This poem, in company with so many others of Mallarmé, concerns the drama of an artist's ambitions and the oblivion which time has brought to his achievements. The evening is the world's forgetting. His feelings are so strong that they form a tomb in an empty cold room. A heavy piece of marble, supported by a console, a kind of ornamental table, literally provides the appearance of a tomb. The table (*console*) shines with some light from its metal ornaments (as vaguely suggestive as the gold in the room of *Ses purs ongles: un or | Agonise*) in the same way as the hair of the child empress in *Victorieusement fui* retains some glimmer of the sun that has set. The poet's burst of pride (*Tout Orgueil*) vanishes into smoke. What the work is to be is as absent as a tomb is empty and isolated.

> *Affres du passé nécessaires*
> *Agrippant comme avec des serres*
> *Le sépulcre de désaveu,*
>
> *Sous un marbre lourd qu'elle isole*
> *Ne s'allume pas d'autre feu*
> *Que la fulgurante console.*[28]

The second sonnet of the series, *Surgi de la croupe et du bond*, concerns ostensibly a vase. (There seems to be less justification for Charles Mauron's interpretation of the object as being a lamp or chandelier.) Mallarmé's constant preoccupation with a room, usually empty, and with pieces of furniture or small objects adorning furniture which are usually empty also, is illustrated in this particular triptych of sonnets. After the empty room of the first sonnet, lighted only by a reflection from the console, the vase of the second sonnet is characterized by a similar emptiness. What might fill the hollowness of the vase becomes the subject of the poem, as what the heir might see if he returned into the ancient room became the subject of *Tout Orgueil*.

The first line, a kind of ablative absolute, describes the shape of the vase as it seems to rise rapidly from its rounded base in a leap upwards. But its 'ignored neck'[29] is broken off or terminated. No flower in it accompanies the evening in its loneliness.

> *Surgi de la croupe et du bond*
> *D'une verrerie éphémère*
> *Sans fleurir la veillée amère*
> *Le col ignoré s'interrompt.*[30]

The poet is alone and looking down at the empty vase as if he were a sylph painted on the ceiling. His evening hours are empty because he has not been initiated to the mysteries and the imaginative powers of poetry. If his mother and her lover had drunk from the same goblet, from the same chimerical source of imagination, he might be different.

> *Je crois bien que deux bouches n'ont*
> *Bu, ni son amant ni ma mère,*
> *Jamais à la même Chimère,*
> *Moi, sylphe de ce froid plafond!* [31]

After the quatrain of the vase's description and the quatrain on the poet's relationship with the vase: his lack of sensitivity due to his ancestors—the tercets, closely joined as is usual in Mallarmé's sonnets, reconsider the vase and imagine its emptiness filled. No water is in the vase. It seems to be dying because of its emptiness. Its empty neck kisses the darkness as if it were trying to draw down some rose into itself in order to join with it in a real kiss.

> *Le pur vase d'aucun breuvage*
> *Que l'inexhaustible veuvage*
> *Agonise mais ne consent,*
>
> *Naïf baiser des plus funèbres!*
> *A rien expirer annonçant*
> *Une rose dans les ténèbres.*[32]

It becomes more certain at the end that there is no light in this sonnet. The shape of the vase is outlined, but immediately its state of emptiness (*Sans fleurir*) becomes the subject of the poem. The waiting of the vase for water and for a flower is comparable to the waiting of the poet throughout the darkness of the night. A rose, placed in the opening of the vase, would have fulfilled the vase in its reason for being, as a poem or some act of creation would have justified the poet's vigil.

The third sonnet of the group, *Une dentelle s'abolit*, is bathed in the whiteness of dawn and lace curtains and a window as if it came in answer or in contradiction to the preceding sonnets on night. But it is attached to them deeply and significantly. It renews and completes the themes of the other sonnets and gives to the preoccupation of the poet as creator a firmer more decisive outline.

The opening quatrain is characteristic of the other two sonnets. It contains a specific word: 'a piece of lace' (*une dentelle*) which turns out to be a lace curtain in the development of the image, and a more abstract word, related to *dentelle*, and around whose meaning the sonnet is to be built. It is the simple word, *Jeu* ('game'), capitalized and mysteriously designated as 'supreme'. In the first sonnet, the room with its trophies and table was joined with the key word *Orgueil* (pride), likewise capitalized and significant, and in *Surgi de la croupe*, the only capitalized word, *Chimère*, bears an obscure but necessary relationship with the more obvious object of the vase. The lace curtain, in half disappearing at the window, reveals a room without a bed. It buries therefore nothing but dangles uselessly in conflict with itself against the pale glass of the window.

Une dentelle s'abolit
Dans le doute du Jeu suprême
A n'entr'ouvrir comme un blasphème
Qu'absence éternelle de lit.

Cet unanime blanc conflit
D'une guirlande avec la même,
Enfui contre la vitre blême
Flotte plus qu'il n'ensevelit.[33]

The tercets re-enact a process which occurs in the other sonnets. The real object, or the absence of the real object, is abandoned for one of pure imagination which in its metaphorical right assumes responsibility for the poem. In *Tout Orgueil,* the literal console was converted into a tomb, image of the oblivion into which the poet had sunk. In *Surgi de la croupe,* the empty neck of the vase is filled with the imagined rose flowering in the darkness. In *Une dentelle s'abolit*, the image of the bed, no longer in the room, is translated into the symbol of a mandoline, with its empty round shape which the poet sees in a dream as if it were a maternal womb from which an expression would be born in the full light of the window.

Mais chez qui du rêve se dore
Tristement dort une mandore
Au creux néant musicien

Telle que vers quelque fenêtre
Selon nul ventre que le sien,
Filial on aurait pu naître.

The commentator, Camille Soula, considers the *Jeu suprême* the game of love. The 'doubt' would be the troubled feeling accompanying the experience and its indecisiveness. Mme Noulet, in her more recent study of Mallarmé's poetry, suggests very ingeniously that the *Jeu* is God's game or the return of light in the morning. The 'bed' would designate therefore solely the place of birth. In the light of the other sonnets, the *Jeu* might be more convincingly transcribed as the game of creation, and particularly the poet's creative art.

The word 'Pride' in *Tout Orgueil* contains all the overtones of the artist's pride whose past achievements or past efforts toward achievement have come to naught. What has been denied him is like a tomb in a cold room. The word 'Chimera' (*Chimère*) in *Surgi de la croupe,* from whose waters the poet's ancestors never drank, contains the power he might have possessed in his imaginative work. The word 'Game' (*Jeu*) in *Une dentelle s'abolit* might well be the very 'pride' which comes from an initiation to the rite of the 'chimera', from a participation in the world of the imagination. A poem is a willed search for analogies and metaphors. In each of the three sonnets is an example of this kind of search, of this 'game' of relationships which is the very substance of poetry. In the first is the analogy between the vanished pride of a poet and the flame of a torch which has been extinguished by a sweeping movement of the arm. In the second is the analogy between the desire of the poet to create, to seize the image of some relationship, and the yearning of an empty vase to be filled with a flower. In the third is the analogy between the forming but confused hope of the poet to give birth to a poem and the image of a musical instrument which is not being played. The birth of a poem is the coming together of something real and something imagined: 1. a console, heavy with a marble slab, and a tomb containing the poet's aspirations and work that have gone unheeded and forgotten; 2. a glass vase without water whose neck gapes empty, and a rose that might have adorned the vase; 3. a room, with lace curtains at its window, that reveal no bed, and an instrument, unplayed, whose round shape recalls a womb.

When considered together, the three sonnets seem to celebrate a disposition or a potentiality. The theme of the void is perhaps thus best described as the propensity of an empty room or of an object that is empty. In the two examples of the room, the principal idea is recapitulated in an object: a tomb, suggested by a marble top console (*Tout Orgueil*) and a mandoline, suggested by an absent bed (*Une dentelle s'abolit*). The sequence of sonnets begins with the extinguishing of a torch when the darkness accentuates the emptiness of the room, and it ends with an imagined impulse toward a window through which a pale dawn is beginning to stream. Between these two limits: the extinguishing of light in a void and the coming of light into another void, one observes a series of experiments on absence and on vacuity.

The 'window' with which the 'mandoline' tries to communicate, in order to give birth, is part also of the poem, *Sainte*, where the musician saint appears accompanied by a *mandore*. But the window is stained glass. The window of *Une dentelle* is associated with birth (*on aurait pu naître*) and the window in *Les Fenêtres* is associated with rebirth (*et j'aime | A renaître*). The familiar image of wings: the *plumage instrumental* of *Sainte* and *mes deux ailes sans plumes* of *Les Fenêtres*, seems to be taken over into the image of lace curtains (*Une dentelle*) and designates the same uselessness or frustration as it does habitually in Mallarmé's poetry (cf. *Eventail; aile* and *vol* in *Le vierge; aile saignante* in *Don du Poème* and *Hérodiade*).

Silence falls everywhere in these poems of windows and emptiness. It is the tomblike silence of waiting and anguish. In *Les Fenêtres* the sick man cannot speak in his intoxication. He can only look through the windows at the golden mirage of early morning, and the poet faints when he sees himself an angel in the same window. All the description of *Sainte* is music, but she is the musician of silence (*Musicienne du silence*). Nothing can be said by the poet in *Tout Orgueil* because all has been disavowal (*Le sépulcre de désaveu*). Nothing is exhaled from the neck of the vase in *Surgi de la croupe*. Its kiss with the darkness is funeral (*Naïf baiser des plus funèbres!*) The instrument in *Une dentelle*, from which sound might come, is asleep (*Tristement dort une mandore*). As soon as an object in these poems is declared, it incites and exacts silence. The principal verbs in the last sonnet, for example, all designate death and silence: *s'abolit, ensevelit, dort*. And the final verb of birth (*aurait pu naître*) is cast in the conditional tense of improbability.

(d) conclusion: SYMBOL OF THE CLOSED BOOK

The group of three sonnets, published by *La Revue Indépendante* of January 1887, and later interpreted by Soula as a triptych of three periods in time: sunset, night, dawn, was followed by a fourth sonnet written in Alexandrine lines, *Autre sonnet,* which is now known by its first line, *Mes bouquins refermés sur le nom de Paphos*.

In the edition of Mallarmé's *Poésies*, brought out in the same year, he placed the sonnet at the end of the collection, as if the initial words, *Mes bouquins refermés*, might naturally allocate it to that position. The first quatrain states with unusual clarity and simplification, the poetic method of Mallarmé, the practice of substitution, which is the practice of the metaphor.

> *Mes bouquins refermés sur le nom de Paphos,*
> *Il m'amuse d'élire avec le seul génie*
> *Une ruine, par mille écumes bénie*
> *Sous l'hyacinthe, au loin, de ses jours triomphaux.*[34]

Mes Bouquins refermés

The most obvious book containing the word, Paphos, which Mallarmé might have been reading, is *Les Fleurs du Mal* of Baudelaire where in the poem, *Lesbos*, for example, there is specific mention of the island and in *Un Voyage à Cythère*, another island of Greece is evoked. With the name of Paphos in his mind, the poet describes, in a game of wit or imagination (the word *génie* comes from the Latin, *ingenium*, which means a game of the mind) what occurs to him. It is a picture of beauty and serenity, a Greek temple in ruins under a blue sky and beside a sea covered with sun-lit foam. The mention of hyacinth colour is also evocative of Baudelaire, in his *Invitation au Voyage* (*D'hyacinthe et d'or*), but the general scene is vastly different from the dark tragic picture of a gibbet which Baudelaire sees in his *Voyage à Cythère*)

> *je n'ai trouvé debout*
> *Qu'un gibet symbolique où pendait mon image* . . .[35]

The second quatrain justifies the creation of the imaginary scene.

> *Coure le froid avec ses silences de faux,*
> *Je n'y hululerai pas de vide nénie*
> *Si ce très blanc ébat au ras du sol dénie*
> *A tout site l'honneur du paysage faux.*[36]

This is the real scene of a Northern land whose cold is like the movement of a scythe cutting close to the surface of the ground all growth of verdue. All is white[37] with snow which refuses the image of such a landscape as that evoked in the first quatrain. But even with this refusal, the poet will not lament like some bird of mourning the loss of the imagined scene.

The tercets recapitulate with a completely different image the same process of substitution.

> *Ma faim qui d'aucuns fruits ici ne se régale*
> *Trouve en leur docte manque une saveur égale:*
> *Qu'un éclate de chair humain et parfumant!*
>
> *Le pied sur quelque guivre où notre amour tisonne,*
> *Je pense plus longtemps peut-être éperdument*
> *A l'autre, au sein brûlé d'une antique amazone.*[38]

The poet's hunger, which originally converted the word, Paphos, into the picture of a ruined temple, is not real and therefore the two kinds of fruit it might satisfy itself on, a real woman and an imaginary woman are both absent. At first, both create an equal fascination for him. But then, the one who appears real to him in her body, as she breaks through the dream, or the poet's prolonged contemplation, holds his attention less ecstatically than the other, an Amazon of antiquity whose breast has been burned off. As in the quatrains where a real landscape was effaced in order to create an imaginary one, so in the tercets the image of a real woman at a hearthside is effaced in favour of an imaginary figure. *Paphos*, the magical word at the beginning, unites the two parts of the sonnet. From it rises up the image of ruins beside the sea, as well as the memory of the Amazons who founded the city of Paphos, on the eastern side of the island of Cyprus. In order to perform the skill of pulling the bow, Amazon women used to burn off one of their breasts. The analogy with the poet is obvious. As the Amazon was willing to undergo suffering and disfigurement in order to perform her skill of archer, so the poet accepts whatever suffering may permit a clearer vision and a deeper comprehension of his world. Man is or becomes what he contemplates. The poet elects the imaginary landscape. The closing of a book is like the closing off of the real world. Ecstasy (great importance is accorded to the adverb, *éperdument*, in the sonnet) is the contemplation (*Je pense . . . longtemps*) of what grows in the mind, of what is created imaginatively from something real. A poem is an absence.

As far back as the years spent at Tournon, and even before, Mallarmé had fixed upon his conception of the symbol. Throughout his career, his art developed within this conception. By 1885, Mallarmé was considered by the circle of young poets around him as the high priest of the symbol. The Tuesday evening gatherings and the publications of that year and the following years are sufficient evidence that Mallarmé was the centre of a 'cult' of the symbol. The conversations of Mallarmé and his writings at that period were looked upon almost as revelations. The example of Wagner joined with that of Mallarmé and confirmed and strengthened the poetic belief of those years.

In January of 1885, *Prose pour des Esseintes* appeared in *La Revue Indépendante*. It was the object of mockery for the uninitiate and an example of pure mystery for the initiate, an example of the powerful suggestiveness of the symbol. *La Revue Wagnérienne* began appearing in the same year, and in the issue of August 8, Mallarmé published his essay on *Richard Wagner: rêverie d'un poète français*. On the 16th of November, he wrote for Verlaine the long autobiographical letter in which he describes the Work he hoped to write, *un livre qui soit un livre,* which will be the Orphic explanation of the earth. This explanation Mallarmé calls the 'sole duty of the poet and supreme literary game'. (*le seul devoir du poète et le jeu littéraire par excellence*). The year 1886 began with the publication of Mallarmé's sonnet, *Hommage à Wagner,* in *La Revue Wagnérienne* (8 January). He wrote a preface (*avantdire*) for René Ghil's *Traité du Verbe,* one of the first attempts to elaborate the literary doctrine of symbolism. On the first of January 1887, in *La Revue Indépendante,* appeared the triptych of sonnets on the theme of absence and *Autre sonnet* or *Mes bouquins refermés.* By this time the Mallarmé legend was fully developed and his disciples were fully aware that a literary battle was on. Mallarmé himself refused to participate, although the struggle centred about his work.

The first obvious aspects of a battle showed up in connection with the publication in *La Revue Wagnérienne* of January 8, 1886, of eight sonnets of homage to Wagner. The contributing poets were Mallarmé, Verlaine, Ghil, Stuart Merrill, Charles Morice, Charles Vignier, Teodor de Wyzewa and Dujardin. A hostile press derided this publication. Dujardin has described a dinner of journalists where the sonnets were made fun of, especially Verlaine's *Parsifal,* in which the word *symbole* is used to designate the Holy Grail, and Mallarmé's *Hommage,* written in his purest and most difficult style. Dujardin points out, however, that the sonnet had made such an impression on many of those present at the banquet, that they knew it by heart and recited it in unison. In the history of symbolism, the importance of the publication comes from the joint collaboration of several poets, united around a single figure and a unified theory of art. The term of 'school' is almost applicable at this time to symbolism. Several literary magazines were founded in order to defend and support the young writers. The first number of *Le Scapin* appeared in December 1885. In the following April, *Le Décadent,* directed by Anatole Baju, announced its programme of destructive revolution. More important than these, *La Vogue,* founded also in April 1886, and directed by Gustave Kahn and Leo d'Orfer, published poems of Laforgue, *Les Illuminations* of Rimbaud, Mallarmé's sonnet, *M'introduire dans ton histoire,* and articles by Teodor de Wyzewa, a young theorist of the group who was strongly influenced by Mallarmé and who was writing at the same time articles on Wagner for *La Revue Wagnérienne.* Wyzewa was one of the first critics to consider Mallarmé an intellectual, to call him a 'logician' who was also an artist. He stressed the seriousness of Mallarmé and the excessive labours of the poet. He described Mallarmé as the poet who first transcribed ideas and then suggested the emotions of these ideas. Wyzewa speaks of the 'poetic emotion' which comes from the art of Mallarmé.

Mallarmé's preface he offered to write for René Ghil's *Traité du Verbe* (Paris, Giraud, 1886) is only a page or two long but it is one of the most fecond sources for the theory of French symbolism.[39] Speech is of two kinds according to this statement: it may be 'immediate' or 'essential'. The first is an elementary use of language, a kind of reporting or description which is an exchange of thought. But the other is a transposition of some natural fact into its purest kind of notion. This is a game or a trick whereby something is changed into its absence (*en sa presque disparition vibratoire*). When the poet says: 'a flower!' the idea of a flower rises up, and precisely the one absent from all bouquets. The great power of speech: dream and song, is constantly being rediscovered by the poet in his art. The word *Paphos* in the sonnet, *Mes bouquins refermés*, acts as the beginning of an incantation in which the lines of poetry will be separated from ordinary speech. This isolation of poetry is a denial of chance because it follows laws of meaning and sound.

The symbol is a world of knowledge that bears only the most tenuous relationship with the real world. Its major law is never to conclude, never to offer a logical conclusion. Whether it be a window or a mirror, a head of hair, an empty room or a closed book, the Mallarmé poem testifies to a disappearance of the poet and an effacement of the object named so that only the idea, a kind of musical elocution, remains. It is lighted up by myriad reflections of night, of dawn, of metal, of roses, of ruins. The school of the symbol was not named until long after Mallarmé had learned that the poet has to leave the initiative to the words themselves which reduced the lyric bombastic utterances of other schools of poetry to the barely perceptible breathing of the words forming a symbol.

NOTES ON CHAPTER I

1. 'Il croyait, en vrai poète qu'il était, que le but de la poésie est de même nature que son principe, et qu'elle ne doit pas avoir eu autre chose qu'elle-même.'

2. Written in London, probably in May 1863. Mallarmé refers to the poem in a letter to Cazalis of June 3, 1863. The poem was not published until 1866, in the May 12th issue of *Le Parnasse Contemporain*.

3. In a vast indifference heavy with memory!

4. I flee and clasp all the window panes
   Where we turn our backs against life.

5.   and, blessed,
   In their glass, washed with eternal dew,
   Gilded by the chaste morning of the Infinite
   I mirror myself and see an angel! and I die, and I love
   —Be the glass art or supernatural—
   To be reborn, bearing my dream as a diadem,
   In the former sky where Beauty flowers!

6. The world below is master.

7. Is there a way for me, knowing all bitterness,
   To break through the crystal insulted by the world
   And escape, with my two plumeless wings
   At the risk of falling for all time?

8. 12 Jan. 1864. cf. Mondor, *Vie*, pp. 104-106.

9.   And what wild night
   Can I throw, O shreds, over that disheartening scorn?

10. For I want—since my brain finally, emptied
    Like the jar of rouge lying at the foot of a wall,
    Has no longer the skill of bedecking the sobbing idea,
    To yawn mournfully toward an obscure death . . .

11. cf. *Château de l'Espérance* (Sens, 1862-63); *Apparition* (London, 1863?); *Angoisse* (Tournon, 1864); *Tristesse d'Eté* (Tournon, 1864); *Phénomène Futur* (Tournon, 1864; in *Divagations*); *De l'orient passé des Temps* (1868, published in *Fontaine*, No. 56); *La chevelure vol d'une flamme*; *Victorieusement fui*; *Quelle soie aux baumes*; passages in both *Hérodiade* and *L'Après-Midi d'un Faune*.

12. In a very early poem, *Le Château de l'Espérance*, which seems to be transcribed in *Quelle soie*, Mallarmé compares a woman's hair to the silk of a flag waving. in the sun. cf. B. Fleurot, *La chevelure vol d'une flamme*, Les Lettres, 1948, pp. 178-187.

13. What silk softened by time
    Where a figured monster is fading
    Is equal to the twisted native cloud
    Which you extend beyond your mirror!

    The holes of the meditative flags
    Are exultant in our street:
    But I have your naked hair
    Where I can press my contented eyes.

    No! The mouth will be sure
    Of tasting nothing in its bite,
    Unless your princely lover

    Makes expire like a diamond
    In the rich hair
    The cry of Glory he stiffles.

14. The hair flight of a flame in order to unwind it
    In the extreme Occident of desires
    Rests (I could say à diadem dying)
    On the crowned brow its former hearth

15. But without gold sighing that this living cloud
    Continues the igniting of the always inner fire
    Originally the only one
    In the jewels of the real and laughing eyes

16. The word, *nue*, is used in *Quelle soie* to designate the hair.

17. A tender hero's nakedness belittles
    The hair which—moving no starred or jewelled fingers
    Nothing but simplifying with glory the woman—
    Accomplishes with its head dazzlingly the exploit

    Of sowing with rubies the doubt it grazes
    Like a joyous and protective torch.

18. First published by Verlaine in *Hommes d'Aujourd'hui*, 1885. The definitive version, to which only two minute changes were to be made, appeared in the 1887 edition of *Poésies*. cf. article of Bonniot, *La Genèse Poétique de Mallarmé*, Revue de France, 15 April 1929.

19. Always more smiling at the more beautiful disaster,
    Sighs of blood, murderous gold, fainting, celebration!
    A thousandth time my solitary love
    With ardour prepared to conquer the tomb.

20. Victoriously fled the beautiful suicide
    Brand of glory, blood in foam, gold, tempest!
    O laughter if over there a purple prepares
    To extend royal my absent tomb.

21. Owned by Mlle Ch Lebey. cf. Pléiade edition, p. 1481.

22. What! from all that sunset, not even a dear shred
    Remains, it is midnight, in the poet's hand
    Except an over-playful treasure of a head
    Pouring into it its light diffused without a torch!

23. What! from all that brilliance not even a shred
    Tarries, it is midnight, in the darkness which welcomes us
    Except that a presumptuous treasure of a head
    Pours its caressed indifference without a torch.

24. Yours, ever so frivolous! it is yours,
    One token which holds from the vanished evenings
    Something of the sad struggle in arranging your hair

    With grace when on the cushions you place it
    Like a warrior helmet of an empress child
    From which, in order to depict you, roses would fall.

25. Yours ever such delight! yours
    Yes alone which withholds from the vanished sky
    A little childish triumph as you arrange your hair

    With light when etc.

26. All Pride of evening smokes,
    Torch stifled in a turn
    Without the immortal motion
    Making up for the abandonment!

27. The old room of the heir
Of many rich but fallen trophies
Would not even be heated
If he happened along the corridor.

28. Necessary anguish of the past
Seizing as with claws
The sepulchre of disavowal,

Under a heavy marble which it isolates
Is not lighted by any other fire
Save the shining table.

29. *le col ignoré* seems to be an Anglicism since the usual meaning of *ignorer* is 'not to know'.

30. Rising from the hump and the leap
Of an ephemeral glass
Without flowering the bitter evening
The ignored neck is interrupted.

31. I the sylph of this cold ceiling
Believe that two mouths never
Drank, my mother nor her lover,
From the same Chimera!

32. The pure vase of no potion
Which the endless widowhood
Slowly kills but does not consent,
Naive kiss of the most death-like!
To expend anything announcing
A rose in the darkness.

33. A lace is effaced
In the doubt of the supreme Game
By revealing as a blasphemy
The eternal absence of a bed.

This one white combat
Of a garland with itself
Pressed against the pale glass
Waves more than it enshrouds,

But in him who is gilded with the dream
Sadly sleeps a mandoline
With its empty hollowness of sound

Such as toward some window
From no womb but one's own
As a son one might be born.

34. My books, closed on the name of Paphos,
I play at choosing solely by means of my imagination
A ruin, blessed by a thousand specks of foam
Under the hyacinth blue, at a distance, of its triumphant days.

35.   I found standing
Only a symbolic gibbet where my image was hanging.

36. Let the cold come with its silences of a scythe,
I won't moan with empty lament
If this very white game level with the ground refuses
Every site the honour of the false landscape.

37. Before choosing *blanc*, Mallarmé hesitated between *pur* and *vierge*. *Pur* occurs in the *Revue Indépendante* publication. *Vierge*, in *L'Album de Vers et de Prose*, was changed to *blanc*, in the handwriting of Mallarmé in the text prepared for the edition of Deman.

38. My hunger which here is satisfied on no fruits
Finds in their learned absence an equal savour:
Let one of them human and sweet-smelling burst through its flesh!

My foot on some andiron where our love stirs the coals,
I think for a long time perhaps in ecstasy
Of the other one, of the burned breast of an ancient Amazon.

39. cf. Pléiade edition, pp. 857-58.

CHAPTER II

METAPHYSICS OF NIGHT

THE THEME of absence or vacuity furnishes Mallarmé, paradoxically, with his richest theme. It generates the other accompanying themes of impotency and artificiality. It relates the philosophical lesson of idealism to that of the emptying tomb of poets. Whether it be the image of a sunset sinking into its subsequent darkness or that of a clown plunging into the icy waters of a lake, the poems of Mallarmé deal consistently and successively with the vanishing of one kind of life into another. The ultimate seems always to be night. And the one illumination which characterizes man's fate is the light in darkness, the afterglow or the piercing ray coming at midnight and serving to define the vastness of the black. The frequently recurring words in Mallarmé of 'emptiness' (*vide*), 'abolish' (*abolir*), 'tomb' (*tombeau*), 'pure' (*pur*), 'absent' (*absent*) and the various negative locutions, are all signs of the perpetual preoccupation with the work of the artist which is a mysterious alchemy, successful only when death takes place. The meaning of night itself seems to have been taken as a clue by Mallarmé for the paradox of the artist's work, which becomes real when an absence is consummated. The purity of night, together with its quality of absoluteness, has its counterpart in the human soul, where we learn to know, darkly and dimly, strands and fragments of absolute truth.

Mallarmé consecrated this theme of night and made it into something very personal and unique in his own work. But he was born into a century of artists, many of whom were preoccupied with the same theme. Nerval, Poe, Baudelaire, Balzac, Goya, Delacroix and Daumier are all artists of a night world. And especially Baudelaire, whose tragedy is staged in darkness, whose experience of evil is projected throughout *Les Fleurs du Mal* by means of a symbolic and choreographic use of night.

Mallarmé discovered Baudelaire in 1861. *Les Fleurs du Mal*, published for the first time in 1857, was the only book of poems, with Poe's poems, which influenced Mallarmé's own writing to any profound and significant extent. The early poems are replete with

Baudelaire's vocabulary and images, and with at least one aspect of his theme of impotency. Mallarmé never met Baudelaire personally, and there was never any exchange of letters between the two poets. But throughout Mallarmé's career, long after he had evolved his own style and found his own voice, Baudelaire remained close to him and revered by him as the great source poet of the age. A letter of Mallarmé has been recently published[1] which was written to Villiers de l'Isle-Adam on the 30th of September 1867, one month after Baudelaire's death, and in which the poet seems to consider himself the successor to Baudelaire, at least in the domain of translator of Poe.

The dandyism of Baudelaire, which was infinitely more profound than a mere pose or attitude, was bequeathed to Mallarmé in a somewhat altered, but still recognizable, form. In its spiritual sense, Baudelaire's dandyism was the artist's heroism of concentration, the almost fatal need to adorn himself in so special and personal a way that he will be separated from all other men. The artist must be unique, or he has failed. He must discover the costume and the words which will mark him off from all other modes of attraction and communication. Dandyism is the effort to suppress all instinctive impulses and to forge a studied personality, to show to the world only the reflective and the critical thoughts. Originality has to be cultivated and prepared before it can be exhibited. The dandy is the aristocrat of the spirit because he is really the actor playing the role of critic.

Baudelaire believed that his character, his own being, when submitted to the scrutiny and the discipline worthy of a dandy, when trained and chastised by his highest critical faculties, would emerge infallible. As an artist, he applied the same principle to his work. But here, Mallarmé went even farther than Baudelaire. There is certainly something of the dandy in Mallarmé's composed and serene manner; in his speech, which so often was doctrinal exposition couched in a language well-nigh esoteric; in his general attitude of sage and high priest and martyr. But much more than Baudelaire, although here he was initiated and directed by the example of Baudelaire, Mallarmé became the dandy as artist. His poems are like distilled essences. He worked over them for years until they attained a degree of infallibility. If meticulousness of dress was for Baudelaire a sign of aristocracy and distinction of spirit, the verbal and exterior communication of a poem was for Mallarmé the symbol

Charles Baudelaire

of an idea and the artifice resulting from the effort to translate or adorn the idea.

Baudelaire was infinitely more isolated from human beings than Mallarmé. And he liked to consider his book as essentially useless. Distinctiveness for the dandy would lead to ostracism in a social sense and to esoterism in an aesthetic sense. Baudelaire was more successful in the first of these, in his remoteness from human beings, and Mallarmé in the second, in the hermetic quality of his published work. Mallarmé's early sonnet, *Angoisse*, originally entitled *A une putain*, is purely Baudelairian in theme and texture. The legend of the poem does not go farther than stating the moral dilemma of the anguish. Vice has marked the poet as well as the prostitute by its repetitive, and hence sterilizing, characteristics. The poet has grown to fear death (*Ayant peur de mourir lorsque je couche seul*), because of the particular understanding of death which sin has given him. The sonnet describes Baudelaire's world and his moral struggle. It relates to very little in Mallarmé's life, save his initial tendency to imitate Baudelaire. The moral connotation of sterility was soon transposed by Mallarmé into the artist's dread, first, of not being able to produce, and second, of all art's fundamental incapacity to translate the idea or the dream or the experience.

Angoisse, of very direct Baudelairian inspiration, was probably written about 1862.[2] Almost at the end of his life, in 1895, Mallarmé published his sonnet of homage, *Le Tombeau de Charles Baudelaire*[3] which is a mature expression of his art, containing all his idiosyncrasies of style. The sonnet is a uniquely Mallarmé piece, but it reveals the poet's essential role of critic. It stands by itself, in its own particular kind of beauty, but it bears, as does every great lyric, a terrifying weight of relationships with the past and the future, with Baudelaire, with all poets, and with man in general.

> *Le temple enseveli divulgue par la bouche*
> *Sépulcrale d'égout bavant boue et rubis*
> *Abominablement quelque idole Anubis*
> *Tout le museau flambé comme un aboi farouche*
>
> *Ou que le gaz récent torde la mèche louche*
> *Essuyeuse on le sait des opprobres subis*
> *Il allume hagard un immortel pubis*
> *Dont le vol selon le réverbère découche*

Quel feuillage séché dans les cités sans soir
Votif pourra bénir comme elle se rasseoir
Contre le marbre vainement de Baudelaire

Au voile qui la ceint absente avec frissons
Celle son Ombre même un poison tutélaire
Toujours à respirer si nous en périssons.[4]

First quatrain.—The temple, symbol of consecration, the place where time and eternity join, where man and the absolute discover their relationship, is revealed by a sewer mouth. Out from this aperture pour mud and rubies. The image of the hidden temple reveals the idol Anubis, god of death, composed of a man's body and a jackal's head. With smoke pouring out from its nostrils, as if it barked, an object to be worshipped. These four opening lines treat the problem of duality: the religious aspiration of man's life, on the one hand, and its crass realism, on the other. They depict the disproportion between the secret spiritual reality of man's heritage throughout the ages (one thinks here of ancient Egypt) and the immediate viciousness and imperfection of any given life, especially of Baudelaire's, where spleen (*boue*) and ideal (*rubis*) vied with one another. The calm, remote beginning (*le temple enseveli*) is soon covered up and forgotten by the harshness and heaviness of the excessive alliteration of *b*: *bouche, bavant boue et rubis abominablement, Anubis, aboi.* Thus the treasures of the spirit and our aspirations issue forth from us irreparably transformed by all our attendant vices. And for the poet especially, for any artist, there exists the vast chasm between the idea and its realization, the discrepancy which belabours him and opposes him and to which he submits rather than continue the strife. In the temple stands the hideous Anubis, so revolting when contrasted with the god it represents; and in the world stands the body of man, the vessel of purity and hope, now sullied, now mutilated and abused despite its spiritual alliance and its duty.

Second quatrain.—Follows, then, a picture of modern Paris, and particularly of Baudelaire's Paris: that is, night and streets now lighted for the first time by gas lamps. The wick in the lamps gives off a flickering flame because of the insults heaped on it. But we realize the insults were directed on what the flame illumines: the body of a prostitute. She is the walker in Baudelaire's nocturnal Paris, who goes from lamp to lamp and whose shadow moving down the street resembles the flight of a bird. The image comes to us clearly because of the adjective, *hagard*, a mediaeval word used in falconry and derived from *haga* or *haie*, the *hedge* where the pursued bird takes refuge from the falcon and, terrified, conceals itself in the branches. The statue of the idol, half-man and half-animal, belonging to antiquity, is replaced by its modern prototype, the prostitute, half-human and half-bird, who receives insults rather than prayers.

The tercets—Since the invention of gas and since the decline of prayerfulness and religious practice in the life of modern man, the nights have lost both their physical aspect of darkness and their spiritual significance. The shade of Baudelaire, returning to sit by its marble tomb, will not bless the withered wreath of flowers and leaves it may find there. The shade is the absence of the poet. Only a fluttering veil, which may well be a night shadow, suggests the returning shade. But even the shade of such a poet as Baudelaire was, is a poison which maintains our own maladies derived from his. Even if they ultimately cause our death, we breathe them in as we receive our very heritage.

Summary.—The many images of this sonnet combine with one another like the construction of a tomb itself on which a bas-relief would depict symbolically the achievements of a life. The images are grouped, and each group is dominated by one centralizing and fortifying image, which assumes the metaphorical strength and responsibility. First, the *Anubis*, the god of death, in the temple, whose mouth is open like a sewer's. The smoke from the temple sacrifice, coming out from the mouth and nostrils of the idol, is related to the image of the sewer, out of which oozes the mud incrusted with the lost gems of the city. The Anubis is the image of the poet's relationship with the Eternal. In the world of fictional freedom, Baudelaire was attached to God and immobilized by his thoughts on God. His response to God may at times have been that of a puppet (cf. *Au Lecteur*) and the cowering of a primitive child before the mystery of God. But Baudelaire knew profoundly the experience of religious aspiration and felt, as he did in other kinds of dramas, his incapacity to move out from the magnetic attraction to God. He was immobilized in the temple, not so much as a man is but as an idol is.

Second, the 'pubic bone', of the belly of the prostitute, with the concomitant images of the gas lamps, which illumine the body and the movement of flight down the street. Like the night scene of sacrifice in the temple, the body of the whore is stylized into a skeletal apparition, immortal, too, because the desire of the flesh is the other aspect of man's aspiration. It, too, is an image toward immortality. It, too, is a prayer, but of such subtlety and trickery that it may bend man toward the eternity of death rather than toward the immortalness of life.

Third, the 'poison' emanating from Baudelaire's shade. The night, in the image itself, is pervaded with it, as the poets of our contemporary world have been transformed by experiencing the form of Baudelaire's art, by smelling his flowers of evil. The paradox is vast and absolute. Art is at once human experience and the form given to it. And the particular beauty of tragic experience bears with it a deeper spiritual significance than any artistic depiction of attainment to holiness.

In all three images there is an alliance of horror and beauty, of what Baudelaire termed *spleen et idéal*: 1. the sewer mouth and the Anubis; 2. night opprobrium and the immortality of the pubic bone; 3. the fatal poison and the poet's shade. Mallarmé has used in the sonnet his favourite method of describing the poet: he has evoked the absence of the poet—the shade which is an effulgence, the leaf which has withered, the prostitute who has become a pubic bone and whose form disappears down the street as each lamp is lighted, the temple which has disappeared underground. The marble tomb, like the literary work itself, is but a fragile receptacle: it can hardly contain the spiritual reality of the poet. Night is the permanent symbol of the poet. Whether it be symbolized by the darkness underground of the buried temple or by the inclosed obscurity of the tomb, the signal greatness of Baudelaire, or of any comparable poet, is measured by his ability to live in the night, to see, to worship, to love, in the world of night.

Mallarmé's sonnet on Poe, another 'tomb' like that of Baudelaire, was read at Baltimore, on November 7, 1875, on the occasion of the unveiling of the poet's tombstone.[5]

The history of Poe's influence in France is totally unlike that of his influence in America. Baudelaire read the first French translations of Poe about 1846-47 and felt instantaneously that he had discovered a spiritual brother, a fraternal genius whose particular destiny in America helped him to understand his own in France. When Baudelaire read a translation of *The Black Cat* in *La Démocratic pacifique* of January 27, 1847, many of his aesthetic principles were

Edgar Allan Poe

already clear to him, but he sensed such a close affinity with Poe that he began a transformation of the life and works of the American that permitted him a self-identification with the poet on the other side of the Atlantic.

He discovered in Poe sentences that had been thought out by himself. In this shock of recognition, Poe's life grew to represent for Baudelaire a tragic duel between the poet and his country. Revolt was the only possible attitude for the artist. Alcohol and drugs provided a method of work for the genius and an escape from his hostile surroundings. But all this is slightly false. Poe was neither such a revolutionary nor such an alcoholic as Baudelaire made him appear to the French, and even to many Americans. The violence and deep sense of tragedy of Baudelaire's spirit were not in Poe. The French poet did not deliberately falsify the facts of Poe's character, but he practised a wilful obsession to see himself in Poe.

In the realm of aesthetics, it is beyond doubt that Baudelaire owed much to the American. Baudelaire's translations of Poe actually created a new artistic movement in France. *The Poetic Principle,* a lecture which Poe delivered twice in November 1848, in Providence, Rhode Island, and in Lowell, Massachusetts, is the main source for the aesthetics of 'pure poetry'. This lecture, unheeded in America, became in France a manifesto for the poets. Baudelaire was its illustrator and champion.

The main ideas in *The Poetic Principle,* which Baudelaire incorporated in his aesthetics, having already felt them to some degree before knowing Poe, might be stated under three headings. First, since the beautiful is perceived only fleetingly and fragmentarily, the poem, which is the fragile receptacle for this perception of the beautiful, must be brief. The poet's thought must be cast into a condensed image. Second, the didactic is non-poetic. There exists a basic incompatibility between poetry and practical usefulness. Boston puritanism had made poetry resemble sermons destined to edify and instruct. Poe opposed this in his cult for pure beauty (even if there might be a transcendental moral in it). Third, the beauty in a poem offers a means for spiritual perception or awareness. Through poetry we can perceive the beauty of the spiritual universe. The poet is a translator. Both Poe and Baudelaire had studied Swedenborg's system of correspondences, in which the material world is considered a key to the spiritual world. Poetry is therefore, according to Poe's poetic principle, the 'rhythmical creation of beauty'. It is the revelation of a world existing outside the logical rules of reason. *Le principe de la poésie est l'aspiration humaine vers une Beauté supérieure et la manifestation de ce principe dans un enthousiasme, un enlèvement de l'âme,* Baudelaire writes in his *Art Romantique.*

Many of these theories are in Baudelaire's *Salon* of 1846, written before he had discovered Poe. But the American helped to give precision and force to Baudelaire's tendencies. He helped the French poet to separate himself from the theories of Gautier, Banville and Ménard. Such phrases as these, from *Marginalia,* must have been dear to Baudelaire, and later to Mallarmé: 'I know that indefiniteness is an element of the true music—I mean of the true musical expression. Give it any undue decision—imbue it with any very determinate tone—and you deprive it, at once, of its ethereal, its ideal, its intrinsic and essential character.'[6] And the sentence, 'I believe that odours have an altogether peculiar force, in affecting us through association.'[7] It is true that Poe's sentimentalism was vastly different from Baudelaire's sensuous realism, but the latter's deep need of finding himself in someone else justified that somewhat fictional Poe he created.

Mallarmé continued Baudelaire's cult of Poe and derived from the example of the American a lesson nearer the actual truth. Temperamentally, Mallarmé was closer to Poe than Baudelaire was. Although he accepted Baudelaire's two explanations for Poe's drunkenness (an effort, first, to escape from the horror of his destiny and, second, to attain a spiritual vision), he saw in Poe the image of his own flat and pale bourgeois existence. Like Poe, Mallarmé believed in the alliance between poetry and the arts and in the secret meaning of the world. Both Poe and Mallarmé relegated passion to an obscure position in their cosmos. The purity of ideas and symbols and Poe's atmosphere of supernatural strangeness are in the poetry of Mallarmé (especially in *Prose pour des Esseintes*). The preciosity of tombs and deathlike objects, unusual and rare words, themes of sterility and obscurity, are in Poe in some degree, and in Mallarmé in a degree that is all-important.

LE TOMBEAU D'EDGAR POE

Tel qu'en Lui-même enfin l'éternité le change,
Le Poète suscite avec un glaive nu
Son siècle épouvanté de n'avoir pas connu
Que la mort triomphait dans cette voix étrange!

Eux, comme un vil sursaut d'hydre oyant jadis l'ange
Donner un sens plus pur aux mots de la tribu
Proclamèrent très haut le sortilège bu
Dans le flot sans honneur de quelque noir mélange.

Du sol et de la nue hostiles, ô grief!
Si notre idée avec ne sculpte un bas-relief
Dont la tombe de Poe éblouissante s'orne

Calme bloc ici-bas chu d'un désastre obscur
Que ce granit du moins montre à jamais sa borne
Aux noirs vols du Blasphème épars dans le futur.[8]

First quatrain.—The opening line, perhaps the most celebrated single line of Mallarmé and the most quoted and used in contemporary criticism, is, when taken singly, an entire sermon or discourse on the fate and the function of the poet. This succinct and condensed statement, which here Mallarmé applies to the individual fate of Poe, the object of his celebration in verse, might well be applied to himself and to any poet. Its theme is the universality of the poet's fate, the hostility and the lack of comprehension of the artist's time. The living accept the mediocre man who tells them what they wish to hear. Only the future generation will read and understand the poet who is superior.[9] 'Eternity' in this passage is time, all that time beyond the lifetime of the poet, when he will exist not in his body and temperament and individuality but in his work, which becomes absolute only at the death of its creator. That is death's triumph; the passing of the poet is the event which makes his voice complete. The poet is like an angel, and his work is like a bared and flaming sword. After his generation has passed, this angel with the sword, like a magician with a wand, can resurrect a century which once was terrified at not having recognized its real voice. The age, without its poet, is inexplicable and unjustified. This quatrain contains Mallarmé's central philosophy or doctine on the poet. An absolute statement in itself, it might serve as introduction to all the poems of Mallarmé and to the work of all the poets. It is almost the condensation of one hundred years' thinking about the poet, about the strange alchemy of time, which ends by revealing the true stature of a poem and which illumines the images of his poetry. The poet himself, during his own lifetime, could not behold that luminosity, which is always future.

Second quatrain.—'They' are the contemporaries of Poe, who incapable of understanding the poet, made him into a pariah and ostracized him from society. The image of Mallarmé is just, because the strangeness of Poe is not in his life (as Baudelaire might have stated) but in his work, in the words, the recognizable familiar words in everyone's speech, which the poet used in so particular a way that they revealed a new purity. Like an angel, Poe instructed his generation in the original purity of words, but they loudly called his art witchcraft and the raving of a drunken poet.[10] They seized upon a weakness in his personal life and used it to explicate and denounce an art which lay beyond their sensitivity. How could an angel or a prophet, clothed in his habitual whiteness, rise up in the body of a man who had lost himself in the black potency of alcohol?

Tercets.—A strong vibrant line opens the tercets forming the second part of the poem and parallels the initial line of the sonnet. This is a song of grievance and accusation. Great opposing forces of matter and spirit, of the earth and of the clouds, are at war in every man, but to an extraordinary degree in the poet, who is able to give voice to the hostility. The old mediaeval debate between the body and the soul, which Villon wrote in the 15th century, is in Poe, too, particularized by his moment in history. Mallarmé evokes this grievance, this source of personal tragedy and art, as one other poet whose life-history and lifework may add to Poe's tomb one more legend or figure. The literal stone of the monument seems to have fallen from the sky itself. It was once a star (*aster*), a flamingly brilliant life. Now it is a cold, hard substance (*disaster*), having fallen from its orbit. The work of a poet always forms at a great distance from the earth and then, when transmitted, becomes fixed and cold in its durable form. The granite, so established on the earth as a testimony and marking place, may, as its slightest function, reveal to mankind what was sacrificed to blasphemy and accusation against the creative spirit of one age. In the future, when this spirit of blasphemy is again aroused, it will see, as if it were a bird of prey in the heavens, this tomb of Poe, a permanent reminder of one of its past victories.

Summary.—Commencing with the word, 'eternity', and concluding with the word, 'future', the sonnet on Poe invokes the drama of time, which, first, at the moment of the poet's death makes absolute his poetic work and which, second, initiates the period of no termination when the meaning and the power of the work develop and change as the work, rendered absolute, is comprehended or rejected or reflected in the poetic consciousness of each succeeding temporal period. The poet's tomb is the poet's life. The final physical immobility coincides with the adventure of communication which a work of art must endure and risk. The strange words spoken by the poet to his own age are the only ones which future ages will remember and hear. The once incomprehensible becomes in time the revelatory. The years interpret the poet's message and unveil his art. After all, he had used the words of his own people, but language is a combination of words, and they must cohabit a long time, in a metaphorical bond, before they yield their simplicity.

So concealed and unrecognizable is purity, at first, that it has to be matched by a pure kind of contemplation. The pivotal metaphor of the sonnet on Poe is the stone tomb, the block of granite which may have fallen from the sky when the meteor of fire burned out its course through space. The hardened matter, fixed in the earth's surface like a boundary mark, on which the words and the figures of a legend are engraved, was once a burning substance in time, comparable to the living body of a man. Both bodies rushed toward an eternal immobility. The body in the tomb and the experience in the verse attain a state of absoluteness after their race through the night.

The night imagery of these two sonnets is that of an expansive exterior night. For Baudelaire's tomb the scene is, first, a city street and then a vaguely defined area by the marble monument, where the poet's ghost returns only to find the coolness of the earth and the withered flowers and the lack of prayerfulness in the night that was once his prayer. For Poe's tomb the scene is the endless hostility between the earth and the sky, in the centre of which the granite block shines, but in a darkness from which it has fallen, through some astrological or fatalistic law. The expanse of blackness, so threateningly exposed in the final line of the sonnet, obscures the human drama unfolding both on the earth and in the skies.

The expense and the expanse of night are images suited in each case to designate the drama of the dead poet. The stars in the sky and the stars fallen from the sky (*désastre*) describe the life-cycle of the poet and the work's culmination. The night setting, particularly that which is endless and shapeless, is the metaphorical equivalent of the poet's vain search for a place in his world, as well as the search for his work, for the cosmos created by the power of words.

73

Mallarmé, by the persistent use he makes of this imagery, implies that this poet's cosmos, constructed with words, is, at best, tenebrific; is at best the mere shadow cast by the unformed work in the poet's mind.

Thus are established the Baudelairian-Swedenborgian correspondences. As the world bears a spiritual analogy with heaven, so night teaches, by negation, the meaning of day. We see darkly in the imperfect light, which is the absence of day. The dream of the poet, his creative idea, clings to him and threatens him like the obscuration of night. The creative idea has no position in space because it lives like a desire. It is always ready to disappear: night would welcome and consummate its dissolution. If the idea of the poem did vanish, before becoming a poem in words, it would mount to the starry garlands in the sky or to some comparable distance, where it would become just barely visible, as some diminished memory, to the lonely poet.

Night is a celebration. But the celebration is invisible to the man who inhabits the night. In the tercets of Mallarmé's sonnet, *Quand l'ombre menaça de la fatale loi*,[11] the poet evokes the dazzling light which the earth must manifest at a tremendous distance from itself when it is still covered with the darkness of night.

> *Oui, je sais qu'au lointain de cette nuit, la Terre*
> *Jette d'un grand éclat l'insolite mystère*
> *Sous les siècles hideux qui l'obscurcissent moins.*[12]

But this natural and physical celebration of night, carried on at a vast distance from the earth, serves as a setting for another celebration, that of the poetic genius. The fires of a star or the light of the earth seen as a star is nothing by comparison with the radiancy of a genius.

> *L'espace à soi pareil qu'il s'accroisse ou se nie*
> *Roule dans cet ennui des feux vils pour témoins*
> *Que s'est d'un astre en fête allumé le génie.*[13]

By the phrase, *le génie d'un astre*, Mallarmé creates an analogy between the time it takes the light of a star to reach the earth and the time needed for an artistic work to grow into a visible reality for men. If the age when a genius lived does not perceive his work, succeeding ages may see more clearly.

A poetic creation is a struggle against night. Because night has the power of pervasiveness, of limitlessness, of formlessness (*vaste comme la nuit*), the work of art, conceived in an atmosphere hostile to itself, must oppose all these qualities of night by its need of condensation and form. Night is a macrocosm: temporally and spacially extending for ever and everywhere. A poem is a microcosm completed, condensed, reserved. They move in different directions: night, outward and beyond all limits; the poem, inward toward the limitation of words and the compression of meanings.

One of Mallarmé's most achieved sonnets, *Tombeau*, written to celebrate the first anniversary of Verlaine's death, January 1897, which was just a year before Mallarmé's own death, contains a brilliantly conceived combination of the themes of night, the poet, and the poetic work. This is almost the last poem Mallarmé wrote, and in it he is still concerned with the aspect of exterior night which floods all space. Almost all the elements are familiar, having appeared in the earlier sonnets on Baudelaire and Poe: the stone itself of the tomb, the star, the public. But there is, in the testimonial to Verlaine, a new conception of movement and flight through the darkness. The waywardness of Verlaine's life is symbolized by the rolling rock of his tomb. This rock has taken on the aspect of human woes and will not stop in its motion, even if pious hands touch it in order to feel the legends of disaster engraved on it and to bless it as if it were a mould of human fate.

> *Le noir roc courroucé que la bise le roule*
> *Ne s'arrêtera ni sous de pieuses mains*
> *Tâtant sa ressemblance avec les maux humains*
> *Comme pour en bénir quelque funeste moule.*[14]

The second quatrain condenses the three sonnets heretofore discussed. In the night scene, if the voice from the branches (that is, the voice of nature, which is the poet's voice) continues to speak, the darkness itself (that is, the sign of mourning) will hide by its shadows the luminosity of the poet's work (that is, luminosity for the future, when the work can be seen in perspective) and, from the light growing with time, some ray will be appropriated from the world of men who, at first, denied it.

> *Ici presque toujours si le ramier roucoule*
> *Cet immatériel deuil opprime de maints*
> *Nubiles plis l'astre mûri des lendemains*
> *Dont un scintillement argentera la foule.*[15]

The two tercets amplify the first line of the sonnet by contrasting the vagabondage of Verlaine's real life with the flight adventure of his work through the world after the poet's literal death. After the initial question, 'Who now looks for Verlaine by following the footsteps of his solitary life?' comes the answer, 'He is hidden in the grass.' Which seems to mean: he is continuing his existence even after death. His work is like the surface of the shallow river, which bears the reflection of his face. The river of death, the Lethe river of extinction or oblivion, has been slandered because the lips reflected therein, like those of Narcissus, even if they do not drink of the water, will remain in fixed immobility. The reflected face, which is comparable to the poetic creation, henceforth steadfast in time, is in profound harmony with death, which has made possible the final achievement. The ultimate simplicity or naiveté is thus attained by death which is the eternalization of a lifework. The artist does not drink of the river of death, as an ordinary man does; he looks into it and thus he is able to continue his existence in an extraordinary mode, after the accident of death. Verlaine, in the sonnet, is not buried, and he has not drunk of the river of death. After all, death is a shallow river, grossly slandered.

> Qui cherche, parcourant le solitaire bond
> Tantôt extérieur de notre vagabond—
> Verlaine? Il est caché parmi l'herbe, Verlaine
>
> A ne surprendre que naïvement d'accord
> La lèvre sans y boire ou tarir son haleine
> Un peu profond ruisseau calomnié la mort.[16]

This sonnet to Verlaine is not so strong a unity in itself as it is a composition uniting all the sonnets on the 'dark night' of the poet. The rolling rock of the first quatrain, which bears all the marks of human woe and deepens them as it continues its career through time, becomes, in the second quatrain, the constellation expending its light throughout the future and, in the tercets, becomes the river, not of death, but of Narcissus. It is a sonnet of three symbols: rock, star, water, all of which symbolize the work of the poet and are characterized by movement through time and space.

The four Mallarmé sonnets, which illustrate the 'dark night' of the poet, all describe the immensity and formlessness of night. That is the ambiency and the challenge of the artist, who, out of formlessness, must create form. In each sonnet there is allusion to a tomb or

funeral monument which, as if it were a stage property, is illuminated by some sharp distant light. In the sonnet on Baudelaire, the
tomb is marble, and the light falls, at some distance away, from the
gas lamps which line the street. The sonnet on Poe describes the
monument as being of granite but also as having fallen from the sky
as if at one time it had been part of a meteor. In the sonnet beginning, *Quand l'ombre menaça*, the sky itself is black and tomblike,
but from its zenith a star radiates its light (*astre en fête*). And, finally,
in the sonnet on Verlaine, where the rock of the tomb is constantly
moving, the matured star (*astre mûri*) appears fixed in the sky.

But in each of the poems the poet himself is evoked as well as his
tomb. For Baudelaire, it is the ghost whose breath is poisonous as if
the spirit of evil continued in his work. For Poe, it is the poet with
a bare sword who continues to play, even after death, the role of
man in revolt. In the sonnet, *Quand l'ombre menaça*, the poet appears
as a solitary figure dazzled with his own faith; and in the sonnet to
Verlaine, the poet is a kind of Narcissus, reflecting himself in the
waters of a river.

Darkness spreads everywhere throughout these four 'tombs' or
'nights', and the four figures of the poet stand alone in the midst of
the darkness as if they were the only principle of unity or order.
Night, because of its vastness, seems to become in the Mallarmé
sonnets the symbol of chaos; and the poet, because of his work to be
achieved or already achieved, represents the opposing symbol of
order. Creation is a struggle against night but must inexorably take
place within night. Even when the conscience of a particular poet is
destroyed, in the event of his death, his works preserve the conscience
or the meaning of night which he had experienced. The obscurity of
a work of art is only a little less obscure than the darkness in which
it was conceived.

Each of the night sonnets of Mallarmé is an example of a self-con-
tained vast world. Each translates some aspect of the depth of night
and provides at the same time, by the determined boundaries of the
sonnet form, a limitation of night, a framework for its experience.
It is curious how the concept of night, in a poem or in a painting,
has to be outlined, and often transfixed, with light and colour. The
sonnet beginning with the words, *Ses purs ongles,* is built around the
light-filled and light-growing expansiveness of night. It is one of the
most remarkably wrought of the night sonnets, in that, what appears
in the opening quatrain as the human experience of anguish, moves

out, by the end of the poem, into the experience of night where it is diluted or metamorphosed into the expansiveness of the sky and the constellations rising there.

This is one of the two or three poems which Mallarmé has himself commented on explicitly. Yet his statements have far more to do with the origin of the sonnet, with the original idea of the piece than with the finished sonnet. The opening quatrain contains a personification of night which may well be one of the important clues to Mallarmé's preoccupation with the entire theme.

> *Ses purs ongles très haut dédiant leur onyx,*
> *L'Angoisse, ce minuit, soutient, lampadophore,*
> *Maint rêve vespéral brûlé par le Phénix*
> *Que ne recueille pas de cinéraire amphore.*[17]

The torchbearer, a Greek personage, holds above his head his hands whose nails reflect the blackness of night. This solitary figure personifies Anguish because his dreams have been burned out by the sun (Phoenix) which in their disappearance leave no trace. The descent of night over the earth joins with the dreams of the poet as they rise up to meet it, and of their commingling no trace remains. The word, 'Anguish', has a strong Baudelairian connotation in this context, but the image itself, or the personification, is Mallarmean. A torchbearer at night holds up his hands with no torch in them, and what he supports is a void created by the dreams that have been burned so completely that no ashes remain. The solitary figure has no memory because the evening dreams have merged with the night itself. The same image of emptiness and useless extension exists in the earliest version of the sonnet, of 1868[18] where the evening is described as being abolished by the sun and the night approving of its total emptiness.[19]

The second quatrain, especially in its rhymes, repeats the Greek overtones of the first quatrain: *onyx, lampadophore, Phénix, amphore.* But the dominant character of the torchbearer disappears, and one visits an empty room.

> *Sur les crédences, au salon vide: nul ptyx,*
> *Aboli bibelot d'inanité sonore,*
> *(Car le Maître est allé puiser des pleurs au Styx*
> *Avec ce seul objet dont le Néant s'honore.)*[20]

So far has the theme of emptiness progressed, that the entire stanza concerns an object that is not even in the room. The salon is empty and no *ptyx* is on the tables. When Mallarmé used the word in the first version of the sonnet, he didn't know what it meant. It was a rhyme. He asked his friend, Lefébure,[21] to discover the meaning of the word, but he preferred that it have no meaning and exist in the poem by its sound alone. Since a poem is created by its need of sound and imagery, there is no reason why a single word shouldn't come into existence by the poem's need for it. But much effort has been spent on finding a meaning for *ptyx*. Its original Greek meaning is 'fold', and by extension can signify a conch shell, the kind of shell which, if held up to the ear, like a portable radio, resounds with the murmur of the sea. The fortuitousness of the word is therefore exceptional because of the verse in apposition, where Mallarmé called it, in the early version of 1868, *Insolite vaisseau d'inanité sonore.*[22] The first two words of the line finally became *Aboli bibelot,* more precise and more applicable to the meaning of shell. The salon is empty, the shell is empty, and the shell is not even in the salon. The Poet has left his room and has descended to the Styx, river in Hades, where he is trying to fill the shell with tears. Hell is the absence of living and is honoured by such an object as a shell. With the opening words of *crédences* and *salon*, we leave the faintly suggested Greek world of the *lampadophore* and seem to be in Mallarmé's own room. But the reign of night confuses time. The *ptyx* itself contains the sound of centuries, and the master poet of the 19th century, when his absence is actually described, stands like a shadowy figure of antiquity by a river of the underworld. As the shell contains the sea sound of past centuries, so it is used by the Poet to draw up water from the Styx, formed by the tears of all those who have lived and died in the imprisonment of eternity. But the ocean and the river which flows into it remain in the emptiness of the conch shell.

The Poet finds himself at the river of death at the precise moment of midnight, the time when the states of being and non-being seem to fuse. The unusual quality of the entire sonnet comes from the paradox of presence and absence. We are told that the Poet is not in his room, and yet it is he who describes it and who in the tercets sees it invested with a special kind of life and colour and movement.

> *Mais proche la croisée au nord vacante, un or*
> *Agonise selon peut-être le décor*
> *Des licornes ruant du feu contre une nixe,*[23]

If the room has emptied itself of presences, it has become alive with the reflections of light in a mirror which stands near to an opened window. The 'gold' shining there (and diminishing in its intensity) might be a dying fire or a metal ornament or even the light of the stars outside. Whatever it is, it shows in some ornamentation the picture of unicorns attacking a nymph. The 'fire' may be in their spirited action or in the literal hearth.

> *Elle, défunte nue en le miroir, encor*
> *Que, dans l'oubli fermé par le cadre, se fixe*
> *De scintillations sitôt le septuor.*[24]

The naked nymph appears dead because she is seen only as a reflection in the mirror. A mirror is a perfect symbol of emptiness, of oblivion. It is a framed void, but contains the reflection of two movements: the unicorns' attack on the nymph, which transpires within the room; and the mounting of the seven constellations of the Big Dipper, which transpires outside of the room, in the Northern sky. Thus, by the end of the poem, even the emptiness of the room recedes, and we are left with the mirrored reflection of two kinds of light, one inside and the other outside the room. The semblance of a human figure, with which the sonnet begins, has been suppressed. The Poet, referred to as an absent figure in an unreal setting, has also disappeared, and all that remains is a reflection of furniture and stars.

Mallarmé himself has described, in a letter of exceptional precision, the effect he wanted to produce in this sonnet. The particular kind of night, which is the subject of the poem, is one composed of absences and questionings. No furniture is described, but there is the suggestion of forms and a fading frame of a mirror containing the stellar reflection of the Big Dipper which provides a bond between the abandoned room and the sky.[25]

Ses purs ongles is a sonnet of exceptional poetic rigour. It provides the picture of a void reflecting the universe. In the profoundest sense, it is a poem about poetry, about the power and the plenitude of speech. The final image of the septet of constellations mounting in the sky is analogous to the mounting of words to the consciousness of the poet, or the renascence of the idea. The poem, in fact, opens with a similar movement of the torchbearer holding up high his onyx-coloured fingernails. And yet, despite this opening and concluding image of dedication (*dédiant*) and stellar illumination (*se fixe*), the sonnet is perfectly organized around three images of vacuity. First, the torchbearer (*lampadophore*), whose flame at midnight seems to be extinguished, because his nails have the colour of blackness and the evening dreams he supported have been burned out by the extinct sun. Second, the shell (*ptyx*), empty of the sea animal it once sheltered, resounding with the past murmur of the ocean, and no longer in place on the table. Third, the mirror reflecting scenes thanks to some dying light from the fire and some mounting light from the sky.

The anguish of the Master, whatever its origin in the Baudelairian sense of personal frustration and closed-in hopelessness, has become in *Ses purs ongles* the Mallarmean anguish of poetic creation. This was of course also an ingredient in Baudelaire's anguish, but with Mallarmé it becomes the permanent personal drama, the spectre of the poet's imagination. It is most real when the feeling of sterility is the most complete in the artist, and yet the poet seems to arise from the most perfect void. The image of the Phoenix at the beginning of the poem is closely associated with the torchbearer. Whether it be interpreted as the fabulous bird rising from its ashes only to be burned again after a certain time, or as the sun itself rising in the sky toward its maximum light and then sinking into darkness, it conveys the idea of a poem mounting toward its complete form and significance out of a seeming emptiness and lack of form.

The picture of the poet's room, emptied of presences and objects, is reminiscent of the effect obtained by Keats in his *Ode to a Grecian Urn* where the description of absence has the power of evoking its opposite, life and animation, a peopled town: 'What little town is emptied of this folk?' In both the sonnet and the ode, absence becomes a very positive and real quality, and the reader is given the experience of fullness.

If the idea of a poem has its origin in the poet's total subconsciousness (which would correspond to the picture of night emptiness), its realization or the actual composing of the poem takes place in the poet's total consciousness when he is fully aware of all poetic devices and word values. And this second part would correspond to the power we feel in the sonnet itself even if it is built around images of the void. To know the complete meaning of an object, we have to destroy it. For the Phoenix to rise in its full feathered glory, it had first to be consumed and reduced to ashes. The idea of a poem first appears in the form of ruins, of fragmentary débris, before its images may be fabricated artfully and wilfully by the poet. A poem is always a union between the poet and the word, but the word is the absence of the thing it designates, and the poem is therefore the poet's entrance into a kind of night or hollowness where he becomes prisoner. By leaving his room where he was first a prisoner, Mallarmé becomes a prisoner of his own poem.

In each of his sonnets on the creative genius, Mallarmé seems to examine his problems by means of the concept of darkness. Almost in the role of an astrologer, he looks into the night sky and in the blackness with which the sky covers the earth, as if there he will discover a precious correlation between the physical black of night and the dark secret of language and artistic expression. In each sonnet, a total image of blackness provides a solid background: 'the buried temple' (*le temple enseveli*) in the poem on Baudelaire; 'the black waves of blasphemy' (*noirs vols de blasphème*) in the poem on Poe; 'the funereal ceilings' (*les plafonds funèbres*) where the Poet's dream perishes, in *Quand l'ombre menaça* 'the black rock' (*Le noir roc*) of Verlaine's *Tombeau;* the Master-Poet by the shores of the Styx in *Ses purs ongles*. The preoccupation seems always to be with the threatening aspect of night. And yet in each of these sonnets some image of light divides or traverses the night. The black is more absolute or the work is more mysterious thanks to the intervention of a flash of light: the rubies and the gaslight in the sonnet on Baudelaire; the dazzling tomb (*la tombe de Poe éblouissante*) in the apotheosis on the American poet; the great burst of light (*un grand éclat*) thrown out by the earth in *Quand l'ombre menaça;* the shimmering (*un scintillement argentera la foule*) of Verlaine's future star; the shining septet of stars (*De scintillations sitôt le septuor*), reflected in the mirror of the empty room.

An almost identical principle is followed by Mallarmé in his *Hommage* to Wagner,[26] written also in the form of a sonnet. Its total effect has perhaps less strength in the coupling of night with the genius than the other pieces, but its organization and imagery follow the same pattern and point to the same conclusion.

Wagner had occupied a central position in Mallarmé's meditations on the theatre and modern art. The sonnet, which contains more difficulties than most, represents to a more marked degree than ever, a tremendous ellipsis. The first quatrain is a unified image but behind it one senses a lifetime of reflection on the history and the art of the theatre.

Le silence déjà funèbre d'une moire
Dispose plus qu'un pli seul sur le mobilier
Que doit un tassement du principal pilier
Précipiter avec le manque de mémoire.[27]

The silence of an empty theatre whose stage appears spectre-like with covered furniture will enter a still deeper silence when the building collapses and a generation passes. The single word, *pilier*, might justify the interpretation of a theatre, and the single word of its rhyme, *mobilier*, might justify the interpretation of the 'realist' stage which the advent of Wagner was to change. But at least the stanza is built around the darkness of a building and the presentiment of oblivion.

The second quatrain calls attention to the art of the poet and precisely that art destined for dramatic use.

Notre si vieil ébat triomphal du grimoire,
Hiéroglyphes dont s'exalte le millier
A propager de l'aile un frisson familier!
Enfouissez-le moi plutôt dans une armoire.[28]

This is Mallarmé's private vocabulary for poetic speech: a poem seen as a linguistic tournament which continues for years (*notre si vieil ébat triomphal*); poetry which first appears as the strange characters and condensed formulas of a sorcerer's book (*grimoire—hiéroglyphes*). But when he evokes the crowd of spectators excited by the poetry (*dont s'exalte le millier*) who feel in it a familiar resonance transmitted by the voice of the actors, we realize that he is thinking more specifically of dramatic art than of his own poems. He seems to refer to an old work which he prefers to see put away in a closet as if it were no longer appropriate for a contemporary presentation. After evoking the darkness of the theatre in the first quatrain, Mallarmé evokes in the second quatrain the darkness of a book no longer capable of illuminating. The two stanzas prepare the advent of the new god, Richard Wagner, who is the subject of the tercets.

The two concepts of theatre and book are joined in the particular art of Wagner which acts as a light piercing the darkness of colder and obscurer forms.

Du souriant fracas originel haï
Entre elles de clartés maîtresses a jailli
Jusque vers un parvis né pour leur simulacre,

Trompettes tout haut d'or pâmé sur les vélins,
Le dieu Richard Wagner irradiant un sacre
Mal tu par l'encre même en sanglots sibyllins.[29]

The legend of Wagner and his moment typifies the genius, detested at first by his predecessors and his early public (*fracas originel* might be the theatre public as well as the music played in Paris when Wagner first came there). But the new art is a new light (*clartés maîtresses*) and it is destined for the theatre. There the actual performance, in the high piercing sound of trumpets, will consecrate the art contained in books. The ancient stories on velum, re-written with the fresh ink of the new genius, will relive in the sounds of Wagner's music, secretive still in its newness. Poetry and music are joined in the new art of the theatre. The first blackness of the empty theatre and of the old poetry to be kept in a closet is replaced by the obscurity of Wagner, which is not literal darkness but sibylline mysteriousness. The critic, Charles Mauron, has pointed out[30] how the word, *sanglot*, for Mallarmé, here applied to Wagner's music, is always associated with the concept of paradise and ecstasy. The hieroglyphic aspect of art, whether it be ancient manuscripts or the writing of contemporary artists, has to be translated by performance in order for it to reveal its beauty.

The world is a dark place for the genius. The image of the darkened funereal stage in the sonnet on Wagner is comparable to the buried temple in the sonnet on Baudelaire. The gaslight in Baudelaire's modern Paris is sufficient to illuminate the night pictures of the city, as the high pitched trumpets in Wagner's music transmit and illuminate with their gold the stories once consigned to ancient books. Wagner, who was the uncontested master of the French symbolist movement, left in his *Lettre sur la Musique* doctrines studied and explored by the poets. His belief that poetry is a substitute of the abstract conventional value of words for their original and sensual meaning[31] might be applicable to the most difficult line of the Mallarmé sonnet:

Trompettes tout haut d'or pâmé sur les vélins.

in which a correspondence is established between the book (*vélins*) and the music (*Trompettes*), between the obscurity of an art fallen into disuse and the piercing light of its rediscovery and renewal. The black sky of the other sonnets and the dark tomb is in the *Hommage* to Wagner transcribed by the image of the darkened theatre. The element of darkness, in every case, whether it be the sky or the tomb or the theatre, is waiting for the future art which will bring that kind of light capable of giving depth and validity to the darkness itself.

There is physical darkness in the world: the fall of night and the extinguishing of light; and there is also mental darkness: intoxication, ecstasy, sleep. Night may be conceived of as a maternal encompassing force or as the blinding experience of love. It might well typify the sadness of a world which is unknowable and unredeemable. Night is the picture of death and the sign of the end of all things when darkness will encompass the universe. In its experience we know something of the chaos which must have preceded the Creation. All creations of men are a struggle against the power of night and the power of dissolution. Night is a terrifying ordeal because in it the vision of the world disappears and man is forced to turn into himself, to effect the tremendous distance between the macrocosm of the universe and the microcosm of the heart and to accomplish thus a strange allegory which is nothing less than the allegory of death itself.

During the day man is supported by the vision of the universe when he can move out of himself in contemplation of the beauty of appearance and forms. But the advent of night limits him drastically. His only realities then are his dreams outside of which everything has dissolved. Mallarmé, and every other artist who has felt as intensively as he the anguish of the void, knows that the only way for him to bear such an experience, is the use and the creation of the word. He knows that the power of the word is that of Creation itself. The power of the word is that of calling into existence. The word is associated with life, with all that opposes dissolution and night. The word contains the very concept of becoming, of growth and expansion. It is the defeat of death and the beginning of eternity.

The role of poet as creator of the word contains always something of the philosopher and the mystic, and Mallarmé, without being in any real sense a philosopher or a mystic, strove in his consciousness of night toward a very high degree of development, toward what might justifiably be called a metaphysical and cosmic development. In each of the night sonnets we witness a celebration of death. That is the immediate use of the night symbol. The one who has died is always the master or the poet. But the living poet who is celebrating death is also in each sonnet, vigilant in the darkness he describes, overcome by the feeling of strangeness in the very celebration he is performing. Through the anguish of the living poet, generated by the half-articulated questions on being he asks, every object takes on a strange primitive appearance. The world has been modified, first in the descent of night, and then in the tiny flames and shafts of light which traverse it, and which seem to designate the cosmic anguish of a solitary man. The gaslight flame in the city murkiness of the sonnet on Baudelaire, for example, seems to be allied with the religious sentiment in its modern form of diminished power. The great poetic voice speaks of death and that is what terrifies the world, according to the sonnet on Poe. In the darkness the poet does see something, even if it is the vaguest outline of a cosmic catastrophe, and that vision is his fearful lucidity. He sees and measures in the light of a small flame which is his genius trying to pierce the value and meaning of existence.

NOTES ON CHAPTER II

1. H. Mondor, *Sur une lettre de Mallarmé, Revue de Paris*, Nov., 1948. 'Vous aurez dans l'un des premiers numéros quelques poèmes de Poe auxquels je me remet-trai: j'accepte cette tâche comme un legs de Baudelaire.'

2. First published in *Le Parnasse Contemporain*, May 12, 1866, under the title, *A celle qui est tranquille.*

3. First published in *La Plume*, 15 Jan., 1895.

4. The buried temple divulges through the sepulchral
   Mouth of a sewer drooling mud and rubies
   Abominably some Anubis idol
   Its whole muzzle aflame like a wild bark

   Or the recent gas twists the squint-eyed wick
   Which has been submitted to countless insults
   And illumines terrified an immortal pubic bone
   Whose flight moves from lamp-post to lamp-post

   What dried leaves in the cities without votive
   Night will bless the shade as it sits down
   Vainly against the marble of Baudelaire

   In the fluttering veil which covers it absent
   For it is a protective poison
   To be breathed in even if we perish from it.

5. Sara Sigourney Rice, *The Poe Memorial*, Baltimore, 1877, p. 93.

6. *Complete works of Edgar A. Poe*, ed. James A. Harrison, New York, 1902, XVI p. 29.

7. ibid., p. 31.

8. Like as into Himself eternity at last changes him,
   The Poet resurrects with a naked sword
   His century terrified at not having known
   That death triumphed in that strange voice!

   They, like a mean twist of a serpent hearing once the angel
   Give a purer meaning to the words of the tribe
   Proclaimed out loud the witch charm drunk
   From the honourless wave of some dark mixture

   Of the hostile earth and cloud, O grievance!
   If our understanding does not carve a bas-relief
   With which Poe's wondrous tomb may be adorned

   Stable block fallen here below from an obscure disaster,
   May this granite at least for ever show its position
   To the black flights of Blasphemy scattered in the future.

9. M. Jacques Crépet has recently pointed out (*Fontaine* 61, pp. 495-6) a possible source for the first line of Mallarmé's sonnet : the end of *Jugement Dernier* in D'Aubigné's *Tragiques:*
   > Ainsi le changement ne sera la fin nostre:
   > Il nous change en nous-même et non point en un autre.
   > Et l'homme qui raisonne une gloire éternelle
   > (Hoste d'éternité), se fera tel comme elle.

10. cf. the lines in the second part of T. S. Eliot's *Little Gidding*:
    Since our concern was speech, and speech impelled us
    To purify the dialect of the tribe,
    And urge the mind to aftersight and foresight,
    Let me disclose the gifts reserved for age
    To set a crown upon lifetime's effort.

11. Published in 1884 in *Les Poètes Maudits*, by Verlaine; in *Lutèce*, No. 95, Nov. 24, 1883, with the title, *Cette Nuit*.

12. Yes, I know that far off from this night, the Earth
    Casts the unusual mystery of a great brilliance
    Under the hideous centuries which darken it less.

13. Space like to itself whether it increase or deny itself
    Rolls in that boredom vile fires to witness
    That the genius of a star in celebration has been lighted.

14. The black rock angry that the wind rolls it
    Will not stop not even if under pious hands
    Feeling its resemblance with human woes
    As if to bless some ill-fated mould.

15. Here almost always if the dove sings,
    This immaterial mourning hides with many
    Nubile folds [clouds] the matured star of tomorrow
    Whose scintillation will whiten all men.

16. Who seeks, stalking the solitary figure
    Just now literal of our vagabond—
    Verlaine? He is hidden in the grass, Verlaine

    While experiencing, naively in agreement
    His lips without drinking or stopping his breath
    So shallow a slandered river, death.

17. His pure nails very high offering their onyx,
    Anguish, this midnight, holds up, a torchbearer,
    Many evening dreams burned by the Phoenix
    Which no bowl for ashes receives

18. The sonnet appeared in its finished form, in the edition of 1887. The early manuscript belonged to Henri Cazalis and was sold in Paris on June 24, 1935. It bears the title, *Sonnet allégorique de lui-même*.

19. La nuit approbatrice allume les onyx
    De ses ongles au pur Crime lampadophore,
    Du Soir aboli par le vespéral Phoenix
    De qui la cendre n'a de cinéraire amphore.

20. On the side tables, in the empty parlour: no shell,
    Abolished object of sonorous inaneness,
    (For the Master has gone to drain tears from the Styx
    With that sole object which honours the Void).

21. Letter of 3 May 1868: ' . . . comme il se pourrait toutefois que rythmé par le hamac, et inspiré par le laurier, je fisse un sonnet, et que je n'ai que trois rimes en -ix, concertez-vous pour m'envoyer le sens réel du mot ptyx: on m'assure qu'il n'existe dans aucune langue, ce que je préférerais de beaucoup afin de me donner le charme de le créer par la magie de la rime.'

22. Unusual vessel of sonorous inaneness.

23. But near the window opened to the north, a gold
    Shimmers perhaps because of the setting
    Of unicorns rushing with fire on a nymph.

24. She, nude and dead in the mirror, while,
    In the oblivion closed by the frame, the septet
    Is immediately fixed with glimmerings.

25. Letter to Henri Cazalis, of July 1868, quoted by Mondor, *Vie*, p. 267. ' . . . une
    fenêtre nocturne ouverte, les deux volets attachés: une chambre avec une
    personne dedans, malgré l'air stable que présentent les volets attachés, et
    dans une nuit faite d'absence et d'interrogation, sans meuble, sinon l'ébauche
    plausible de vagues consoles, un cadre belliqueux et agonisant, de miroir
    appendu au fond, avec sa réflexion stellaire et incompréhensible, de la Grande
    Ourse, qui relie au ciel seul ce logis abandonné du monde.'

26. The sonnet, written after the prose piece, *Richard Wagner, rêverie d'un poète
    français*, in 1885, was first published with the title, *Hommage à Wagner*, in *La
    Revue Wagnérienne*, of Jan. 8, 1886. Edouard Dujardin, founder of the review,
    had solicited Mallarmé's collaboration as early as Jan. 1885.

27. The silence already funereal of a veil
    Covers with more than a fold over the furniture
    Which a collapse of the principal pillar
    Will efface with the loss of memory.

28. Our so old triumphant exercise of the conjuror's book,
    Hieroglyphs with which the crowd is excited
    At propagating on its wing a familiar thrill!
    Rather hide it for me in a closet.

29. Hated by the original smiling noise
    There burst forth from master lights
    To the stage born for their representation,

    Trumpets high of gold fainted on velum,
    The god Richard Wagner radiating a consecration
    Ill-silenced by the very ink in sibylline sobs.

30. cf. *Mallarmé l'obscur*, p. 150.

31. 'Le poète cherche, dans son langage, à substituer à la valeur abstraite et con-
    ventionnelle des mots leur signification sensible et originelle.' *Lettre sur la
    Musique*.

CHAPTER III

MEANING OF THE POET

1 THREE MASKS

(a) CLOWN (*Le Pitre Châtié*)

THE CONDITION under which man is permitted to live demands that the kind of existence he leads contradict the deepest desire of his heart. No matter what vocation is elected or imposed, the gulf between the way one lives and the way one would like to live widens tragically with time. To some degree, every man feels the torture of constraint and caresses the idea of revolt. More clearly and more tantalizingly than other visions, the experience of love, or the hope for the experience of love, provides man, oppressed by his way of existence, with the remedy for his serfdom. Man innately believes that love will turn him more truthfully into himself and will permit him to see more clearly that kind of life he should lead in order to realize himself. If it is the artist who speaks of this problem, it is always difficult to know which means more for him: the pure experience of love or the revelation which that experience makes to him concerning his vocation. Love is opposed to the monotonous routine of living, but art is also. Both are means of deceiving life, or at least of engaging upon an activity which will convert a seemingly futile existence into a rich experience of significance and excitement.

The profound subject of *Le Pitre Châtié* seems to be an insurgence against the state of tension which comes from any accepted and practised vocation. The clown is the symbol of the experience, one destined for constant use in European art after Mallarmé's period and one which may well have been suggested to him by Baudelaire's prose poem, *Le Vieux Saltimbanque*.[1] Throughout his career, Mallarmé was tempted by the theatre and bewitched by its particular art. The role of the actor or the clown would be an obvious symbol for him of the artist. Baudelaire makes a very direct comparison between an old decrepit mountebank he sees standing beside his improvised stage, and the ageing writer who has survived the generation in which he figured brilliantly. In the picture which precedes the comparison, the poverty and sadness of the clown are contrasted with the hilarity of the circus stalls. Baudelaire's clown, like one of Rouault's paintings, seems degraded in his isolation. His destiny is over and he has abdicated on the very spot where other clowns are trying to incite laughter in the Parisian spectators.

The earliest version of *Le Pitre Châtié* goes back to the spring of 1864, when Mallarmé was living at Tournon and suffering from the tedium of a small city and the onerous tasks of school teacher. It was first revealed to the public in *La Revue de France* of April 25, 1929, by Mallarmé's son-in-law, Dr. Edmond Bonniot, long after the appearance of the definitive version in the edition *Poésies* of 1887. It would be false to depend completely on the first version for an understanding of the final form of the sonnet. In tightening the language and developing the initial images, the poet unquestionably discovered new meanings or new aspects of meanings. The mysterious and bold opening of the sonnet: *Yeux, lacs*, was, in the early form, *Pour ses yeux—pour nager dans ces lacs*,[2] and Dr. Bonniot deduces that the eyes must be those of the beloved, compared to lakes where the clown will swim. This meaning still adheres to the sonnet, but in its remarkable contractions more meanings than one are engendered, and the complications of a heart, which are often comparable to the complexities of a symbol, become visible. If the first version is obviously a love sonnet, the final version remains that, but not obviously, and in its rigorous language it hides the inital experience of the poet in order to reveal the fuller and deeper experience of the metaphor.

The first quatrain describes both a real and an unreal setting, as well as the central action of revolt for which the clown is to be punished.

> *Yeux, lacs avec ma simple ivresse de renaître*
> *Autre que l'histrion qui du geste évoquais*
> *Comme plume la suie ignoble des quinquets,*
> *J'ai troué dans le mur de toile une fenêtre.*[3]

Only the fourth line seems to be totally clear. It is the action of Petrouchka who with his hands tears a hole in the tent walls. The marionette hangs there unable to escape completely from his cell. What of Mallarmé's clown? Does he execute the same gesture for the same purpose, to escape from a puppet-master into the arms, unwilling to receive him, of a ballerina? There is assuredly something of that. The 'eyes' may well be 'her eyes' and comparable to lakes which will bring about the desired purification of love. On the inter-pretation given to *yeux* and the word in apposition, *lacs*, depends the meaning of the sonnet. After the first quatrain, the rest of the poem is given over to the metaphor of the lake. Its first mention, a kind of explosion of desire at the very beginning of the sonnet, stands in con-trast with all that follows in the first stanza: the tent canvas, the artificial lighting, the evocation of the actor's stage. The lake, what-ever it symbolizes, is opposed to the mimed existence of the clown. . . But from all time, in his vocation of actor (*histrion*), the clown has performed for the eyes, the hundreds of pairs of eyes which have watched him. Those who live on a stage often use the cliché of a 'sea of faces' to designate the public, and this second possible meaning of *yeux* gradually joins with the first. The problem of vocation, of 'per-formance', cannot easily be dissociated from the experience of love.

The intoxication (*ivresse*) which the clown feels in the presence of the 'eyes' is of a spiritual order. To be reborn (*renaître*) has even a religious connotation. To become something else than one is (*autre que l'histrion*) may mean both a change of vocation—the shift from clown to lover, according to the first version of the sonnet—and a deepening of one's initial role. To consider that the eyes watching him represent a liberating force, a power that will convert him into a great actor, is related to the conviction that the two eyes of his be-loved are outside of the tawdry show in which he plays nightly. As the actor conveys the meaning of his role by gestures and miming, so his plume or whatever property he employs for his part is seen in the illumination of the footlights which leave a base soot on their glass. There seems to be a parallel on the one hand between the actor (*histrion*) and the soot of the stage lamps (*la suie des quinquets*), and on the other hand between the miming of the art and the plume or the costume necessary to create the illusion of the role. The entire sonnet is constructed on the idea of escape and of a punishment inflicted because of the escape which is related to what is being escaped from. If a man escapes from himself by becoming a clown, he imitates in his role of a clown all the actions of a man.

Swiftly the action proceeds, and the image of the lake, which was the unreal setting in the first quatrain, becomes the real setting in the second quatrain.

> *De ma jambe et des bras limpide nageur traître,*
> *A bonds multipliés, reniant le mauvais*

Hamlet! c'est comme si dans l'onde j'innovais
Mille sépulcres pour y vierge disparaître.[4]

Thus the metaphor becomes the experience, with full setting and strong action. In the early version of this stanza, the lake is described realistically and the clown's costume is seen on a tree trunk as he swims in the forbidden waters.[5] The word traitor (*traître*) is already there and the clown plunges naked into the water. Otherwise, the four lines are completely transformed. Rather than swimming gracefully, a curious movement is performed in the water which most of the words relate. Frog-like, his legs held together, the clown leaps jerkily through the water. After each spurt, he sinks down as into a tomb. The water closes in around him and he disappears from sight, always virginal. If he is a traitor to the tent, he has preserved in his aquatic freedom and despite his nudity, the aspect of the clown and the capers of the comic figure. His movements are still the caricature of normal movements. He has not altered his nature. He is still a virgin, if love were the goal of his escape. One thing only has been accomplished. By leaving the tent, the clown repudiated the hamletism in his nature, the incapacity to act, to make up his mind and will a change in the ordinary course of events. He was a 'bad Hamlet' once, the mimic of the hero frustrated and troubled who circled about the same stage without finding a solution. But when the eyes of his temptation became a lake in which he could swim, he renounced the role of Hamlet. If one sees in the eyes solely the temptation to love, the description of the clown's swimming in the lake would seem to indicate a failure to realize the experience of love. Rather than discovering a new life and the expending of himself in the act of love, his repeated efforts are deathlike because in them he preserves his virginal intactness.

The tercets, which are one sentence, describe the punishment and provide at the same time an explanation for it.

Hilare or de cymbale à des poings irrité,
Tout à coup le soleil frappe la nudité
Qui pure s'exhala de ma fraîcheur de nacre,

Rance nuit de la peau quand sur moi vous passiez,
Ne sachant pas, ingrat, que c'était tout mon sacre,
Ce fard noyé dans l'eau perfide des glaciers.[6]

The opening line of this section, which doesn't exist in the early version, gives to the entire conclusion the aspect of a rite, of a mystery being performed. As in a circus, when a sharp gong or bell announces a new act, the abrupt sound of a cymbal marks a shift in poetic or metaphorical attention and at the same time reminds the naked swimmer that he is still the clown who has lost something of his consecration. The first half of the line (*Hilare or de cymbale*) contains the words of a psalmist, and the second half (*à des poings irrité*) throws the image back to the circus tent. In this single line Mallarmé evokes the vocation of the clown transpiring in its native atmosphere and its deepest analogy with a religious sacrament. In its final word, *irrité*, it prepares the punishment which is about to fall, and in its opening words, *Hilare or,* it explains why the punishment must be swift and absolute.

The sun, whose gold was already in the brass instrument of announcement, strikes against the nakedness of the swimming body. It is the picture of vulnerability. The escape from the eyes of the public has taken place as well as the approach to the eyes of the beloved, but there the illumination of such an approach reveals the clown divested of what made him a clown: both costume and make-up. The greasepaint, darker than his white skin, is compared to a night turning rancid. It is dissolving into the new element of the water and disappearing around him. In the sunlight, whose illumination is a cruel punishment, so different from footlights (*quinquets*) of the circus, whose illumination is strategy and performance and realization of a role; and in the water of the new experience where his body shows its white nakedness and where his greasepaint disappears, the clown knows finally the value of his consecration which he has now lost, the supremacy of his mask which permitted him to be seen and not to be seen.

Love appeared to the clown as a salvation. He went to it: he literally plunged into it, and found it to be a force of destruction. The image of water, like that of a mirage, is simultaneously salvation and destruction. It purifies and drowns. The experience of love in its usual sense is both liberation and death. But from it, the conscience of man learns something about his own mystery and greatness. Only in revolting against one's faith, does one learn its value. The clown had to leave his tent and lose his travesty in order to comprehend the mystery of his calling and the deep kind of liberty which resides within one's restrictions and patterns of living.

The sonnet of *Le Pitre Châtié* is succinctly contained within the two words, *yeux* and *glaciers*, the first and the last words, which designate the same thing: the mirage and the reality of the same temptation. In between the first and the last words, one other word is explored, that of *lake* which is suggested by the *eyes* and which ends by becoming congealed in the *glaciers*. All the temptations of the world follow that same pattern and the same evolution. And the temptation of the poem, for such a poet as Mallarmé, is the same myth of yearning to seize the idea (*yeux*), of attempt to recreate it in an image (*lacs*) and of the final experience of sterility and frustration (*glaciers*) which prevents an adequate transmission of the Dream.

The moral problem in *Le Pitre Châtié* is the remorse which torments a man throughout whatever vocation he has elected. No one is exempt, whether he be monk or clown, from the gnawing doubt that he chose badly his way of life. The human spirit never ceases demanding a higher state for itself and from time to time it breaks out in some violent revolt or denial of what provides it with dignity and stability. Baudelaire treats the same theme in his poem, *L'Irréparable*, but directly and forcibly, as opposed to the complicated conceit of Mallarmé's sonnet. Curiously enough, in the last two stanzas of Baudelaire's piece, occurs the image of a commonplace theatre:

> *J'ai vu parfois, au fond d'un théâtre banal*

where the poet sees a winged fairy light up a tawdry backdrop with the colour of dawn and destroy with her pure luminosity the spirit of evil. He compares his heart to a theatre which continues to wait for its transformation:

> *Mais mon cœur, que jamais ne visite l'extase,*
> *Est un théâtre où l'on attend*
> *Toujours, toujours en vain, l'Etre aux ailes de gaze!*

The theatre, which is a source of metamorphosis, is the image for both Baudelaire and Mallarmé to designate man's will to change himself and the terrifying illusion of change when it is recognized as being an artificial and a temporary change. The contrast between what man is and his loftiest spiritual ambition forces him to see his existence as that of a comedy, an absurdity where he moves about as an irresolute Hamlet. Even love, which appears as the surest means to self-renovation, accentuates also in the lover the realization of his original state and of his permanent drive to something even higher than love. If the mask of the clown is put off, he will be punished all the more in his need to recover it.

(b) SWAN (*Le vierge, le vivace*)

The 'swan' sonnet, for thus it is called, has become Mallarmé's most popular poem, the first choice in anthologies, the poem to explicate in survey courses. It is well on its way to becoming the hackneyed piece, the *Vase Brisé* of symbolism, used both for recitation and for pedagogy to elucidate a poetic method. It is regrettable that such a poem, whose beauty is in its freshness and originality, should be so weighed down with explanations. Readers who know only this single sonnet are able to see in it a striking metaphor which is fairly easy to interpret. But only those who know the complete work of Mallarmé can begin to realize how central it is in his art, how each word and each part of the elaborate image represent aspects of the poet's sensitivity.

It was first published in March 1885 in *La Revue Indépendante,* and then two years later in the edition of *Poésies* of 1887, where it appeared without any changes. No manuscript exists and no date of composition can be ascertained. But by its form and the mastery of its technique, it belongs to the great sonnets written around 1885. It takes its place with them by its ellipsis and condensation, by the dramatic quality of its metaphor whose suggestiveness seems to invite varieties of theories and elucidations.

The picture of Mallarmé's swan, caught in the ice of the lake and looking at it disdainfully, places the creature in the familiar romantic menagerie where there are so many examples of animals designating the poet crushed by the world and hating it. Whether it be Musset's pelican or Vigny's wolf (or his Moses), the ivory tower theme of the poet's isolation and his scorn for the world that ostracizes him, had been sounded countless times before Mallarmé invented his swan. Closer to Mallarmé than the romantic poets was Baudelaire whose own albatross and swan should count among the ancestors of the frozen bird. In *L'Albatros*, Baudelaire describes the bird imprisoned on the deck of a ship by his own wings so large that they are unable to elevate him from the flat surface. In *Le Cygne* the same frustration is described where the bird appears exiled from its lake and unable to exist in the mud of the city street.

Almost every role or interpretation has been ascribed to Mallarmé's swan. For most critics the swan typifies poetic stoicism, and the lake the hostility of the world toward the artist. This is a traditional theme in modern letters and especially in the romantic movement. Albert Mockel[7] gives the sonnet a philosophical interpretation by seeing in it an example of the Platonic myth (cf. *Phaedrus*) of the soul fallen from the ideal and aspiring to return to it as to its native land. Albert Thibaudet[8] sees in the 14 rhymes in -*i* the power of a sound able to reproduce the vastness and coldness of monotonous white space. Mme Noulet[9] opposes the interpretation of the swan as romantic prisoner caught in the contingencies of life and exiled from a native purity. She sees him not as a prisoner of the world, but as a martyr of the ideal, as one haunted by the blue of the sky. She sees the sonnet as an answer to the earlier piece, *L'Azur*. Charles Mauron[10] also feels that the explanation of stoicism is insufficient, and very suggestively attaches the swan to the lineage of Hérodiade. The swan would be the final metamorphosis of Hérodiade, her petrification and disappearance into the ice. The themes of the phantom and the mirror would thus reach their full justification. Pierre Beausire,[11] in an arresting and lofty page of analysis, sees the sonnet as a study of the hostility between being and becoming. The swan would represent a consciousness attempting to vanquish time, but the world cannot be surpassed no matter how insistently one is called toward the absolute.

The pure verbal beauty of the sonnet is so strong and so convincing that one hesitates before attempting an analysis. The art of Mallarmé, more insistently here than elsewhere, defies a breaking down into ideas and concepts. The poem is unique and the form is inseparable from the content. And yet, in the presence of so achieved a form, one discovers meanings in the relationship between man and the universe which go deep and far.

First quatrain. The subject of the poem, 'today' (*aujourd'hui*), is prepared and announced with three epithets.

> *Le vierge, le vivace et le bel aujourd'hui*
> *Va-t-il nous déchirer avec un coup d'aile ivre*
> *Ce lac dur oublié que hante sous le givre*
> *Le transparent glacier des vols qui n'ont pas fui!*[12]

The poet wonders at the beginning of a new day about its possibilities and its promises. Since he is a poet, he wonders especially whether something permanent in terms of art may be extracted from the purity and the growing power of the dawn. And immediately, again since he is a poet, the concept, 'dawn', or 'today', appears to him invested with the power of an image, of a winged creature trying to escape from a frozen lake. The image will become clearer for him in the second quatrain. In the first, the image is forming and demanding attention. It composes itself in accordance with the wonderment and fear it translates: what freshness and what beauty will be liberated from this day? The poet's desire to create resembles the helpless wings of a bird flapping underneath the ice which is forming over them. The whiteness of the day as it stretches endlessly over the earth is deceptive. Purity may turn quickly into frigidity. The idea, as it first occurs in its vast promise, may be lost by its very vastness. The wings beat, but the bird doesn't rise, as the idea palpitates without finding a form in which to assure its life.

Second quatrain.—The problem, posed first as a question and given the vestment of a nascent image, now becomes solidly and fixedly the metaphor which grows of itself assuming all responsibility for the problem.

> Un cygne d'autrefois se souvient que c'est lui
> Magnifique mais qui sans espoir se délivre
> Pour n'avoir pas chanté la région où vivre
> Quand du stérile hiver a resplendi l'ennui.[13]

The image rising up to the full consciousness of the poet and assuming the form of a bird encased in ice, seems to come from a distance in time. The bird, once the image is clear and autonomous, names itself a swan and remembers back to the moment when it gave itself over to the beginning of defeat. Its beauty at that moment was perhaps even enhanced by its despair. We learn in what way it was captured by the cold: it stayed in the lake at a time when it should have been elsewhere, when it should have been singing of some other more propitious region. But we do not learn why it willed to remain. The full action of the metaphor, beginning with the initial question of 'today', implies that the strangulation of the will and the ultimate immobility were brought about with the consent of the poet, with the approval of the swan. I have the feeling that the explanation is hidden in the second line of the quatrain, *Magnifique mais qui sans espoir*, from which one might deduce an important aesthetic consideration. Beauty is tragic because of its transitoriness, because of its unseizableness. By its very principle, whether it be a woman, a bird or an idea, it has no power to remain unchanged, and when it is transposed into a poem or a painting, it is likened to that which dies. The sonnet of Mallarmé is concerned precisely with the change from freedom of movement (*va-t-il nous déchirer ce lac?*) to an immobilization (*où le plumage est pris*), but what is most important in this destiny of frustration is that it is willed by the swan in order to insure a maximum pathos of beauty.

First tercet.—Briefly a struggle is engaged against the very force longed for by the bird.

> *Tout son col secouera cette blanche agonie*
> *Par l'espace infligée à l'oiseau qui le nie,*
> *Mais non l'horreur du sol où le plumage est pris.*[14]

By now the image is totally clear. The neck of the swan is free above the ice, but if it is undying (cf. *vivace* of the first line), the body is held under the ice. The freedom of the air has been replaced by the frozen lake, once another element of freedom, but which has become, with the advent of winter, a prison. Since the fight is waged between two degrees of whiteness: the winter frost and the plumage, the scene takes on the aspect of a fantasy, of a spectral silenced combat.

Second tercet.—The opening word and the final word of this tercet are long sounds translating audibly the eeriness of the visual scene.

> *Fantôme qu'à ce lieu son pur éclat assigne,*
> *Il s'immobilise au songe froid de mépris*
> *Que vêt parmi l'exil inutile le Cygne.*[15]

The swan is spectre because his whiteness merges with the colour of the snow and ice. Only his moral force, his Pascalian knowledge that he is being crushed, remains to distinguish him from the elements. This exile into hardness and immobility may well be useless —he could have gone elsewhere—but it has given him an inner self-reliance, a hardness of his own, a scorn which he puts on as if it were a mask to cover his suffering.

The dominant sound of -*i*, in all the rhymes of the sonnet, penetrates the last two lines, as if by pure insistence it will bring about a resolution. The final line,

> *Que vêt parmi l'exil inutile le Cygne*

might be a play on sound and meaning,

> *Que vêt par mille exils inutiles le Signe*

which in itself would be a gloss on the sonnet. In the single syllable, *Cygne* (*Signe*) is the essential word of the metaphor and the proof that it is a metaphor. A metaphor is a word, a sign in exile, masking some human experience, but not masking it in a futile game. The entire poem is a Sign, exiled from the ordinary speech of man. And yet every part is recognizable and familiar. Only the composition, the coming together of the words is new, and that is why it appears as a metaphor, as a speech exiled from all the lakes which have not frozen.

The action of the sonnet is totally simple. Within the brief space of a few minutes a barren winter landscape turns into an icy immobility. As the day dawned, there was one moment of hope for liberation and achievement, as if the day were a bird about to fly up into the sky. But the rigidity of death settled down over the land, and what was to be a burst of creative life ended by becoming a stark ghost-like pattern mingled with the colourless surface of the lake.

The sonnet is the story of human destiny reduced to the final decisive moment when it appears controlled by some implacable law of matter. Can it be that the profoundest adventure of the human will, the one which concerns life itself and creation, may end with the reign of matter? A poet is present in the world, asking his eternal question about his chance for poetic achievement, for poetic self-realization. And in answer, the best that he achieves is a picture of the very moment in which the material world closes off his existence, crushes, with the heaviness of a glacier, the will to live and move.

The image is so mythic, so charged with the oldest desire of man to rise above the world of matter to which he is chained, and to become a pure spirit, angelic and bird-like, that we are able to recognize in it a monument to existence itself, an epitaph in the form of a metaphor into which the adventure of destiny is condensed. It is a monument also to the power of the word, which, alone in a world of immobilization produces a vision of freedom.

In whatever appalling solitude man finds himself, he sees at some distance the appearance of other worlds. (Even as the clown, in *Le Pitre Châtié*, believes in the possibility of other vocations beyond the limits of his tent.) He wills then to flee his solitude, or whatever world he inhabits, without knowing exactly what purposes he may accomplish in the distant world of appearances. He seems to be obeying some original or primordial urge to purification. But the tragedy occurs when he realizes that one does not leave one's solitude, that the past cannot be forgotten or left behind. Man lives by bearing

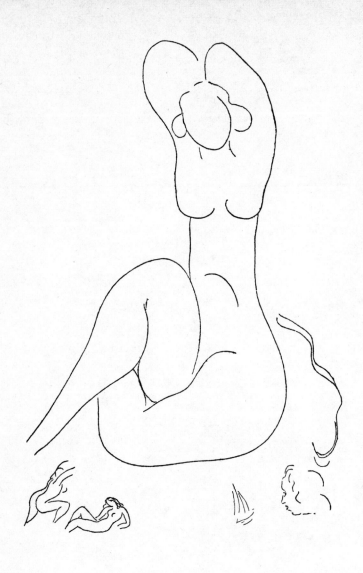

M'introduire dans ton Histoire

everything at once: the weight of the past, the reality of his solitude and the desire for his world of appearances. The swan and the clown are one: the lake will either freeze and immobilize them or it will dissolve the camouflage which made them real in the world. The absolute must remain for man, no matter how passionately he desires it, a terrifying duty, a goal seen as a mirage. The tent of histrionics and the lake of ice testify to the kind of world we have to inhabit. The lake of multiple deaths in which the clown swims and the region which the swan failed to sing of are all that we can know of our approach to the absolute. Man's tragedy comes about from his inferiority to his mission, from his incapacity to redeem his spiritual necessity. He is simultaneously flesh and vision. He has to learn how to live his role: that of permanent self-destroyer.

(c) HERO (*M'introduire dans ton histoire*)

The initial line of the sonnet, *M'introduire dans ton histoire*,[16] repeats an important action in the sonnets of the clown and the swan. In each case the protagonist seeks to introduce himself into some place, to move out from a closed-in oppressive setting into one of freedom. The clown leaves his tent for a lake; the swan wants to break through the ice of the lake to reach the freedom of the sky and the south; and the hero of the third sonnet insinuates himself into the story of someone he addresses familiarly. He mentions the new place as if it were a fertile land and yet we know also that it is a person. It is the most obscure of the three sonnets because it translates an experience of joy, which, far more incommunicable than that of tragedy, has to be recast into an elaborate conceit.

This sonnet also is more closely knit together than the others. Without punctuation and with no stanza demarcations, it has to be read in one breath.

> M'introduire dans ton histoire
> C'est en héros effarouché
> S'il a du talon nu touché
> Quelque gazon de territoire
>
> A des glaciers attentatoire
> Je ne sais le naïf péché
> Que tu n'auras pas empêché
> De rire très haut sa victoire

Dis si je ne suis pas joyeux
Tonnerre et rubis aux moyeux
De voir en l'air que ce feu troue

Avec des royaumes épars
Comme mourir pourpre la roue
Du seul vespéral de mes chars.[17]

The mysterious 'introduction' with which the poem begins, opens up immediately into an image, of mythic reminiscence, where the hero is timid and touches with his bare heel a plot of grass so verdant and warm that it melts the glaciers resting on it. The idea of conquest, associated with a hero, is therefore transcribed with delicacy as a treading of his bare foot on green grass. The first word, 'to introduce myself', is thus recapitulated in the image of touching with a bare heel; and the second word, 'your history', is converted into the image of grass capable of threatening the existence of ice. The hero is represented as being terrified at the moment of his conquest, when his bare heel touches the grass. The allusion to Achilles, vulnerable only in his heel, is obvious. If the allusion is maintained with any accuracy, the moment of conquest will therefore be for the Mallarmé hero a mortal wound or a dying.

But no one part of the sonnet can be understood without the other parts. The next three lines (6-8) complete the image of conquest and confront the hero or protagonist with the character addressed as *tu*. The one word, 'sin' (*péché*), juxtaposed with its adjective 'innocent' or 'virginal' (*naïf*), elucidates the particular meaning of conquest which the sonnet treats. The victory of such an act is precisely of such a nature that it is not followed by jubilation in the form of laughter. The existence of the woman with whom the act is accomplished stifles whatever shout of triumph might have been uttered.

The elation of the naive hero has to be expressed in some other way. The cry of joy which he would have uttered upon the achievement of any other act of conquest turns within him in his physical release, and he converts what he feels of triumph and death of triumph into a high sky image of constellations and a sun chariot. The myth of Achilles' vulnerable heel (unquestionably a transcription of the virginal phallus, as the *gazon de territoire* is the pubic hair of the unnamed woman) turns into the myth of Apollo's chariot mounting the sky and then sinking into a ruddy glow. In such a sonnet, the metaphor appears substantially as a condensed myth. The mounting of the chariot, in its power and beauty, is narrated in a single line in which we hear the thunder of conquest and the sacramental red flashes of combat: *Tonnerre et rubis aux moyeux*. 'Thunder' and 'rubies' are not only appropriate for the image of chariot wheel, but they also illustrate the existence of opposites, of matter and spirit, of imprisonment and deliverance, which seems to characterize any profound experience.[18] What the poet sees in the image (*De voir en l'air*) is really what the hero has felt in his experience of physical conquest. The entire sonnet is an avoidance of any direct narration, of any specific allusion to the original experience. It is a celebration of an experience, especially in the tercets where the tone of exaltation mounts and diminishes.

The protagonist looks up into the sky and sees there depicted a celebration of what he has felt of triumph in his nudity on the warm grass. He sees a flame piercing the air and scattered kingdoms or constellations round about. And then he sees the wheel of the flaming chariot die in the centre of a deepening colour as evening invades the sky. The course of the sun is the myth whose action seems to follow in all its particularities a sexual performance. The triumph is explosion and release, and it is described in terms of a flaming sunset sinking into its own death, comparable to the suicide of another sunset of Mallarmé, *Victorieusement fui le suicide beau*. But *M'introduire* is concerned with a triumphant conquest and not with its aftermath. It is the sonnet of a hero and not of a lover. Innocency, inexperience and discovery are its themes. A wide-eyed wonderment characterizes its hero, who, Achilles-like, takes off the dresses of his disguised adolescence and discovers a new power in his feelings.

I can see in the sonnet no allusion to the luxuriant hair of the girl on which Soula, Mme Noulet and Beausire centre their comments. (And I am well aware that in another sonnet, *La chevelure vol d'une flamme*, which does describe hair, occur many words which are in *M'introduire: héros, joyeux, feu, rubis*.) The wheel which dies in a purple colour (*Comme mourir pourpre la roue*) is first the sun of the metaphor. The verse following it and with which it is joined: *Du seul vespéral de mes chars*, continues the sky metaphor of sunset and sun suicide, and clearly substantiates the sexual connotation of triumph. But the 'wheel' belongs to the 'chariot'. It is the 'fire piercing the air' which contains scattered remnants of its explosion (*Avec des royaumes épars*). The sonnet concerns the hero, timid, virginal, successful in his attack, for whom the experience is so cosmic that he sees it written over the heavens as a primitive sun ritual. The female partner of the experience is described by means of a pronoun, as far as the poem is concerned, and by the one image of grass, although one senses her becoming the air and the vastness of the sky at the end. An action is ascribed to her, that of preventing the hero from signalling the victory of his sin by laughing out loud.

> *Je ne sais le naïf péché*
> *Que tu n'auras pas empêché*
> *De rire très haut sa victoire*

This is perhaps the most difficult passage of the sonnet. No word in it seems to justify the interpretation that the hero stifles his laughter in the girl's abundant head of hair. The very nature of the conquest prevents laughter. The hero hardly realizes what he is doing: *Je ne sais le naïf péché*, but it is so tremendous that it centres him in an inexplicable sidereal solitude. It resembles a flash of lightening across the sky. A single individual, timid and inconspicuous, is suddenly transformed into an agent of power. He becomes more than himself, an actor, a swan of some metamorphosis, a hero.

(*d*) THE THREE SYMBOLS

Each of the three symbols seems to manifest the poet as hero, the poet as protagonist according to the classical definition. The symbol in each case unfolds as a constricted tragedy, as a reminiscence of tragedy.

At the beginning is a flash of greatness, power, heroic beauty. The clown feels an intoxication (*simple ivresse*) which is going to direct and strengthen his will. The swan remembers a former magnificence (*magnifique*) which will help him to bear the state into which he is entering. The character associated with a victory, even if he is timorous, is a hero in the surpassing of himself (*c'est en héros*). Thus, initially, the poet appears with a mask magnifying him, intoxicated with an action to perform, glorious in his beauty, heroic in his accomplishment.

When the action prophesied is actually begun, it bears a resemblance with the dream of the action but it also appears strangely impeded, annunciatory of some fatal defect. The clown does plunge into the water of his lake, but there his movements are performed erratically and almost comically. The wings of the swan are out-stretched in their expansive beauty, but over them has grown a coat-ing of ice which they are unable to break through. The triumph of the hero cannot be articulated exultantly. It can only be compared to the flash of a flame piercing the sky in a moment of distant cosmic silence. The heroic action does not therefore correspond exactly to the promise of heroic beauty and heroic dreaming.

The conclusion of each sonnet is quite in keeping with the tragic dénouement. Coldness is the final climate of the hero: glaciers for the swimming clown in the water where his make-up has dissolved; the ice freezing over the swan and causing to form over his head a cold mask of disdain; the red glow of the hero dissolving into the night as if the glaciers, mentioned previously, were about to be re-formed. In the clown sonnet, the sun is the instrument of punishment striking the nudity of the hero and revealing his strange pallor when the greasepaint has been washed away. In the swan sonnet, the sun is hidden behind the low clouds of winter. It is shining in that place where the swan should be. There is no sunlight where there is no movement. In the hero sonnet, the hero becomes the sun and dies after its greatest flash of brilliance. After playing the role of revela-tion and punishment, either by action or by absence, the sun joins the two roles in revealing itself by a burst of triumph and punishing itself in its suicide. The legend of the hero remains strangely the same in all three sonnets. His story falls into its three parts of in-toxication, when everything can be accomplished, of action mysteri-ously impeded, of death which is always the loss of original beauty and power.

2 IGITUR : Mallarmé as Hamlet

PREPARATION FOR THE WORK

Mallarmé never published his prose work, *Igitur*, and doubtless never intended publishing it, at least in the form in which it was found. Ever since its posthumous appearance in 1925, made possible by the editorship of Dr Bonniot, it has exercised an increasing at-traction for students of Mallarmé who find in it the poet's most pro-found metaphysical statement. Although it was written between the years 1867 and 1870, it contains themes and problems which are never absent from the subsequent writing of Mallarmé. The manu-script, discovered in 1900 by Bonniot, bears after its title, *Igitur*, the word, *déchet*, which Mallarmé was in the habit of using to designate writing left over from a completed work, the unused material or the material which had been recast into a more permanent form. It is curious that a work which Mallarmé had never wished to publish, although he had read it once to Catulle Mendès and to Villiers de l'Isle-Adam, in 1870, has become for contemporary readers a work of considerable importance.

The letters of Mallarmé, written between 1862 and 1870, which have in part been published, are of great aid in the understanding of *Igitur*, and in fact, somewhat control its interpretation. The work seems to be a human drama of marked poignancy which is almost explicated by the fragments of Mallarmé's correspondence now available. *Igitur* is perhaps the essential document on Mallarmé's deepest personal crisis.

The theme of impotency in his early poems not only reflects an influence of Baudelaire, but corresponds to a permanent trait in Mallarmé's own nature. As far back as 1862, Mallarmé, in a letter to Cazalis,[19] spoke of a three months struggle against a feeling of sterility, and said that his first sonnet[20] was a denunciation of his malady. Worry over artistic sterility never ceased for Mallarmé. But it prevented him from accepting anything facile in his art and provided a theme, which, paradoxically, opened up into many poetic utterances. If it caused anguish, it also shaped his particular sensitivity and helped to formulate his aesthetics. To fear one's impotency is at the same time to be profoundly conscious of oneself. To suffer from an excessive self-awareness is to see so clearly that there is always the chance of becoming hero of one's conscience.

Endless passages in the letters written between 1864 and 1866 speak of a constant discouragement and of a physical torpor into which the poet would sink. At the age of 23, he felt like a corpse or an old man. He feared idiocy and used to observe his traits in a mirror.[21] Already the symbol of a mirror, destined to play an important part in *Igitur*, preoccupied him. The three years spent at Tournon (Nov. 1863-summer, 1866) can be called, without exaggeration, a period of crisis. The designation 'les nuits de Tournon', tends to equate the experience of Mallarmé with Pascal's, of a more purely religious nature. But the equation, in terms of intensity and significance, is not without meaning. Three months, in late winter and early spring, were spent in persistent meticulous labour over *Hérodiade*. The work presented such difficulty that Mallarmé saw ahead of him three or four further winters of work before the poem would attain its form. In the same letter[22] in which he chronicles this tremendous expense of effort, he refers to an 'eternal discouragement' victimizing him, and then develops in three paragraphs an explanation of an 'abyss' he has come upon, and which he names *Le Néant*. The letter combines a physical discouragement and a metaphysical impasse that go far in preparing the poet's state of mind which was to conceive *Igitur* and in adumbrating themes which were to be employed in the work.

Man he believes to be a 'vain form of matter', having an awareness of being (*ayant une conscience d'être*) and forcing himself toward a Dream which he knows cannot be. In singing the soul and the age-long impressions of the soul, the matter (*matière*) of man is simply proclaiming lies. But the poet must continue to sing, even if he sings as a man in despair. By such an experience, Mallarmé shows to what extent the new kind of poetry he is writing (different from the earlier Baudelairian verse) is really an approach to the absolute and to its synonym, the void. *Igitur* is going to depict a personal and willed disappearance of the poet.

Another letter to Cazalis,[23] written the following year, in May 14, 1867, appears of the utmost importance. In true mystic fashion, he begins by saying that everything which has transpired during the difficult year that is just ending is unrelatable. He has died during it, he says, and the most impure region where his mind can go is Eternity. He defines his spirit as the 'solitary inhabitant of his own Purity' (*ce solitaire habituel de sa propre Pureté*). He has passed the stage of anguish and struggle, and is now desirous of clothing himself with an exterior indifference. One day, after the harsh period of struggle and agony, he looked at himself in his mirror (*ma glace de Venise*), and knew that he still had great need of looking at himself and that if the mirror were not in front of the very table on which he was writing the letter to Cazalis, he would himself become the Void (*je redeviendrais le Néant*). This he calls his state of impersonality. Self-observation in his mirror permits him to think. He is no longer a person but an 'aptitude' which the universe has of seeing itself through him. The universe has to rediscover in him its identity. He feels that the poems on such themes (*Hérodiade,* for example) may be too difficult to be realized. Will he have enough time to attempt their realization? All that remains for him to believe in is Beauty and its most perfect expression: Poetry. This letter, written at Besançon, to which he had been sent in a kind of disgrace, to teach in the lycée, and where he stayed only for the school year 1866-67, re-affirms Mallarmé's extraordinary belief in poetry which for him takes the place of love, because he sees it as beauty in love with itself.

The Avignon period began in October 1867. The early Baude-lairian poems had been followed, in Tournon, by the first drafts of *Hérodiade* and *L'Après-Midi d'un Faune*, composed in the first peculi-arly Mallarmean style. In Besançon he evolved, largely by medita-tion, his still fuller personal style which was to find its expression in the poems of Avignon, where *Igitur* also was to be composed. His writing was soon to become definitively difficult and rare. His ex-perience of a poet was gradually embracing and absorbing his experience of a man. His perseverance which was to end by produc-ing poems chiselled and hard, exact and condensed, was made possible by a tremendous psychic effort, by insomnia and agony. He often felt close to madness,[24] and his only consolation was the belief that his suffering would either diminish or end by killing him.

However Mallarmé's state of mental health may be designated, either as neurasthenia, or, as Dr Mondor believes the specialists would call it, psychasthenia[25], it continued to grow worse during 1868 until in early 1869 it reached a kind of climax, described in an important letter to Cazalis[26] of February 19. For some time he had had to dictate to his wife whatever he wanted to write because of palpitations which would occur whenever he took up a pen. But now the palpitations would return even if he dictated. In order to avoid what he calls 'hysteria', he announces that he will not write again until Easter. He describes his mind as being invaded by a Dream, and, refusing its usual functions, about to perish in a perma-nent kind of insomnia. It was then he called upon night and a total blackness. The actual phrase is difficult to cast into English: *J'ai imploré la grande Nuit, qui m'a exaucé et a étendu ses ténèbres*. This marks for Mallarmé the end of the first phase of his life. Only with the excess of darkness was his conscience able to reawaken and a new man to rise up, one able to see his Dream after having created it. The writing of *Igitur* may well be the effort to escape from the hold of his psychic dilemma, to get beyond the first night of darkness by going through it and explaining it to himself as far as he is able to. All writing, but especially poetry and writing of poetic expression, is a kind of exorcism. *Igitur* seems to be an exercise undertaken by Mallarmé to explain to himself a state of mind from which he is determined to escape. Self-knowledge is a liberation. The act of writing is a remedy. (The act of reading, to a lesser degree, may also be a remedy.) By itself, *Igitur* may be a work of an importance and a meaning far different from its importance to Mallarmé and the meaning it had for him. A note written to Cazalis on Nov. 14, 1869,[27] is sufficient proof that the poet thought of his new work as a story by means of which he was going to annihilate the old monster of impotency. If he succeeds in completing it, he will be cured.[28] He writes *Igitur*, therefore, as if he were exorcising an evil spirit in him.

ANALYSIS

Rolland de Renéville states in *L'Expérience Poétique* that the title, *Igitur*, comes from the second chapter of *Genesis: Igitur perfecti sunt coeli et terra.* He says also that the word, *Elbehnon*, in Hebrew, means the son of the Elohim, creative potentialities of Jehovah.[29]

The brief introduction, or *ancienne étude*, is practically in the form of notes. The subject of the three paragraphs is 'he', who is not named until the final sentence, separated from the paragraphs: 'Igitur, as a child, is reading his exercise to his ancestors'. The fragment seems to be notations for a stage-set. (We are told in an epigraph to arrange the setting ourselves.) The ancestors in the tomb are about to blow out the candle which illuminates the letters of the sorcerer's book (*grimoire*), but Igitur says, 'not yet!' He is fascinated by this knowledge that he can cause the darkness by blowing out the small flame. After that act the absolute will exist outside, the absolute which denies immortality.

Another kind of introduction follows, which has been given the title, *Argument*, by Dr Bonniot, and which has guided him in arranging the order of the manuscript fragments. It is a plan of the work, written by Mallarmé later than 1870, which names the four principal sections, and which stands as sufficient proof that what we are to read as chapters is far from completed.

The first scene, *Le Minuit*, is described in the 'Argument' as that moment when the dice are to be thrown. Igitur goes down the stairs into the tomb. His descent is really that of the human spirit into its greatest depths where it will know itself the most lucidly. The 'presence of midnight' is the theme of the meditation. The ringing ot the clock (*révélateur du minuit*) has made pure this moment, an absolute present of all things. Its presence is in the room itself, in the furniture whose immobility seems to arrest the movement of thought. The pure ego, dreamed of for so long, is realized at last. As time is confused or compared with the draperies of the room (both time and draperies contain an oblivion), so the abundant hair around a woman's face is seen to harbour time as contrasted with her eyes reflecting only the present moment.[30]

Midnight is both an actuality, a recognized light, and the deep shadows around it. An opened book on a table presents a kind of pallor and silence of words spoken long ago. It also resembles the setting of night. But a hero has entered the room, Igitur, who becomes the pure time of the present. An object in the room, a chimera, reflects some light. It, as well as the book now closed and signifying the absence of light, will illumine an idea that wants to come to life and absolve midnight.

The darkness and the draperies are caught in the permanent form of all time. But the clock, with its diamond decoration of a chimera, has produced a light which marks both the survival and the beauty of Eternal Night. Time, or the hour of midnight, speaks in a kind of echo to the night and bids it farewell. Time was once night and therefore its own sepulchre. Now, in its surviving shadow it will be metamorphosed into Eternity.

The second scene, and the longest of the four fragments, is called the *stairs* in the table of contents. Rather than sliding down the banisters, Igitur has lost his way on the stairs. The striking of the clock has continued in the pulsations of night, which means that night is being perceived not only by the light of its shadows but by the sounds which, although fallen into the past, continue to be heard. This is at best an equivocal position. Even when all sound is over, a movement in the air seems to prolong the experience. The sound of the tomb doors closing over the visitor seems never to come to an end, as if it were a spiral of sound unwinding. What is reminiscence remains real. The sound of the clock and its mysterious prolongation resemble a night bird which, startled by a flash of light, beats its wings and circles endlessly around the closed-in tomb.

The sound, now described as a panting (*halètement*) does not come from the doubt of one being moving his wings in some chance passage, but the rubbing of an earlier and better age whose innumerable genii carefully collected their ageing dust in order to see themselves in their own remains. The paragraph beginning, *Car, pour le halète-ment*, is one long sentence, Proustian in its multiple divisionings, which by its very form reproduces the image of the Arachnean thread it describes. The thread is not wound up but seems to attach all the night apparitions and hold them in a hand. The volume is the other unit shining with its escutcheon clasp. All nights are in its contents. The Shadow itself (the only capitalized word of the paragraph) casts a shadow extended flat behind itself which it walks over, while ahead of it, in a well, it casts another carpet of shadows, become pure night, formed by all the nights which have already existed. But all of these apparitions and layers of shadows are the prolongation of the noise caused by the closing of the tomb doors.

An assurance becomes clearer with the deepening of experience. The two parts of the door have closed over Igitur. He sees a reminiscence of a place, a kind of interval where he waits, but he can no longer be deceived. The place where he is is his conscience, his ever-increasing awareness of self. This is clear to Igitur in the two parts of the door. With one hand he touches one side, the panel which seems illuminated with actual knowledge; and with his other hand, the second panel representing the closed volume of his nights, those units of time containing the past and the future. What is unexplored all around him, ahead and behind, is the infinite, the darkness formed by all the apparitions together. It is they which have fallen and caused the noise continued now in his own heart beats.

But the sound is not pleasing to Igitur.[31] An excess of certainty is comparable to an excess of light. He prefers to return within the Shadow which exists inside him and which had existed before his new self-awareness. There he would like to strip off the disguise he wears through the necessity of living in the heart of his race. That heart he now hears beating. It is the last remnant of ambiguity. Since neither of the two openings represents the future, Igitur finds them equivalent and fears his old enemy chance (*le hasard*) which divided him into darkness and created time. Both are now pacified in the same sleep. Everything has come to an end and his fear, which once resembled a bird, is over. What he was is now reflected (in the mirror?) and he is pleased at watching the reflection in order to liberate his dream from its costume.

The last three paragraphs of the passage speak again of the noise which Igitur continues to hear as a kind of scansion (*scandement*) or metrical beating. The spiral stairway is a graphic representation of the recurrent beats. A bird has perhaps grazed him (*ce frôlement*) in the darkness. But now he doesn't believe it to have been a hairy-bellied creature inferior to himself which flew away, but rather a velvet-covered bust of some superior personage. The face of the character may be Igitur's, separated from his body by a spider-web collar, the same thread perhaps that was just now unwound. The hero's duality is for ever separated, and since the head is unable to hear the progress of the body, the ego of the poet is going to forget everything because of the body's separation, and dissolve in itself. The beating of the noise lessens because it is now a remembered measure prolonged by the echo in the corridor of time and hallucination. In the same way as the tomb door was really closed, now it is going to be opened for the explanation of the dream. The time has come for Igitur to leave the room, when the mirror will arrange itself without the character before it. The furniture will be abandoned and the Dream will return to the pure glass containing the substance of the Void.

In the third section, *Vie d'Igitur*, the hero gives an accounting of his life to his ancestors before they are to blow out the candle. His life, he says, has been concentrated on the clock. In order that time might remain present in his room, he thickened the curtains and tried to catch the atoms of time in heavy materials as he sat in front of his mirror.

But Igitur was projected outside of time by his race. What his race was is the sensation of the finite in him. With this sensation, the hours of the clock convert boredom into heavy time. But boredom cannot be, and it returns into its element: closed pieces of furniture. When Igitur feels himself threatened with becoming eternal upon seeing his features fading in the mirror as if he were going to dissolve into time, he opens up the pieces of furniture so that they will release their memories of human impressions. By this act, he believes he resumes his being which had been on the point of disappearing. The horror of disappearing into eternity had been so great for Igitur that he had placed his hands over his eyes in order not to see into the mirror. When he opened his eyes again, he saw in the depths of the mirror the terrifying phantom gradually absorbing the elements of feeling and sorrow in the glass and feeding on the shafts of light from the chimeras on the furniture and on the instability of the draperies, until it became so purified that it was separated from the mirror, and even the monsters of the furniture became fixed in a death-like immobility and the draperies also fell into a permanent form.[32]

The fourth section, *Le Coup de Dés,* deals with an act in which chance is at stake. Whether affirmative or negative, chance accomplished its idea. The box (*le cornet*) in which the dice are shaken is the horn (*la corne*) of the unicorn. (One further example of Mallarmé's predilection for empty objects filled with a mysterious absence.) By performing an act, chance is denied and the Infinite is fixed. Before joining the ashes of his ancestors, Igitur shakes the dice. He closes the book, blows out the candle, and lies down on the ashes of his ancestors. At that moment, it would seem that the sound ceases, and Igitur speaks to his 'immemorial race'. He is the anachronism, the character who has felt in himself the existence of the absolute. He has forgotten human speech by reading in the magician's book (*grimoire*), and he has forgotten thought in his contemplation of the light (reflected from the chimeras). The sorcerer's book of magic formulae predicted the negation of chance, and the illumination in the room revealed his dream.

The brief epilogue, separated in the published text as part V, depicts Igitur lying on the astral undivided ashes of his family. He has drunk the drop of pure nothingness. The flask is empty and it is all that remains of the castle. Purity and vacuity are identical.

INTERPRETATION

The very multiplicity of themes and objects in *Igitur* makes it a work difficult to follow with any logic or precision. It is cast in the form of a story, but also in the form of a dream. Both forms, however, appear only approximated. The passages are still close to a state of notes where the work is half visible. The intention of the poet seems clearer than the intention of the work. A time comes in the creation of a literary work when the writing is independent enough to reveal its own intention and move toward its own elucidation. It is the moment when the artist becomes artisan and has only to compose and order a work whose intention is sufficiently developed to control the pure technical consideration. What is published under the title of *Igitur* seems to belong to the period of writing previous to this state of independence. In its notes Mallarmé is still too close to the guiding idea of the work, too involved in its conceptual state for the writing to have its own form, its own life. The sentences never give the impression of finality or adequate transmission. They are searching for themselves and their own expression.

Most of the pages deal with Mallarmé's particular hallucinations: the 'dream' and the 'void'; and at the end, he adds certain considerations on the theme of 'chance'. The action of Igitur seems to be a necessary and inevitable impulse toward death. As in a tragedy, the hero dies at the end. But the movement toward death is extremely slow, as in a dream. He forces himself into a dream consciousness, a disinterested kind of living where he is narcissistically in love with himself and where he is able to live a part that he is not ordinarily. He wants to know an existence which is not an existence, which is precisely the absence of existence. The dream he is living becomes therefore equivalent to the void or to a denial of being or ontological reality.

Man ordinarily lives in accordance with the time of his thought, with the flow and the change of his thought. Igitur tries to stop time and to crystallize his thought in the form of an idea. The mirror is the object by which he tries to accomplish this. If man is unable to cause his own beginning, he is able to cause his extinction (as he is able to blow out the light of a candle). *Igitur* raises the question of whether he is able to arrest his being somewhere between his beginning and his end.

By living 'in the heart of his race', as he defines it, Igitur has covered himself with layers of disguise. These he must divest himself of as he descends more deeply into himself. The image of the stairway is that of the descent by degrees and stages into a purer reality. At the bottom is the well, the abyss of original water where, if he reaches it, he will come to an end of his introspection. There he will no longer hear the beating of his heart, the flapping of the wings, the striking of the clock. There he will have removed the last vestige of his personality and plunge into some cosmic underground fluid.

To prove that he isn't is the tempting idea that Igitur is trying to manifest. If it is manifested, Igitur will prove himself right and logical, but he will at the same time bring about his death. At the beginning (*Le Minuit*) he turns over the idea in his mind as if he were engaging upon some kind of intellectual narcissism. He lists the objects that contain a memory of life, that once were life: the book, now closed; the light reflected from a chimera or some metal ornamentation or furniture; the draperies along the wall where the darkness accumulates as if it were a substance; the clock, an echo of time and a survival of all previous nights. With them he undertakes a self-hypnosis. By divesting himself of the various costumes of his personality, he undergoes the reaction of a psychic chemistry by which all the manifestations of night surrounding him are metamorphosed into Eternity. To free oneself of all the past forms of the ego is to reach something that approaches the primal essence of one's being. Igitur is the adventurer of what is most primal in oneself. The stairs lead down to that region.

After reaching the decision to descend the stairs (the need to see the pure self), which is the subject matter of the first section, the major scene is rightfully that which transpires on the stairs. His moving through the darkness is the effort to cause a disintegration or a fragmentation of his personality. There are two parts to the tomb door, two massive surfaces of darkness, which are really two facets of his conscience, and he doesn't know through which one to pass. They appear equal. To choose is to run a risk, Chance is the old enemy. How can it be annulled?

Before shaking the dice and accomplishing the act, Igitur gives an accounting of his life to his ancestors. The word which dominates this passage of an interlude is *ennui*. His life has been characterized by boredom and impotency. What he has been has really been his ancestors, his race, who have born down on him and given him the sensation of the finite, of the malady of living and feeling always the power of determinism and time. Igitur wants to separate himself from time, to project himself outside of the realm of time, but he is also terrified at accomplishing this. He watches with horror his reflection in the mirror as it seems to turn into an aspect of eternity. In a sense, this marks the development of the poet-hero. In order to create a poem, the genius has to reach a state of independence, of autonomy. Although the artistic work reflects the universe and needs the help of the universe, it is completely separated from it. The artist is the 'ego projected absolute' (*un moi projeté absolu*) outside of time. The act of creating something isolates the artist from everything that is created. And so, the objects in the room, the furniture, the monsters and the curtains, become fixed also and eternalized when they figure in the created work.

The throwing of the dice seems to be the act of artistic creation by which the work is projected outside of the artist and chance annulled. The poet is thus relieved of chance and his work is fixed for eternity. When Igitur lies down in the tomb over the ashes of his ancestors the work is really born. It is the castle of purity, whereas the one who created it is reduced to nothingness and absorbed into it.

Throughout all the sections of *Igitur*, one follows, almost intuitively, so obscure are the logical sequences, a strange conflict between a metaphysical problem concerning the being of the poet and an aesthetic problem concerning the work of the poet. An identification is established between the Absolute and the Void. The absolute of the work is fixed when the artist is absorbed into the void. It would seem that two kinds of torment prepared this particular conflict: the torment about the work to be achieved: Mallarmé's familiar mirage of the white page; and the torment about the artist's eventual death: Mallarmé's other preoccupation with the theme of absence. To describe an object in a work is to describe its absence. The real creator is he who disappears so that the work may begin its own truncated and autonomous existence. This idea Mallarmé is going to develop more fully in *Toast Funèbre* and in the night sonnets, but it exists already, although obscurely, in *Igitur*.

The very constructions of the poet, which are his triumphs over chance, contain an element of the absurd in them because they are monuments to the Void; they are built in the Void. There is something both prodigious and desperate about Mallarmé's intellectual adventure of *Igitur*. And our reaction to it will either be that of Mendès or of Villiers de l'Isle-Adam to whom the poet first read the manuscript in 1870. Mendès, the impatient and perhaps false friend, expressed his lack of comprehension and lack of belief in his impolite nervousness and in his irritability. Villiers, respectful and attentive, showed later in his drama, *Axel*, completed in 1872, to what extent Igitur had influenced him.[33] Paul Claudel sees in the work of Mallarmé, in what he calls *La Catastrophe d'Igitur*[34] a reincarnation of Hamlet, a complacency with disaster, a kind of communion between the darkness of night and the misfortune of being a man. Although Claudel considers Igitur the matrix out of which Mallarmé's art emerged, he chides the poet at being too exclusively the hero of the closed room filled with Victorian bibelots. But with his two predecessors, Poe and Baudelaire, Mallarmé is for Claudel the poet whose art developed out of a metaphysical comprehension of night. Night was the ambiency and the spiritual climate for the greatest realization of the poetic word in the 19th century.

A penetrating reading of *Igitur*, even an accurate reading, is perhaps impossible because the work is too close to the experience. And such an experience of thought, as it half forms on the few pages of *Igitur*, appears so tremendous that its articulation and our understanding of it can at best be only approximate. The poetic act is reasonable and necessary because human life is not eternal. The poet speaks of his mortality of man. Igitur's primal urge seems to be the will to abolish his own personality and time. He will succeed in abolishing the very void toward which he moves by living, if he creates the eternity of words. His one chance for survival, the one risk involved in throwing the dice, is the creating of his poem.

The guiding phrase of the work is perhaps that of the first fragment: *C'est le rêve pur d'un Minuit.*[35] *Igitur* is the story of a dream, of an imaginary dream in sleep and of the artist's dream. Both kinds of dreams are transpositions of reality and efforts to transcend it. As in a dream, where the subconscious constructs scenes and creatures bearing a strong resemblance with the universe, so in a poem the technique of artifice and art aims at establishing some reminiscence of the word's form. If all men are dreamers, according to André Breton (*l'homme, ce rêveur définitif*), the poet is a special kind of dreamer, who consciously applies the laws of a technique of words and at the same time yields to the insistence and the initiative of the words themselves. His mind often resembles the course of a river where images flow by quickly, impatient at not being seized. Every poet is eager to possess the image in its original and inner purity. To cast it into a form is always to run the risk of losing its primal power and beauty. As every colour tends to vanish into white or the absence of colour, so every object of mental images tends to melt into a void, and so every syllable of mental words tends to disappear into silence. Words are all endowed with a basic or essential power which has more to do with their resonance, their power of suggestion, their colouring than with their more limited meaning.

The poetry of Mallarmé often resembles a chemical agent applied to objects, which, dissolving them, precipitates them into a void. But this artistic stratagem is performed in order to throw into unique prominence the *idea* of the vanished object. The idea of the object is its absence and its purity. Mallarmé's dream is the creation of a world of this kind of purity. Igitur, in the same way, divests himself of passions and affections in order to comply with the exigency of the absolute. He becomes a part of the pure present which is actually a participation in eternity. Mallarmé's magic, performed with incredible accuracy, results in a transparency where the object is seen and seen through. Igitur himself ends by sustaining no weight and is mingled indistinguishably with the ashes of his ancestors. The poet's will to transfigure the real was pushed farther by Mallarmé than by any other poet. The prose of *Igitur* may be considered a close note-taking on Mallarmé's dangerous psychic crisis between 1865 and 1870, which was in many ways the dream of self-annihilation. The literary work and the psychic experience both approached that margin of absurdity or insanity where words no longer bear their recognizable traits. At times the experience of living and the experience of writing become inhuman in their faculty to discredit or sever all human bonds of attachment and affection. This is a dream like others, but where the darkness grows absolute.

To live, in the most simple way, from day to day, is for each man to participate in an adventure of dissolution. The poet's work rescues man for a second of time from this daily adventure. The poem is a solution, if life is a dissolution. *Igitur* is close to being a treatise on the dream of the poet and especially on its dangerous temptations. A dream is the common way for man to separate himself from the appearances of the world in order to reach what some like to consider the essential Being. A dream is therefore a voiding of the sensible world. The poetry of Mallarmé, in its close association with the dream and the motif of absence, is a way of knowledge, a way of knowing, whose goal would seem to be the total dissolving of images. After passing through one kind of night, the poet enters another night. After the night of the dream comes the night of the poem.

NOTES TO CHAPTER III

1. First published in *La Revue Fantaisiste*, of Nov. 1, 1861.

2. For her eyes—in order to swim in those lakes.

3. Eyes, lakes with my simple passion to be reborn
   Other than the actor who evoked with gestures
   As a plume [of an actor] evokes the base soot of lamps,
   I pierced a window in the canvas wall.

4. With my legs and arms limpid traitor swimming
   By successive leaps, denying the bad
   Hamlet! as if in the water I innovated
   A thousand tombs where I disappeared a virgin.

5. Et d'herbes enivré, j'ai plongé comme un traître
   Dans ces lacs défendus, et, quand tu m'appelais,
   Baigné mes membres nus dans l'onde aux blancs galets,
   Oubliant mon habit de pitre au tronc d'un hêtre.

6. Joyous gold of a cymbal shaken by wrists,
   Suddenly the sun strikes the nudity
   Which pure came off from my white coolness,

   Rancid night of the skin when you passed over me,
   Not knowing, ingrate, that it was my consecration,
   This make-up, drowned in the perfidious water of the glaciers.

7. *Stéphane Mallarmé: un héros*, 'J'y vois la conception platonicienne de l'âme déchue de l'idéal, et qui y aspire comme à sa patrie natale.'

8. Thibaudet, *La Poésie de Stéphane Mallarmé*, p. 250.

9. Noulet, *L'Oeuvre Poétique de Mallarmé*, p. 263.

10. Mauron, *Mallarmé l'obscur*, pp. 157-159.

11. Beausire, *Gloses*, p. 159.

12. Will the virginal, strong and handsome today
    Tear for us with a drunken flap of his wing
    This hard forgotten lake which the transparent glacier
    Of flights unflown haunts under the frost!

13. A swan of former times remembers it is he
    Magnificent but who without hope gives himself up
    For not having sung of the region where he should have been
    When the boredom of sterile winter was resplendent.

14. All his neck will shake off this white death-agony
    Inflicted by space on the bird which denies space,
    But not the horror of the earth where his wings are caught.

15. Phantom whom his pure brilliance assigns to this place,
    He becomes immobile in the cold dream of scorn
    Which the Swan puts on in his useless exile.

16. First published with the title, *Sonnet*, in *La Vogue*, 13-20 June 1886 and reprinted later without any change.

17. Introducing myself into your story
    Is as a timid hero
    If he has touched with his bare heel
    Some grass of a land

    Hostile to glaciers
    I do not know the naive sin
    Which you will not have stopped
    From laughing out loud over its victory

Tell me if I am not happy
Thunder and rubies at the hub
At seeing in the air which this fire cuts through

With scattered kingdoms
The wheel dying purple
Of my one evening chariot.

18. In Mallarmé's sonnet on Baudelaire, the image of the sewer is described as drooling 'mud' and 'rubies': *bavant boue et rubis.*
In T. S. Eliot's first quartet, *Burnt Norton*, part II, two lines seem to reproduce the Mallarmé image of opposites and the axle-tree:
Garlic and sapphires in the mud
Clot the bedded axle-tree.

19. 'Après trois mois d'impuissance, je m'en suis enfin débarrassé.' Letter to Cazalis of June 1862. cf. Mondor, *Vie*, p. 48.

20. *Renouveau.* First called *Vere Novo.* 'Mon premier sonnet est consacré à la décrire, c'est-à-dire à la maudire.' ibid.

21. 'Je me traîne comme un vieillard, et je passe des heures à observer dans les glaces l'envahissement de la bêtise qui éteint déjà mes yeux.' Letter to Cazalis, Dec. 1864. ibid. p. 149.

22. To H. Cazalis, March 1866, ibid. pp. 192-3.

23. ibid., p. 236-8. In collection of H. Mondor.

24. cf. letter to Lefébure, 3 May 1868. Catalogue Giraud-Badin et Cornuau, 1925. Quoted by Mondor, pp. 259-60.

25. cf. Mondor, *Vie*, note on p. 276.

26. A part of this letter is quoted by Mondor, p. 278. A longer portion is given by Michaud, in *L'Aventure Poétique*, p. 187.

27. Mondor, *Vie*, p. 286.

28. 'C'est un conte, par lequel je veux terrasser le vieux monstre de l'Impuissance, son sujet, du reste, afin de me cloîtrer dans mon grand labeur déjà réétudié. S'il est fait, (le conte) je suis guéri; *Simila Similibus.*'

29. The full title is: *Igitur ou La Folie d'Elbehnon.*

30. cf. the passage beginning, 'Et du Minuit demeure la présence en la vision d'une chambre du temps . . . '
translation: And from midnight remains the presence in the vision of a room of time when the mysterious furniture stops a vague trembling of thought, luminous breaking of the return of its waves and their first enlarging, while (within a moving limitation) the former place of the fall of the hour, in a narcotic calm of the pure ego dramed of so long, is immobilized. But from midnight, time is resolved into draperies on which the deadened trembling has stopped, completing them with its splendour, like languishing hair around a face lighted with mystery, with the vacant eyes similar to the mirror, of the guest, stripped of all meaning except presence.

31. cf. the passage beginning, 'Je n'aime pas ce bruit: cette perfection de ma certitude me gêne . . . '
translation: I do not like the noise. This perfection of my certainty troubles me; all is too clear; the light shows the desire for an evasion; all is too shining; I should prefer to return into my increated and former Shadow, and strip off by thought the disguise which necessity imposed upon me, of living in the heart of this race (which I hear beating here), the sole remaining ambiguity.

32. cf. the passage beginning. 'Et quand je rouvrais les yeux au fond du miroir, je voyais le personnage d'horreur . . .'
translation: And when I reopened my eyes in the depths of the mirror, I saw the fearsome character, the phantom of horror gradually absorb what remained of sentiment and grief in the mirror, feed his horror on the supreme tremblings of the chimeras and the instability of the draperies, and shape itself by rarefying the mirror to an exceptional purity, until it was detached, permanent, from the absolutely pure mirror, as if caught in its cold—until finally the furniture, after its monsters had succumbed with their convulsive rings, died in an isolated form, projecting its hard lines into the absence of atmosphere, with the monsters held in their final effort, and until the curtains, no longer restless, fell into a shape which they were to preserve henceforth.

33. Kurt Wais, in his book on Mallarmé, lists seven points in common between *Igitur* and *Axel*: the setting of an old castle, the last scions of a dying family, the hour of midnight, the tomb, the spiral stairway, the noise of steps, the sorcerer's book (*grimoire*).

34. Claudel, *Positions et Propositions,* Gallimard, pp. 197-207.

35. This is the pure dream of a midnight.

PART II

THE WORK ACHIEVED

Hérodiade

CHAPTER IV

HÉRODIADE

ON NO POEM, more than on *Hérodiade*, did Mallarmé expend time, anguish and painstaking care. The poem, or rather the character who gives her name to the poem, was a kind of perpetual muse for the poet. He returned to her intermittently, as to an old fidelity or, at best, as to a well-loved habit, during more than thirty years. Mallarmé composed *Hérodiade* at the beginning of his career, soon after he arrived in the city of Tournon where he occupied his first post as school teacher. At the time of his death, at Valvins, on the Seine, where he spent so many summers, the manuscript of *Hérodiade* was open on his desk and gave evidence to the fact that it was among his last preoccupations.

Mallarmé arrived at Tournon in November 1863, at the age of twenty-one. The following year, in October 1864, he announced in a letter that he had begun work on *Hérodiade*. And he spoke immediately of the terror which this enterprise inspired in him, a terror which seemed to spring from the conviction that the language of the new poem must necessarily come from a new poetics. He attempted in this passage of the letter to give a definition of this poetic theory, 'To paint, not the thing, but the effect that it produces.'[1] This sentence, used by Mallarmé to describe the new writing of *Hérodiade*, has served, more than almost any other definition, to summarize the art of symbolism, and especially that aspect of symbolism, developed by Mallarmé. Thirty-four years later, in a letter written in May 1898, the year of his death, he described a day of work and in referring to *Hérodiade*, put the matter in the future tense, by saying that the poem will come about gradually and that he is somewhat in possession of himself.[2]

Hérodiade is not simply an early poem which Mallarmé recast at the end of his life. It is a poem he lived with or rather struggled with all his life, and it illustrates perhaps better than any other piece Mallarmé's intense love for a poem and the desperate difficulty he underwent in achieving it, in finding for it a form or expression suitable to translate the idea. On one level of interpretation, Hérodiade is a cold virginal princess who stands aloof from the world of men, but she may also represent the poem itself, so difficult to seize and possess that the poet ultimately despairs of knowing it. Hérodiade is therefore both a character whom Mallarmé tried to subdue, and a mythical character whose meaning goes far beyond the comprehension of the poet. She presided over Mallarmé's life as poet in a dual role of princess and myth, of character and symbol.

Hérodiade was the poem of Mallarmé's winters. The three years spent at Tournon were among the most painful, in terms of material discomfort, of the poet's life. But they were also the most fruitful in terms of poetic creativeness. His correspondence of the latter part of 1864 is replete with references to *Hérodiade*, but when the winter is over, he abandons work on it for another new poem, more suitable for spring and summer, on the theme of a faun, which ultimately is to be called *L'Après-Midi d'un Faune*. It is significant that the three major poems of this period: *L'Azur* (written possibly before Mallarmé came to Tournon), *L'Après-Midi d'un Faune* and *Hérodiade*, all composed during the most abundantly productive years of his career, deal with the same theme of artistic sterility. Whether it be the cold bejewelled princess of the winters or the lascivious faun of midsummer, Mallarmé is essentially preoccupied with the problem of fertility and birth, with the staggering impossibility of achieving the perfect birth of a poem. No poet has ever been made so completely a prisoner of his own poem as Mallarmé. He became so much a part of the poem that he was always fearful of being unable to project it outside of himself. Mallarmé's love for his own creation tended to obstruct and obscure any articulation he might give to his love. Mallarmé as a poet was in a certain sense the kind of lover who converts the beloved into a mystery and whose silence is adoration.

Mallarmé's life-long preoccupation with *Hérodiade* is significant not only for an understanding of his own poems, but also for the much wider context of modern literature, especially for the entire movement of symbolism and the so-called decadent literature of the latter 19th century, and for surrealism in the 20th century. Mallarmé's princess Hérodiade has an extensive literary genealogy. The very year that he began the composition of *Hérodiade*, 1864, he discovered Flaubert's novel, *Salammbô*, which was first published in 1862. Salammbô and Hérodiade have the same characteristics of aloofness. Their beauty is mysterious and hermetic. It is shattered or would be shattered by marriage. Midway between the early version of *Hérodiade* and Mallarmé's death, Villiers de L'Isle-Adam published in 1885-86 his symbolist drama, *Axel*, whose leading character, Sara, bears an intimate affinity with Hérodiade. Sara's death is consummated in a blaze of jewels and she wills her own death at the moment of marriage when she is on the verge of happiness, because she, like Hérodiade, is a soul seeking to escape from the state of becoming. She, like Hérodiade, and like Hérodiade's most recent descendent, Valéry's Jeune Parque, is a young girl of a philosophical turn of mind, who is anxious to attain the preferable state of being, even if being takes on for her the form of death.

The principal thought on which Mallarmé's poem seems to depend is that expressed at the beginning of the dialogue between Hérodiade and her nurse: the thought that beauty is death. This doctrine, expounded in its most psychological form in Mallarmé's *Hérodiade,* is the culmination of a century of philosophical inquiry, which is usually defined as pessimism. When the beauty of woman, such as Hérodiade's, is cold and inaccessible, it summarizes the void of life and hence translates a philosophical concept. The splendour and magnificence of Hérodiade's appearance, as well as Salammbô's in Flaubert's novel, and Sara's in the play, *Axel*, symbolize sterility.

This feeling about the void of life is apparent in the very early manifestations of what we call today the romantic movement in Western Europe. Examples are numerous: at the end of the 18th century, the suicide of the young English poet, Chatterton, and Goethe's early novel, *Werther;* in the first years of the 19th century, Chateaubriand's stories which not only express pessimism about life but also give some of the first illustrations of the lonely and hence sterile beauty of woman. The cosmos, felt as a flux and as an eternal movement in each individual soul who seeks to find stability somewhere else, usually in death, is the subject matter of much of the writings of Nerval, Baudelaire, Flaubert, Rimbaud, Mallarmé and the surrealists.

The poem, *Hérodiade*, a creation of a poet, bears of course a strong relationship to the poet, but its theme comes not only from Mallarmé but from many of the poets and thinkers who preceded him. As a human being the princess Hérodiade opposes the flow and the change of life by her studied and concentrated frigidity. Her opposition to normal life and vicissitude is the projection of the mythical role of poet which Mallarmé believed in and practised, of which there exist examples before him in the 19th century and which the surrealists will re-enact in the 20th century. I refer to the magical property of the poet, to his function of hierophant, of priest and miracle worker. The poet feels all the cosmic vibrations and changes of the world, but establishes outside of them, by means of his art, which is the alchemy of language, a reality which by its durability is a denial of flux and change.

The word 'magical' as applied to an artistic creation seems startlingly new in the 19th century. The poet holds the secrets of his creation. He is the new dealer in occultism or hermeticism. Hugo considered himself the *écho sonore* of a world not heard by ordinary ears, of a supernatural world not submitted to the logic of a changing world. For Mallarmé, and, to a lesser degree, for other poets of the century, there is a point where poetry passes into the realm of the unexpressed. In *Hérodiade* he seems to leave poetry just on this side of that point. But in Mallarmé's final poem, *Un coup de dés*, it is quite possible that he takes poetry over into the realm of the unexpressed or the ineffable and hence creates in a very absolute sense a surrealist poem. But the method and principle of surrealism may be more easily studied and apprehended in such a poem as *Hérodiade*.

In considering the main function of the poet as that of magician or symbol-maker, Mallarmé was giving to the symbol an occult power very close to the mystical power of the Word or the Logos. Baudelaire in his doctine of *Correspondances* had stressed the spiritual reality of the symbol. In this doctrine, Baudelaire was perpetuating the lessons of Swedenborg's *Arcana Coelestina*. Novalis also had taught that the poet sees the invisible and feels the supra-sensible.

This definition of the poet's function, which has sometimes been called *angelism*, because in it the poet withholds his secrets, places him in a category comparable to that of the priest, and therefore to the type of individual who is isolated from society, who serves society in his isolation, in his hieratic calling. Nietzsche has said that all poetry is originally hieratic.

Thus poetry becomes one of those activities of the human mind whose nature and purpose are spiritual. The poet finds himself, by the mystery of his vocation, the guardian of creative secrets, in much the same way that Hérodiade wills to make herself into the guardian of her own being. The man who is engaged in the alchemy of his own language, like the princess who is engaged in the benumbing of her senses and emotions, is a poet not only in the creation of his own world, but in the creation of his own divinity as well. The poet in this sense is both priest and god. Here culminate the romantic dream and the romantic temperament. Rousseau had once described this quietistic state of being when nothing exterior to self exists, when one is sufficient unto oneself as God is. The modern poet has revindicated his ancient role of Prometheus and Orpheus, of fire-stealer and mystical singer. He learned once again, during the very century that was copiously consecrated to the definition of the philosophy of science, the meaning of divine madness which Plato had once used in characterizing the poet.

Poetry's esoteric principle was explored by Stéphane Mallarmé and incarnated in his princess Hérodiade. The three leading aspects of this principle: angelism, hermeticism and narcissism, are also the three leading characteristics of the princess. Angelism seems to signify that the poet creates his own world and lives within it. This would correspond to Hérodiade's desertion of the world, her return to the tower and her isolated existence. Hermeticism is on the one hand the secret meaning of poetry, jealously guarded by the poet, and on the other hand, the magical practices of Hérodiade or even the ritualistic manner of her life. Finally, narcissism, by far the most significant and most obscure of the three aspects of the esoteric principle, is a required attitude of every poet who is himself the subject of his poetry, and is revealed in Hérodiade's words addressed to her mirror.

The poem, as it appears in the most recent editions of Mallarmé's work, is in three parts: an overture, *Ouverture Ancienne;* a dialogue between Hérodiade and her nurse, called *Scène,* which is the main part of the poem; and a short detached lyric spoken by St. John the Baptist, called *Cantique de saint Jean.*

The overture was written after the first version of the dialogue, during the years 1865-66, when Mallarmé was still in Tournon, but it was never published during the lifetime of the poet. The poem, which is 98 lines in length, remained among his papers and manuscripts until long after his death when his son-in-law and literary executor, Dr Bonniot, published it in the *Nouvelle Revue Française,* in November 1926. The entire piece is spoken by the nurse as a kind of incantation. It serves to set the scene for the subsequent dialogue. The nurse talks about what she sees from the tower. First the landscape, which is desolate under a dawn now abolished. *Abolie* is the first word of the poem. It had been used previously in the hermetic poetry of Gérard de Nerval, and was to become one of Mallarmé's most frequently used words. The dawn, once golden and red, is now abolished or pallid, and has chosen for its tomb the tower where the nurse awaits the return of Hérodiade. There is the suggestion that the tower had been used by Hérodiade for propitiatory or occult practices, and its present abandonment has spread to the autumnal scene of the landscape. The room and the bed appear empty to the nurse. She wonders if the voice she hears is her own or the empty echo of some voice of the past. Everything is funereal and tenebrific and monotonous. The nurse refers to the young girl exiled in her precious heart—an early very direct allusion to Hérodiade's narcissism—but especially accumulates words of an esoteric import: prophecy, dreams, stars, books of magic. The dominant theme is the emptiness of the present. The setting and the repetition of certain words are reminiscent of Poe. The mood is built up for the strange dialogue which follows.

The cry of the nurse announces the return of Hérodiade. The older woman bends down to kiss the rings of the princess, but Hérodiade, who is to spurn everything, wards her off. In order to explain why a kiss would kill her, she speaks instantly of her blond hair which, immaculate, is the symbol of her immortality. In its fire and light, her hair is opposed to the principle of her cold body. She has just come in from a morning whose splendour is now dying (this theme was announced in the *Ouverture*), in order to be again with her nurse of the winters (*ô nourrice d'hiver*). She had been able to walk among the lions unharmed (according to legend they are respectful of virgins) as if they had represented the dangers of the outer world or the menaces to the integrity of her being. The reminiscences of the world, which she has left, are not in herself but in her hair which she asks the nurse to comb indolently before a mirror:

> *Aide-moi, . . .*
> *A me peigner nonchalamment dans un miroir.*

Her hair imitates the wild manes of the lions and the brilliantly jewelled light of the sun. The beauty and violence of the world have left her intact, but they have been reflected in her hair. She rejects all perfumes because she wishes her hair to resemble not flowers nor the languishing odour of flowers, but gold and the sterile coldness of metals. As a young child her hair reflected the iron weapons and bronze vases of the tower, and now as a virgin princess it must reflect the light of precious gold and jewels.

When the nurse holds up the mirror before her, Hérodiade's actual words addressed to it are very brief, but their meaning pervades the rest of the poem. Deep in the mirror, as in a black hole, she has searched hours on end for her memories and appeared to herself as a distant ghost. On certain evenings, when the mirror resembled an implacable fountain (at this point it is obvious that the myth of Hérodiade is joining with the myth of Narcissus), she realized the bareness or the reality of her dream: *J'ai de mon rêve épars connu la nudité?* Here she interrupts her speech by asking the nurse if she is beautiful. The nurse compares Hérodiade to a star, but when she extends her hand to raise up part of the princess's hair which is falling, Hérodiade turns violently on the woman and accuses her of sacrilege in trying to touch her. This is the third crime the nurse has almost committed: first, the kiss on the hand and rings; second, the offering of the perfume; and finally the attempt to touch Hérodiade's hair. For the princess these constitute three forebodings of disaster for this day in the tower.

The second part of the scene begins when the nurse insinuates that Hérodiade must be waiting for some hero, that she must be reserving her being and her purity for some man. Hérodiade's answer to this insinuation, which is an ironical hope of the old nurse, constitutes the longest speech of the scene. It is a kind of aria in three parts containing the psychological explanation of her life and vocation. It begins like an aria with a line of strong narcissistic import:

> *Oui, c'est pour moi, pour moi, que je fleuris, déserte!*

All the themes, heretofore partially announced, are now commingled and made specific in this aria, which Hérodiade sings not merely to the nurse, but to the world, or at least to the public in the theatre where she is performing the scene. Mallarmé's initial project was to compose a play on the theme of Hérodiade and in this monologue there is something of the rhetoric of the theatre. This element of drama was strong enough to permit Martha Graham to compose a dance on the poem, and the composer, Paul Hindemith, to write a musical setting which follows closely each line of the poem.

Hérodiade is flowering for herself, not in the usual kind of garden, but in a garden of amethysts and precious stones. Her beauty is like the hidden beauty of jewels deep in the earth which contain the ancient secrets of the world. The first part of the aria describes the beauty of Hérodiade's eyes and hair as essentially a sterile beauty.

Her eyes are like pure jewels and her hair is fatal and massive because it reflects the colour of metal. Jewels and metal, originally buried in the earth, are as sterile and useless as the eyes and hair of Hérodiade, concealed in her tower away from the world of men.

> *Oui, c'est pour moi, pour moi, que je fleuris, déserte!*
> *Vous le savez, jardins d'améthyste, enfouis*
> *Sans fin dans de savants abîmes éblouis,*
> *Ors ignorés, gardant votre antique lumière*
> *Sous le sombre sommeil d'une terre première,*
> *Vous, pierres où mes yeux comme de purs bijoux*
> *Empruntent leur clarté mélodieuse, et vous*
> *Métaux qui donnez à ma jeune chevelure*
> *Une splendeur fatale et sa massive allure!*
> *Quant à toi, femme née en des siècles malins*
> *Pour la méchanceté des antres sibyllins,*
> *Qui parles d'un mortel! selon qui, des calices*
> *De mes robes, arôme aux farouches délices,*
> *Sortirait le frisson blanc de ma nudité,*
> *Prophétise que si le tiède azur d'été,*
> *Vers qui nativement la femme se dévoile,*
> *Me voit dans ma pudeur grelottante d'étoile,*
> *Je meurs!*[3]

The awesomeness of Hérodiade's virginity is the theme of the second part. Her chastity burns with the same pallor that the snow casts against the night outside.

> *J'aime l'horreur d'être vierge et je veux*
> *Vivre parmi l'effroi que me font mes cheveux*
> *Pour, le soir, retirée en ma couche, reptile*
> *Inviolé sentir en la chair inutile*
> *Le froid scintillement de ta pâle clarté*
> *Toi qui te meurs, toi qui brûles de chasteté,*
> *Nuit blanche de glaçons et de neige cruelle!*[4]

The night, which is cold and dead, is called the eternal sister of Hérodiade.

> *Et ta sœur solitaire, ô ma sœur éternelle*
> *Mon rêve montera vers toi: telle déjà,*
> *Rare limpidité d'un cœur qui le songea,*
> *Je me crois seule en ma monotone patrie*

Et tout, autour de moi, vit dans l'idolâtrie
D'un miroir qui reflète en son calme dormant
Hérodiade au clair regard de diamant . . .
O charme dernier, oui! je le sens, je suis seule.[5]

This is the third and last movement of the song in which a fusion takes place between the sterile night and the sterile image of Hérodiade in the mirror. The poem at this point reaches culmination in its inner action whereby Hérodiade attains to a oneness of being, to a vain state of beauty in her monotonous kingdom.

It is narcissism pushed one degree farther than the limit which Narcissus reached. Whereas the adolescent in the Greek myth was content with watching in the mirror-fountain the reflection of himself and in the reflected traits the world he loved and the being with whom he wanted to unite himself, Hérodiade represents the other sex, the narcissism of woman. She seeks to establish not merely solitude and her reflection in a mirror, but an absorption of her being (of her beauty and her chastity) with the material world. In order to know the secret of existence, she wants to be as closely absorbed in the cosmos as the diamond is one with the earth in which it is embedded.

Every theme in *Hérodiade* represents some aspect of night: the literal fall of night outside the tower which covers the monotonous landscape of approaching winter; the night inside the tower; the night of necromancy and dark magical rites; the perpetual night inside the earth where the jewels and the metals sleep; the night of the mirror which is like a black hole into which Hérodiade looks in order to see all the remembered and forgotten memories of her life; and the final night of the reflection in which Hérodiade's being becomes useless and sterile.

From these various aspects of the night theme we are led to realize that the poem of Mallarmé involves a vaster and more profound myth than the simple story of Narcissus. It might be called the myth of self-destruction which lies at the core of every human being and which the principle of life and the principle of religious belief are constantly trying to submerge or conquer or forget. The myth of self-destruction is more closely associated with us than we willingly acknowledge. It seems to be an important element of many of the so-called principles of life, such as birth, love, love of God, artistic creation. In order to accomplish anything, we have to destroy ourselves to some degree. *Hérodiade*, which we are considering a mythical poem, is a symbolic or even choreographic expression of an impulse which is deeply and natively human. Mallarmé's princess wills to become an image of herself, unreal and untouched, as each man wills, in his solitude of sleep or love or work or prayer, to become more one with the principle of his being, more harmoniously or intimately himself.

What we have called the principle of self-destruction in the poem, *Hérodiade*, might justifiably be named the principle of transformation or metamorphosis. The eyes and hair of Hérodiade are not only compared to jewels and metals but seem to be converted into the inert material world. One remembers the suicides in Dante's *Inferno*, canto 13, whose bodies have been metamorphosed into tree trunks and one may well be struck by the analogy between Hérodiade's desire for material immobilization and the Dantean punishment accorded to the sin of suicide. Once in the Mallarmé poem, Hérodiade compares herself to an inviolate reptile (v. 105-6). This is a further allusion to transformation which also has its counterpart in the *Inferno*, in the circle where thieves are punished by having their bodies changed into snakes or fused with the body of a snake.

If the deepest aspect of this will or action on the part of Hérodiade is self-destruction, a more immediate aspect is the desire to know oneself and the world, to know the unity of self and the world. During the past one hundred years, and even slightly more if we include works of prose, poetry has been submitted to a philosophical use. The romantic period in the first half of the 19th century, the symbolist period in the second half of the century (at the beginning of which, *Hérodiade* sets the décor and introduces the principal vocabulary) and the surrealist period in the 20th century, might easily be considered as one literary period or one artistic movement characterized and unified by a unique philosophical preoccupation. *Hérodiade* stands therefore midway between the *Correspondances* of Baudelaire and the activities of the surrealists in the 20's and 30's when experimentation is pushed very far in studying the relationships between man and the material world, when the figure of man and objects in the purely material world are commingled in dreams and artistic creations. In the surrealist period the meaning of man and of his existence is deliberately confused with the meaning of art. Never was so much demanded of art and poetry, in terms of knowledge and philosophy, as in the surrealist period. Hérodiade stands as a figure on the threshold of surrealism. The poem is an initiation not so much to the methods of surrealism as to the goal of surrealism. We have seen Mallarmé's princess partaking of the material and the spiritual worlds, joining them, and thus explaining them and the unity which binds them. The action of Hérodiade does not merely involve a fusing of subjective and objective elements, but much more than that, an attainment to surreality, in a literal sense. She enters a domain above or apart from the real world.

No such figure as Hérodiade can exist alone. She must have ancestors and descendents. When related to them, she loses some of her enigmatical character. She is not fully explained by them (no mythical figure is ever fully recognizable) but they help to localize and situate her in relation to our own changing world and our paltry understanding of it. Her immediate ancestors are women created by the romantic temperament and by romantic artists, and her descendents are to be found in the works of the surrealists: in books like *Nadja* of André Breton and in certain paintings of women by Picasso.

A first clue to Hérodiade's ancestors might be in the romantic equation of beauty and death. We saw how Hérodiade and night were fused as sisters in Mallarmé's poem. Beauty and death would be the equivalent abstractions used constantly by the romantics, or at least, on a more elementary level, beauty and sadness. It is quite possible that in the myth of woman the most important factor is the proximity or simultaneity of beauty and sadness. Beauty of woman is real for man only when it is imperilled, threatened with dissolution. The sentiment of the beautiful generates immediately the sentiment of melancholy. Chateaubriand taught us that when we look at nature, at an exotic landscape, we experience both exaltation and melancholy. As pleasure and pain are inseparable, so any intense knowledge of the beautiful is synthesized with a knowledge of suffering. In many poems of Baudelaire, such as *Hymne à la Beauté*, and throughout his personal journals, we read of the inevitable commingling of voluptuousness and sadness.

The implacable cold beauty and virginal aloofness of Flaubert's Salammbô and Mallarmé's Hérodiade would not have been celebrated soon after 1860 if this type of woman-goddess had not been preceded by the type of fatal or persecuted woman. The Medusa head is an example of beauty allied with the repulsive, and there persists an element of the Medusan beauty in the countless examples of beauty allied with physical suffering and torture in the late 18th century and early 19th century heroines. Examples might be chosen from both good and bad literature, and from all countries: Gretchen in Goethe's *Faust,* Atala in Chateaubriand's novel, Antonia and Agnes in Lewis' novel, *The Monk,* Mrs Ann Radcliffe's tales of terror, especially *The Italian,* the Marquis de Sade's stories, such as *Juliette* and *Justine,* where voluptuousness is achieved in scenes of crime and destruction.

This theme of crime and perversion, associated with love and the beauty of woman, is not only an important background for such a poem as *Hérodiade,* but it is also a theme renewed and recapitulated by the surrealists, although not perhaps in their major works. In fact, what has been called the attraction of the horrible and the monstrous in surrealist art is not so apparent or so strong as that in the early and post romantics. The urge to commit a crime or a mortal sin in order to discover in it an innate element of beauty is more easily studied in Sade, Baudelaire and Dostoievski, than in Breton, Eluard and Desnos. In Flaubert's *Tentation de Saint Antoine,* there is a closer identification of lust and death than in the writings of Lautréamont. The richest documentation on the study of beauty as springing from the paradoxical source of horror and suffering would be, first, in the poems and prose of Baudelaire; that is, in the example of his poems and the critical judgements and exegeses of his prose writings; and secondly, in the paintings of Eugène Delacroix whom Baudelaire admired so unreservedly. Beauty, on the canvases of Delacroix, is almost always translated in terms of frenzied action and scenes of sadism. Baudelaire, in his poem on painters, *Les Phares,* in the stanza on Delacroix, calls him a 'lake of blood' *(lac de sang).* Delacroix illustrated some of the more terrifying scenes of Goethe and Byron, and chose as subjects for his paintings: the interior of harems, or drowned Ophelia, or the sack of Constantinople. In the many names with which Baudelaire apostrophized his mistress, Jeanne Duval, we begin to see the transformation from fatal woman or suffering heroine to the type which culminates in Hérodiade: tigress, cruel beast, demon, vampire, frigid idol, black Venus, Amazon. Jeanne is feared by Baudelaire, almost as if she were a Clytemnestra, who, like the women of Lesbos, murdered her husband.

The evolution from early and late romanticism to such a work as *Hérodiade* marks the shift from the drama of sadism, as illustrated in such writers as the Marquis de Sade, Baudelaire and Lautréamont, to the drama of occultism, as illustrated by Gérard de Nerval, Villiers de l'Isle-Adam, Mallarmé and Huysmans. These two dramas cannot be fixed chronologically. Lautréamont, for example, wrote his sadism-permeated cantos after Mallarmé had composed his first version of *Hérodiade*. However, the drama of hermeticism seems to succeed in time the drama of sexual violence, although there always remains an element and a memory of sadism in occultism. These two words might easily be translated by the Nietzschean terms: Dionysos and Apollo. Nietzsche's work, *The Birth of Tragedy*, which states that art contains something of both the Dionysian and Apollonian strains, was first published in Leipzig in 1872, just three years after the first appearance in print of *Hérodiade*. The terms we have been using of sadism and occultism seem to be narrowed and particularized synonyms of what Nietzsche means by Dionysos and Apollo. They represent two traits of distinction or distinctiveness by which the writer is able to isolate himself from the rest of society: first, as a psychological man whose instincts seem shocking and reprehensible; and secondly, as artist whose work is difficult to understand. The artist-Dionysos is the reprobate and pariah in terms of bourgeois society, such as Baudelaire and Rimbaud. The artist-Apollo is the priest and guardian of creative secrets, such as Mallarmé and André Breton. In *Hérodiade* it would be possible to point out elements of sadism, as well as the more obvious elements of occultism, but all these elements appear conventionalized and disciplined. Mallarmé has condensed in a single poem much of the literary and artistic efforts of a century. He has therefore, in a certain sense, applied a classical method to romantic traits and themes.

In the Gothic tales and the so-called *romans noirs* of Sade, Lewis and Radcliffe, the heroine or the beautiful woman is treated as a victim. The scenes of orgy and destruction show her as a kind of sacrificial victim and the means by which man's passion and frenzy are aroused. But, as it often occurs in the evolution of religious practice when the victim becomes god, so in this literary evolution the victimized or fatal woman of the romantics becomes a goddess in such a work as *Hérodiade*. The art form in which she appears is so placid and bejewelled that it resembles Byzantium art and is often referred to by the term Byzantianism. Hérodiade in her final state attains to a closed metallic useless perfection. The very words of the poem take on something of the vain beauty of jewels. The hair of Hérodiade, as the symbol of a cold and golden treasure, became a commonplace in literary symbols of the latter 19th century. It was a facile transcription of the psychological moment when the dream about life had succeeded in exhausting the impulse to live.

The exoticism of such a state of mind as well as the simple exoticism of Hérodiade's appearance are types very easy to confuse with mysticism. At best, Hérodiade's might be called a mystical exoticism since it takes her outside the actualities of time and space. This will be a goal repeatedly announced and described by the surrealists. Whereas the real mystic seeks to move outside the world in order to unite with Divinity, Hérodiade's exotic goal appears much more narcissistic, more closely allied with the enigmatical and androgynous mystery of Leonardo's *Gioconda*, celebrated by Walter Pater, and with the psychic powers of Keats' *La Belle Dame sans Merci*.

> *I saw pale kings, and princes too,*
> *Pale warriors, death-pale were they all;*
> *They cried—'La Belle Dame sans Merci*
> *Hath thee in thrall!'*

The shift from Baudelaire's Jeanne Duval, called tigress and vampire, to Mallarmé's Hérodiade, virgin and priestess, is paralleled in the shift from Delacroix's, painting of women to Gustave Moreau's. After the fiery drama of Delacroix's oils we come to pictures of a cold static state in Moreau. Mario Praz in his book, *The Romantic Agony*, has pointed out how Moreau worships his subjects from outside, how they are all ambiguous and androgynous figures, as Hérodiade is.

Huysmans in his novel, *A Rebours*, imagines that his hero, des Esseintes, acquires two paintings of Moreau: one, *Salomé*, in oil, and the other, *L'Apparition*, in watercolour. These two paintings depict the two aspects of woman emphasized by the romantic and decadent movements of the 19th century. In the watercolour, *L'Apparition*, Salomé is cowering half-naked and horror-struck before the severed head of John the Baptist. In the oil painting she appears as a symbolic deity, reminiscent of ancient Helen, and holds in her hand a Lotus flower, the Egyptian and Indian symbol of fertility. Mallarmé uses for Salomé her mother's name because she is the woman who has conquered terror, who incarnates at the beginning of the modern world female beauty and cruelty, and who thus perpetuates a particular myth of woman which had been fashioned earlier by the Sphinx, by Pasiphae, Leda, Europa.

The same character, in Mallarmé's own time, was treated by Flaubert and Laforgue and Oscar Wilde as well as by Richard Strauss in his opera. But Mallarmé's creation is more significant psychologically. It is in a sense, a synthesis of the entire symbolist and decadent movement in art. His Hérodiade, a kind of Emma Bovary become priestess, represents the anguish of loneliness. One idea dominates Hérodiade: the triumph over all her longings, the effort to make of herself a human star (*un astre humain*). In Picasso's painting of 1932, *Girl before a mirror*, we have an example in painting of what Mallarmé did in poetry: a psychological or even surrealist portrait of an hysterical girl overcome by a kind of hieratic indolence. Mallarmé's *Hérodiade* and Picasso's *Girl before a mirror* both speak to the mirror as if they are speaking to the stars and to the void.

To designate as third part of *Hérodiade*, the poem, *Cantique de Saint Jean*, is fairly arbitrary. It didn't appear in print until long after Mallarmé's death, in the 1913 edition of his *Poésies*. The date of its composition is not known. It appears now, in all recent editions, as a kind of 'vignette' placed after the longer pieces, *Ouverture Ancienne* and *Scène*. Very different from them in appearance and in poetic texture, it is brief and intricately composed in seven stanzas of four lines each. This particular form of versification (three lines are of six syllables and the fourth is of four) is unusual for Mallarmé.

The *Cantique* combines in no intrinsic way with the other sections of *Hérodiade*. At best, it might be considered as the third part of a triptych, whose subject matter would bear relationship with the 'story' of the other two parts and yet which differs from them in style and colour. *Ouverture Ancienne* is spoken by the nurse and she is the principal figure in it. But the canvas of this first part of the triptych is covered with the scene she describes. The colours of dawn are changing to black at the fall of night and sinking into the tower. The season of autumn descends over the earth and the swan lowers its head as everything seems to depict the merger of all colour with its death. *Scène* is a dialogue between the nurse and Hérodiade, but most of the lines are spoken by the princess. She is, in the second part of the triptych, the principal character. We see her covered with her heavy jewels and reflected in her mirror. This is the broadest canvas of the three and contains the full figure of the girl and her mirror-reflection. It dominates the entire triptych by its dramatic intensity and its realism.

If in the first panel we see a setting which combines dawn and twilight, and in the second the full figure of Hérodiade, in the third panel, *Cantique de Saint Jean*, we see a sun interrupted in its course and the head of St. John the Baptist at the moment of decollation.

> *Le soleil que sa halte*
> *Surnaturelle exalte*
> *Aussitôt redescend*
> *Incandescent* [6]

At the solstice (the feast of St. John falls on the summer solstice) the sun reaches its highest peak and seems to stop for a moment, by some supernatural control, and then begins its descent in an incandescent light. St. John, at the moment of his martyrdom, if he were looking up at the sun, would see it suddenly interrupted, and his head, as it fell, would resemble a descending sun. With the beginning of the second stanza, we realize that the hymn is being spoken by the head of the saint as it is truncated from the body.

> *Je sens comme aux vertèbres*
> *S'éployer des ténèbres*
> *Toutes dans un frisson*
> *A l'unisson*

The decollation is first felt by the head as a spreading of darknesses which are joined together. Then follows the sensation of the head rising up into space.

> *Et ma tête surgie*
> *Solitaire vigie*
> *Dans les vols triomphaux*
> *De cette faux*
>
> *Comme rupture franche*
> *Plutôt refoule ou tranche*
> *Les anciens désaccords*
> *Avec le corps*

When the blade descends upon the neck in its violent movement, the head is slightly thrown up and for a second resembles a solitary watcher. When the separation of the head from the body is accomplished, it seems to cut off all the harassing struggles between mind and body. A second of time has been sufficient to push back into a distant time a familiar and recent controversy. In the last three stanzas, the saint speaks of his own head in its new state, and formulates a wish concerning it.

> *Qu'elle de jeûnes ivre*
> *S'opiniâtre à suivre*
> *En quelque bond hagard*
> *Son pur regard*

> *Là-haut où la froidure*
> *Eternelle n'endure*
> *Que vous le surpassiez*
> *Tous ô glaciers*

> *Mais selon un baptême*
> *Illuminée au même*
> *Principe qui m'élut*
> *Penche un salut.*

As the physical action of the knife was felt, the head was thrown upward, and the saint formulates the wish for his glance to continue looking up toward the coldness of the sky, a coldness quite in keeping with the mystic's search for the absolute. The decollation is a second baptism because at that precise moment salvation comes. The head as it turns to fall back is illumined with a halo which is the sign of holiness.

After the picture of the landscape (*Ouverture*) and the picture of the princess (*Scène*), comes the strange picture of the saint's truncated head, described in a monologue, whose effect is surrealistic. By evoking the cruel myth of decollation, Mallarmé has provided a poem which illustrates Jean Cassou's definition of Mallarmé's poetry: 'the philosophy of death, of being and of glory'. This time the syllables themselves bear an extraordinary directness and precision. The mystery comes from the unusualness of a head speaking and at the same time entering upon its state of sanctity. A poem has always some kind of obligation toward a story, a myth or a theme. The form into which it is cast rediscovers and reconsecrates the sacredness of the story. Of the myth of Salomé and John the Baptist, nothing remains but a canticle sung by the head, which is sun and trophy and halo. The element of the myth, denied by *Ouverture* and *Scène*, is here in *Cantique* reconstructed elliptically and surrealistically almost as a vengeance of the myth itself which in its final word of *salut* both cancels itself out and elevates itself to its highest meaning.

The image of the head truncated from the body and rising up into space where it resembles some watcher of the sky (*Et ma tête surgie / Solitaire vigie*), is one more example, from innumerable examples in Mallarmé's work, of 'angelism', of the strange separation of life from life, of experience liberated from life which is both the martyrdom and the glory of the artist. St. John wins his halo by the action of the assassin's knife, and the poet achieves his poem by severing himself from all facile participation in life. What is finally won or created in this mysterious vocation of loneliness, which is, after all, the theme in the three parts of the triptych: the desolation of approaching winter (*Ouverture*), the frigidity of the virginal princess (*Scène*), the decollation of the victim (*Cantique*), is an experience of the void in which the sequestered object appears wan and gory. There is quite possibly a filiation between the crimson sun reflected in the pool of *Ouverture*, and the garden of amethysts buried in the earth of *Scène*, and the head cut off by a triumphant blade of *Cantique*.

This death-like image of colour and violence might be sufficient to attach to the triptych *Hérodiade*, as a kind of prelude, the 14 line piece, *Don du Poème*. It was written at Tournon, in October 1865, when Mallarmé was composing *Hérodiade*,[7] and contains especially the image of the poem separated from the poet (as the head is separated from the saint) in terms of a blood-soaked birth of a bird.

> *Je t'apporte l'enfant d'une nuit d'Idumée!*
> *Noire, à l'aile saignante et pâle, déplumée,*
> *Par le verre brûlé d'aromates et d'or,*
> *Par les carreaux glacés, hélas! mornes encor,*
> *L'aurore se jeta sur la lampe angélique.*[8]

From the title we know that the gift is a poem, but the image signifying it is a dismal birth. The poem is inadequate and the birth is covered with blood. The poem is disinherited as soon as it is created and is thus compared to a child of Edom which was the country of Esau, the brother disinherited in favour of Jacob.[9] Whether or not there is an historical reality in considering Hérodiade, princess of the family of Herods, as one of the Edomite dynasty, there is considerable reason to see in the image of a difficult birth of a poem which might well be, at the date of *Don du Poème*, the creation of *Hérodiade*.[10]

The introduction is interrupted by the long sound of the word,

Palmes,[11] which translates the coming of dawn as it joins with the light of the lamp.

> *Palmes! et quand elle a montré cette relique*
> *A ce père essayant un sourire ennemi,*
> *La solitude bleue et stérile a frémi.*[12]

The poem, as well as the bird, is referred to as a 'relic', as that which remains, and the father, or the poet, feels in himself hostility toward the child or the poem he has produced. The solitude of his night's vigil, sterile for so long, trembles now when it sees the result of the labour.

The end of the poem is in the form of a question which the poet asks of the nurse who is receiving the child at its birth.

> *O la berceuse, avec ta fille et l'innocence*
> *De vos pieds froids, accueille une horrible naissance:*
> *Et ta voix rappelant viole et clavecin,*
> *Avec le doigt fané presseras-tu le sein*
> *Par qui coule en blancheur sibylline la femme*
> *Pour les lèvres que l'air du vierge azur affame?*

The father is separated from his daughter at her birth, as the poet is separated from his poem when he gives it to a reader. The *berceuse* rocks the child and sings to her, accomplishing thereby what the reader does for the poem. In the image of the cold feet[13] which have to be warmed (reminiscent of the poem which has to be recited in order to prolong its life), the ugliness of the birth is reasserted. Then life begins for the child, with the singing of the nurse and the milk from her breast. The image becomes heavy with the particularized vocabulary of Mallarmé: *blancheur sibylline* and *vierge azur*, especially, which force the meaning closer still to that of the poem. After the creation of the poem, it grows into its own secrecy, into its own language which sustains it (as the mother's milk sustains a child). Every poem is avid for its absolute expression and total meaning. Mallarmé is still haunted by the azure perfection of the pure poem.

The birth of Mallarmé's daughter, Geneviève (19 November 1864), and the composition of *Hérodiade* (engaged upon at least as early as October 1864), might be sufficient to explain the combined imagery of *Don du Poème* and the circumstances of its conception. But as always, a true poem surpasses whatever events initiated it.

Don du Poème is not only the dedication of *Hérodiade* but it is a commentary on how to see in all poetry: a birth, horrible in its first form by comparison with what it is to become; a welcoming on the part of the reader who becomes nurse to the poem and feeds it on his own secrets; and finally toward absolute expression and absolute meaning. A poem is always an effort to give a purer meaning to an idea. The images of the sun sinking into the night (*in Ouverture*), of Hérodiade becoming her reflection in the mirror (in *Scène*), of the head becoming its illumination and sanctity (in *Cantique*), and finally of a horrible birth becoming a poem of secrecy (*Don du Poème*) all testify to the poet's perpetual renovation of himself, to the eternal creation by which life is maintained, to that kind of poetry which is ceaselessly being reborn in the art of some men.

1. Letter to H. Cazalis, Oct. 1864: 'J'ai enfin commencé mon *Hérodiade*. Avec terreur car j'invente une langue qui doit nécessairement jaillir d'une poétique très nouvelle, que je pourrais définir en ces deux mots: *Peindre non la chose, mais l'effet qu'elle produit.* Le vers ne doit donc pas, là, se composer de mots, mais d'inventions, et toutes les paroles s'effacer devant les sensations.' cf. Pléiade edition, p 1438.

2. From two letters written from Valvins to his family:
   11 May 1898. 'Je me suis sournoisement mis tout à l'heure à *Hérodiade*, avec espoir.'
   14 May 1898. 'Journée de travail, Hérodiade ira lentement, mais ira, je me possède un peu.'
   cf. Mondor, *Vie*, pp. 788-89.

3. Yes, it is for me, for me, that I flower, alone!
   You know it, amethyst gardens, buried
   Endlessly in learned dazzling abysses,
   Hidden golds, keeping your ancient light
   Under the sombre sleep of a primordial earth,
   You stones wherein my eyes like pure jewels
   Borrow their melodious light, and you
   Metals which give to my young hair
   A fatal splendour and its massive form!
   As for you, woman born in wicked centuries
   For the evil of sibylline caves,
   Who speak of a mortal! according to whom, from the chalices
   Of my robes, aroma of fierce delights,
   Would come forth the white trembling of my nakedness,
   Prophesy that if the mild azure of summer,
   Toward which natively woman uncovers herself,
   Sees me in my shivering shame of a star,
   I die!

4. I love the horror of being a virgin and I wish
   To live in the terror which my hair gives me
   So that at evening, lying on my bed, inviolate
   Reptile, I may feel in my vain flesh
   The cold scintillation of your pale light,
   You who die, you who burn with chastity,
   White night of icicles and cruel snow!

5. And your solitary sister, O my eternal sister
   My dream will mount toward you: such already
   Rare lucidity of a heart which dreamed it,
   I believe myself alone in my monotonous kingdom
   And everything around me lives in the idolatry
   Of a mirror which reflects in its sleeping calm
   Hérodiade with her clear diamond gaze . . .
   O last charm, yes! I feel it, I am alone . . .

6. The sun exalted
   By its supernatural halt
   Immediately redescends
       Incandescent

   I feel darkness
   Spreading through my back
   In a shiver
       And joining with itself

And my head rising up
Lonely vigilant
In the triumphant flashes
   Of that blade

Like a clean severing
Rather represses or cuts off
The former disagreements
   With the body

Drunk with fastings
May it persist in following
In some wild leap
   Its pure glance

High up where the eternal
Cold will not allow
You to surpass it
   O glaciers

But as for a baptism
Illumined by the same
Principle which elected me
   May it bend down a salvation.

7. The poem was first entitled *Le Jour* and sent to Théodore Aubanel who criticized it. The second version, entitled *Le Poème Nocturne*, was also sent to Aubanel who continued to complain of obscurities, in his letter of Dec. 21, 1865. An amusing anecdote about the poem and use made of it by Villiers de l'Isle-Adam is related on pp. 1435-6 of the Pléiade edition.

8. I bring you the child of an Idumean night!
  Black, with a bleeding pale wing, its feathers pulled,
  Through the glass burned with aromatics and gold,
  Through the icy panes.... alas! still dismal,
  The dawn cast its light on the angelic lamp.

9. cf. Denis Saurat, *Perspectives*, Stock, 1935, pp. 113-116. An article which emphasizes the Cabalistic tendencies of the poem. Saurat says that the kings of Edom were sexless and reproduced without women. The poet, also, produces his poem alone.

10. Charles Mauron in his *Commentaires* sees a relationship between the line, *Par le verre brûlé d'aromates et d'or* (*Don du Poème*) and the line in *Hérodiade*, *Mais de l'or à jamais vierge des aromates.*

11. It has been pointed out that the words, *Idumée* and *Palmes*, are both in a line of Virgil: *Primus Idumaeas referam tibi, Mantua, palmas.* (*Georgias* VIII, 12). cf. Noulet, *L'Oeuvre Poétique de Mallarmé*, p. 397.

12. Palms! and when she [dawn] showed this relic
  To the father trying to smile as an enemy,
  The blue and sterile solitude trembled.
  O singer, with your daughter and the innocence
  Of your cold feet, welcome a horrible birth:
  And your voice recalling viola and harpsichord,
  With your faded finger will you press the breast
  Through which flows the woman in sibylline whiteness
  For the lips which the air of the virgin azure famishes?

13. The American poet, Wallace Stevens, has borrowed this image for one of his poems:
   If her horny feet protrude, they come
   To show how cold she is, and dumb.
   Let the lamp affix its beam.
   The only emperor is the emperor of ice-cream.

   (*The Emperor of Ice-Cream* in *Harmonium*).

CHAPTER V

L'APRÈS-MIDI D'UN FAUNE

MALLARMÉ's eclogue for his faun, his longest poem after *Hérodiade*, has become his most renowned largely because of its association with the other arts. At the moment of its earliest version, 1865, it was known, in the poet's circle, to be destined for the stage. The actor Coquelin considered it for presentation at the Comédie-Française, but the work was finally refused in this form. Eleven years later, in 1876, the poem appeared in print in its definitive version, in a small edition published by Derenne. Limited to 195 copies, it was handsomely presented with an illustration by Edouard Manet. Both the poem and the exceptional beauty of its first edition were commented on in Huysman's novel, *A Rebours*, published in 1884. Between 1892 and '94, Claude Debussy composed his musical work inspired by the eclogue, *Prélude à l'Après-Midi d'un Faune*, which was first performed on the 22nd of December, 1894. In 1912, the dancer, Nijinski, drawing both on the poem of Mallarmé and the music of Debussy, arranged a choreography and danced the work during the season of the Ballets Russes in Paris.

The poem itself, which has attracted so many artistic collaborations, is one of Mallarmé's most ambitious poetic enterprises, one of his richest in combination of themes and subtle nuances, one of the central pieces in the development of his art. It stands out from the rest of his work by its very marked erotology. Mallarmé is an erotic poet, but almost never obviously so, as he appears in *L'Après-Midi d'un Faune*. Taken with *Hérodiade* (the two poems were conceived and composed at the same time and are in many ways related with one another), the faun's monologue represents Mallarmé's most significant inquest into the problems of eroticism and especially into the perplexing but omnipresent relationship between the sexual dream world of the poet and his creative life as practising poet.

The history of the composition of *L'Après-Midi d'un Faune* occupies a little more than ten years of Mallarmé's life. In a letter to Henri Cazalis of March 1865, he refers to labours on his tragedy, *Hérodiade*, and complains of the lack of time for such work. His family and

L'Après-midi d'un Faune

pedagogic duties at the lycée of Tournon are constantly interrupting his poet's activity. He insists upon the particular difficulty of his subject and of the kind of verse he writes. The letter contains an allusion to the mysterious Dream and Work which preoccupied him all his life and of the possibility that they will never be accomplished.[1] By June, we learn in another letter to Cazalis, that Mallarmé has abandoned *Hérodiade* to the cold winter behind him and that he is engaged in a new work, an heroic interlude, as he calls it (*un intermède héroïque*), whose hero is a faun. The verses are difficult to create because the poet is adapting them for the theatre, 'not very possible for the theatre', he writes, 'but needing the theatre'.[2]

The new work, therefore, grew out of a period of intense discouragement, which, paradoxically, often seems the necessary ambiency for the creation of art. Discouragement is an experience of renunciation and self-examination from which may come a very clear vision of a work which, by its nature, will be redemptive. Such a work will assume responsibility for the discouragement and the experience of the artist. By July, the new poem appeared sufficiently important to Mallarmé to make him decide to stay on at Tournon through the end of August, and to give only the month of September to relaxation and a visit to Paris. In order to carry out this project and complete a version of the work, called *Le Monologue d'un Faune*, Mallarmé consumed increasing amounts of coffee during the summer weeks and diminished the hours given over to sleep. It is believed that Théodore de Banville, whose works were being performed at the Théâtre Français, had promised Mallarmé an introduction to Coquelin, destined to interpret the role of the faun. But the poem, when presented by Mallarmé to Coquelin and Banville, appeared so denuded of story and action, that it was refused for dramatic use.[3]

During the winter of 1865-66, Mallarmé resumed work on *Hérodiade,* which he then conceived of as poem rather than as tragedy.[4] In March of 1866 he wrote to Cazalis that he planned to begin work again on *Le Faune* by the first of May, reserving it for his summer occupation.[5] A third version of the work, intermediary between *Monologue d'un Faune* and the definitive poem, has recently been made public by Dr Mondor,[6] who discovered it in the collection of autographs of Dr Lucien Graux. Entitled *Improvisation d'un Faune*, it was proposed by Mallarmé to the publisher, Lemeere, for the third volume of *Le Parnasse Contemporain*, in 1875.

The three judges composing the committee, Théodore de Banville, François Coppée and Anatole France, refused the Mallarmé piece. Banville was inclined to accept, Coppée vacillated, but Anatole France was strong in his opposition, saying that if the poem were printed, the judges would be ridiculed. He rejected at the same time poems of Verlaine which he called 'the worst he knew' and which were destined to appear in one of Verlaine's finest volumes, *Sagesse*.

The definitive version, *L'Après-Midi d'un Faune*, was published in March, 1876.[7] The changes made in the text between the second and third version are fewer than those made between the first and the recently revealed second version. All stage directions for theatrical presentation had been eliminated. The work had become a poem. The *Monologue* was a fairly direct scene of eroticism, but it contained many important passages which were not to disappear: the sucking of the grapes, the episode of the two sleepers, the apostrophe to the anger of the two women, the water scene, the abduction of the couple. In *Improvisation*, only the faun speaks and the poetry persistently stresses Mallarmé's tendency toward the mysterious and the suggestive which will become the dominant tone in *L'Après-Midi*. The three openings characterize the three poems. 1. *J'avais des nymphes*: imperious and realistic. 2. *Ces nymphes, je les veux émerveiller*: where already the faun is Mallarmean in his expression of veiled delicacy. 3. *Ces nymphes, je les veux perpétuer*: where the final verb is supremely Mallarmean in its rich thoughtful ambiguity.[8]

The few changes made on *Improvisation* for the definitive version are the most subtle of all. Very often only a single word is changed. The original line, *Ondoie une blancheur éparse de troupeau*, underwent in the second version the fairly radical change to: *Ondoie une blancheur animée au repos*. In the third version only the word, *animée*, was changed to *animale*, which heightens the image seen by the faun.[9] The last line of the eclogue was in its first form: *Adieu, femmes: duo de vierges quand je vins*, which repeated the realism of the opening and made the faun seem like a typical male boasting of his physical prowess. The line was omitted in the second version, but became in the third the expression of pure idealism, *Couple, adieu, je vais voir l'ombre que tu devins*.[10]

A variety of sources have been suggested for this poem on the faun. Thibaudet insists, somewhat dogmatically, that it was inspired by Boucher's painting of the faun and nymphs which hangs in the

National Gallery in London. But the curators give 1880 as the date when the museum acquired the painting, which is 17 years after Mallarmé's visit to London and 15 after his choice of the subject. It is not believed there was any public showing in London of the painting before its acquisition by the National Gallery.[11] Banville's play, *Diane au Bois*, of 1863, has often been cited. Schinz, in an article[12] dealing precisely with the problem of the poem's provenance, holds that it is an expression of the general hellenism of the period rather than of any single work, and refers to many examples, such as Gautier's *Affinités Secrètes*, Banville's *Dieux en exil*, L. de Lisle's *Poèmes Antiques*, Hugo's *Chansons des Rues et des Bois*, Renan's *Prière sur l'Acropole*. Other critics have called upon the poetry of Keats (especially his *Endymion*), the writings of Novalis and Chateaubriand. Mondor has given in his *Histoire d'un Faune* an exhaustive list of works read by Mallarmé in which occurs some version of the faun story. Particularly suggestive would be the condemned poems of Baudelaire, *Lesbos* and *Femmes Damnées*, *Mademoiselle de Maupin* of Gautier, Hugo's *Le Satyre* and Vigny's *La Dryade*.

Rather than engage upon the fruitless quest for a literary or pictorial ancestor of *L'Après-Midi*, I should prefer to evoke simply the well-known myth itself of the satyr Pan pursuing the nymph Syrinx to the shores of the river Lado in Arcady. It will be remembered that there she implores help from the goddess Diana, who changes her and her sisters, the naiads, into rushes. Pan embraces the rushes and his breath gives out a sweet music. It is precisely the music which becomes the bond of his alliance with the nymphs. Satyrs are convenient actors or projections of our more primordial instincts and visions. The myth of the satyr Pan is quite easily explained in terms of the myth of the poet, Stéphane Mallarmé, in the sombre city of Tournon on the Rhône River.

The literal setting was the windy Ardèche in France, and the psychic background was a persistent spleen. Neither his wife nor his young daughter were sufficient company for the disillusioned school teacher who was a poet and who was therefore filled with a relentless appetite for another land than where he lived. The coming of summer in any year and in any city is the releasing of energies and desires in every man. The ancient theme of Pan is always contemporary, and Mallarmé, in the summer of 1865, in composing his monologue for the faun, as Keats in composing his *Ode to Psyche*, relived the myth of the Pagan in love with the sensual beauty of the world and the spirit of nature. Summer with its new light and warmth is each year a renewed solicitation to enjoy the sensations of sight and feeling. The faun spying on the intertwined bodies of two nymphs represents the universal desire to search for the illusion of appearances. The first reaction to such a vision is a flood of erotic desire, which is closely followed, in the poem, in the myth, and in the experience of many men, by the aesthetic desire to create a melody for such a vision. The initial sombre and so-called carnal urge of the faun is transmuted into his breath skilfully blown into two hollow reeds. Mallarmé's winter months had been spent on *Hérodiade*, on the cold virginal princess who represented a sumptuous but sterile and hieratic vision. With the coming of summer, the poet abandoned the priestess in her remote tower, and entered the forest where he followed the traces of the faun, his other self whose very appearance he resembled with wide outstretched ears.

The first line, or rather, ten of the first twelve syllables, which are separated from the rest of the poem, is a condensation of the entire work.

> *Ces nymphes, je les veux perpétuer.*[13]

In the verb, *perpétuer*, Mallarmé seizes and summarizes the myth, his own as well as Pan's, because of the dual meaning he gives to his desire: copulation may well be one significance of the afternoon's quest; and—the word, 'perpetuate', is of refined elegance—preservation by means of art may be the other. From the opening line, which might be said brutally by an aroused faun or meditatively by a meticulous artist, we learn that the poet is going to cast within the strict form of an ancient and well known story the myth known to every man and every poet of self-perpetuation. Desire is always a need or a quest for immortality.

The next two lines, also separated from the rest of the text, give a brief vision of the nymphs asleep:

> *Si clair,*
> *Leur incarnat léger, qu'il voltige dans l'air*
> *Assoupi de sommeils touffus.*

The rose colour of their flesh is so delicate that it seems to float in the air. The heaviness of their sleep resembles the thick wood in which they are lying. The basic problem of whether the faun sees the nymphs or not is already stated in these two lines. How can their flesh be real if it rises up into the air and creates a tinted atmosphere rather than depict two bodies? The full noon quietness in the depths of the woods would give a sufficient picture of sleep. Is it simply nature that is asleep and not the nymphs?

The faun has prepared his question and now asks it.

> *Aimai-je un rêve?*

With exceptional penetration he formulates a negative doubt, strong enough to banish all belief in the reality of the nymphs.

> *Mon doute, amas de nuit ancienne, s'achève*
> *En maint rameau subtil, qui, demeuré les vrais*
> *Bois mêmes, prouve, hélas! que bien seul je m'offrais*
> *Pour triomphe la faute idéale de roses.*

Whatever dream the faun has been enjoying ends when he opens his eyes and sees about him the familiar wood setting of numerous thin branches, real as contrasted with the vanished dream. He is alone in this forest scene when he awakens, and he reasons that he must have been alone as the dreaming faun when he had triumphantly possessed the nymphs. The same branches under which he fell asleep are there when he awakens. The woods contain no sign of the amorous adventure. The bodies (*roses*) of the nymphs must have been creations of a dream; the sin must have been desire (*la faute idéale*). To himself he says: *Réfléchissons:*—which seems to mean, by what follows, 'let me try to recapture the dream, let me try to reconstruct the vision'.

> *ou si les femmes dont tu gloses*
> *Figurent un souhait de tes sens fabuleux!*
> *Faune, l'illusion s'échappe des yeux bleus*
> *Et froids, comme une source en pleurs, de la plus chaste:*
> *Mais, l'autre tout soupirs, dis-tu qu'elle contraste*
> *Comme brise du jour chaude dans ta toison?*

Here the faun speaks to himself as he tries to remember the episode of the nymphs. He calls himself the faun almost as if he had become two distinct beings: both the lascivious faun and the one who wonders if he had been lascivious in some dream world. He even says to himself that he doesn't exist, that his senses belong to a fabulous creature. The memory of erotic senses in a man is always that of a dream, of an experience that never actually took place. The difference between a faun (who triumphed over the nymphs) and a schoolteacher (who uses such a pedantic word as *gloses*) is precisely the difference between the reflective side of a man who is trying to reconstruct the memory of an erotic experience and the physical being who had the experience. In four lines (v. 10-13) the faun reviews the differing temperaments of the two nymphs: one is chaste, blue-eyed and full of illusions; the other, more experienced, sighs for love. Their difference is like that of the warm breeze in the fleece of the faun, the heat of day and body heat. Such psychological finesse is rare in dreams, but what is not rare is the dual theme of facile quest and obstacles. Together the nymphs would easily represent the prolonged difficulty of obtaining sensual satisfaction in a dream and its ultimate attainment.

The first reaction of the faun to his own reasoning is to deny it and belittle it.

> *Que non! par l'immobile et lasse pâmoison*
> *Suffoquant de chaleurs le matin frais s'il lutte,*
> *Ne murmure point d'eau que ne verse ma flûte*
> *Au bosquet arrosé d'accords;*

The fainting of the day (*pâmoison* is usually applied to a person) is its immobile heat, and the morning, if it struggles to recover from the heat suffocation resembles a body trying to recover its senses. No sound accompanies this struggle of day to rise up from its torpor unless it were the notes of the faun's flute which showers its melodies like drops of water over the woods. This is the first mention of the flute which is to play so important a part in the eclogue. It comes after the image of eroticism (*un souhait de tes sens fabuleux*) and the physical exhaustion which follows the erotic act (*lasse pâmoison*). With the recovery of the faun (as with the recovery of day), a new kind of animation is going to fill him, that of the musician (*ma flûte*), and the rest of the passage continues the theme of the flute.

> *et le seul vent*
> *Hors des deux tuyaux prompt à s'exhaler avant*
> *Qu'il disperse le son dans une pluie aride,*
> *C'est, à l'horizon pas remué d'une ride,*
> *Le visible et serein souffle artificiel*
> *De l'inspiration, qui regagne le ciel.*

The faun seems to be watching his own performance and its ultimate dispersal. Quite detached now from the dream and his preoccupation with the two nymphs, he contemplates his breath being blown into the two pipes and sees it, before it showers its notes like rain (arid because, after all, it is only sound), on the clear horizon as a breath of wind inhaled back into the sky. The single breath (*seul vent*), which is to be so divided into notes as to resemble rain drops, exhaled by the faun, is seen to be inhaled (*inspiration*) by the sky. After creating the music, the air resumes its initial form of wind which serenely mounts up in a single line. The analogy between the music and the dream imposes itself and the passage subtly concludes the opening section of the poem. What remains of the music after it has been played? What remains of the dream after one awakens? The problem is the same. The wonder is the same. The faun both as animal and musician is perplexed by the ancient question of appearance and reality, of experience and of what remains after it.

In order to tackle the problem, the faun has recourse to the old stratagem of memory. He goes back in time and place.

> *O bords siciliens d'un calme marécage*
> *Qu'à l'envi de soleils ma vanité saccage,*
> *Tacite sous les fleurs d'étincelles, CONTEZ*
> *'Que je coupais ici les creux roseaux domptés*
> *'Par le talent; quand, sur l'or glauque de lointaines*
> *'Verdures dédiant leur vigne à des fontaines,*
> *'Ondoie une blancheur animale au repos:*
> *'Et qu'au prélude lent où naissent les pipeaux*
> *'Ce vol de cygnes, non! de naïades se sauve*
> *'Ou plonge . . .'*

The faun asks the Sicilian swamp to narrate the event he remembers either from a dream or a real experience. The sun floods with its light the entire scene and envies the faun who proudly takes another kind of possession of it. The phrase, *ma vanité saccage*, gives the image of a boisterous animalistic faun dissipating the calm of the swamp. But then immediately his attention is fixed on the reeds. He cuts them and subjugates them to his talent of musician. At a distance from him, on the water which is of greenish gold, he sees a group of white birds sleeping. With the first notes from the improvised instrument, the white swans awaken only to reveal their real character of nymphs. They recognize the art of the dangerous faun, ravisher of their race, and they scatter through the swamp or dive into the water.

The faun wants the swamp to tell the story and yet he is telling it himself. With the rapid dispersal of the nymphs, he interrupts this style of story-telling and returns more exclusively to himself. He remembers the moment after the flight of the nymphs and his amazement at their terror.

> *Inerte, tout brûle dans l'heure fauve*
> *Sans marquer par quel art ensemble détala*
> *Trop d'hymen souhaité de qui cherche le la:*
> *Alors m'éveillerai-je à la ferveur première,*
> *Droit et seul, sous un flot antique de lumière,*
> *Lys! et l'un de vous tous pour l'ingénuité.*

Again there is mention of the hour, high noon, called now the 'tawny hour' (*l'heure fauve*) when everything burns under the sun. No trace remains of the nymphs, of those with whom the faun would like to have consummated a union (*Trop d'hymen souhaité*) at the very moment when he was engaged in tuning his pipes, in discovering the note A. These congealed verses fuse into one experience the two desires of the faun: that of the musician bent upon discovering the pure note on which all the other notes of his instrument will be formed; and that of the animal whose presence, revealed by his prelude, threw into panic and flight the nymphs of the swamp. As if the faun were actually reliving the story, he tells us next what will happen to him in the sequence of events. He will awaken, he says, to his first fervour. The disappearance of the white bodies of the nymphs has reawakened his animal instincts, his vanity of ravisher already referred to in terms of his pounding course through the swamp (*que ma vanité saccage*). He stands up alone, almost as if he had suddenly become a man, under the full light of the shining sun for countless ages, and sees near by him, at the edge of the swamp, lilies which, erect like him, resemble him. He is in fact one of them, upright in his full beauty and development, as well as pure in his ingenuousness. Mallarmé's faun is inexperienced in love, although he is well experienced in desire for it.

Still in his erect pose and in his exceptional attentiveness, the faun perceives on his chest, virginal of any amorous embrace, the mark of a bite which must have come from the teeth of some proud creature. This is quite different from a banal kiss which might well be perfidious.

> *Autre que ce doux rien par leur lèvre ébruité,*
> *Le baiser, qui tout bas des perfides assure,*
> *Mon sein, vierge de preuve, atteste une morsure*
> *Mystérieuse, due à quelque auguste dent;*

Even the marks of the teeth on the faun's chest do not solve the permanent problem of whether he actually embraced the nymphs or not. Such physical manifestations are known to occur in the wake of intense mental dreams. No one can really tell the power of dreams, and even the faun seems disposed not to give full credulity to a mere physical testimonial. He passes lightly over the problem of the teeth marks but not without suggesting that they were made by some worthy creature. Almost irritated by the mysteriousness of the entire episode, he converts the mystery into the subject of a quasi-meditation.

> *Mais, bast! arcane tel élut pour confident*
> *Le jonc vaste et jumeau dont sous l'azur on joue:*
> *Qui, détournant à soi le trouble de la joue,*
> *Rêve, dans un solo long, que nous amusions*
> *La beauté d'alentour par des confusions*
> *Fausses entre elle-même et notre chant crédule;*
> *Et de faire aussi haut que l'amour se module*
> *Evanouir du songe ordinaire de dos*
> *Ou de flanc pur suivis avec mes regards clos,*
> *Une sonore, vaine et monotone ligne.*

Whatever has happened, known or unknown, may be confided and transformed into the music of the double pipes. In the solo of the pipes the faun may continue his dream of having brought confusion into the woods by means of his naive playing. In the high notes of the flute the entire experience of love may be reduced into a single melodic line, vain and monotonous as all art is when contrasted with the immediacy and necessity of experience. As he plays thus on his instrument, the faun is master of himself and his feelings. He is able to follow inwardly the dream of having seen the nudity of a nymph, her back and side, and to sing of such a vision without experiencing the need of acting upon it.

But the spell of pure creative accomplishment is interrupted also, and the faun addresses his flute as he takes it down from his cheek, and resumes momentarily the posture and the thoughts of the lascivious animal.

> *Tâche donc, instrument des fuites, ô maligne*
> *Syrinx, de refleurir aux lacs où tu m'attends!*
> *Moi, de ma rumeur fier, je vais parler longtemps*
> *Des déesses; et par d'idolâtres peintures,*
> *A leur ombre enlever encore des ceintures:*

Everything goes backward in time, almost as a cinema reel being reversed. The faun imagines the flute, which had caused the flight of the nymphs, reflowering as a simple reed at the edge of the swamp. He sees himself as the proud destroyer of the swamp's calm, and back of that, as the voluptuous hero of his own dreams in which he removes the clothing of goddesses. The faun betrays himself as more and more the dreamer whose dreams possess such exceptional imagery and erotic motifs that he has lost the power to distinguish with any accuracy between the world of consciousness and the dream world.

But the indulgent and exaggerated dream about the goddess cannot last for ever, and we see the faun resume a pose of carefree animal playfulness.

> *Ainsi, quand des raisins j'ai sucé la clarté,*
> *Pour bannir un regret par ma feinte écarté,*
> *Rieur, j'élève au ciel d'été la grappe vide*
> *Et, soufflant dans ses peaux lumineuses, avide*
> *D'ivresse, jusqu'au soir je regarde au travers.*

The pose is classic and yet some of the details characterize the Mallarmean faun. The regret he banishes is that of not having found the nymphs and his pretence was that of being the musician capable of dominating and transmuting experience. Momentarily the faun is the animal who is going to forget having lost the prize of the woods. He laughs and sucks the meat out of the grapes. Then he plays with the empty skins, and blowing in them, looks through them at the changed colour of the sky. Wine and intoxication replace love, and the faun makes the great pretence that this is natural, that this is really what he wanted. Here the faun resembles the clown who plays so sincerely the comic part that his own heart is deceived.

Here ends the first half of the poem. What promised to be drama ends in a farce, but like most farces, it serves to underscore and exhort tragedy.

The second part of the poem begins in almost the same way as the first: *O nymphes* (instead of *Ces nymphes*). The faun wants to assemble all his memories about the nymphs. He wants to blow up the memories as he blew up the empty skins of the grapes. Even the comic gesture of the intoxicated faun leads him back to his principal wonderment. Intoxication is only temporary. He returns to the moment of sight and ravishment, and tells it now in greater detail.

> *O nymphes, regonflons des SOUVENIRS divers.*
> '*Mon œil, trouant les joncs, dardait chaque encolure*
> '*Immortelle, qui noie en l'onde sa brûlure*
> '*Avec un cri de rage au ciel de la forêt;*
> '*Et le splendide bain de cheveux disparaît*
> '*Dans les clartés et les frissons, ô pierreries!*
> '*J'accours; quand, à mes pieds, s'entrejoignent (meurtries*
> '*De la langueur goûtée à ce mal d'être deux)*
> '*Des dormeuses parmi leurs seuls bras hasardeux;*
> '*Je les ravis, sans les désenlacer, et vole*
> '*A ce massif, haï par l'ombrage frivole,*
> '*De roses tarissant tout parfum au soleil,*
> '*Où notre ébat au jour consumé soit pareil.*'

After the introductory line, come twelve lines which are mainly narrative. The faun relates again how he saw the white bodies of the nymphs on the water, and how at the sound of his voice, their hair floating on the water and their bodies sparkling in the sunlight disappeared, as if myriads of jewels sunk into the water. He hastened to the bank and found there two more still sleeping. They were embraced in sleep, so tightly, that it seemed painful for them to be two. Without disentangling the nymphs, the faun lifts them up and carries them to a bed of roses in the full sunlight (and therefore detested by the shadows of the forest) where the perfume is dried up by the rays of the sun and where the struggle between faun and nymphs is comparable to the day consumed by the light.

The narration is interrupted by the passage of seven lines beginning, *Je t'adore*, which is less narration than meditation. The faun briefly analyses the shock and terror of the nymphs and their differing reactions to their ravisher.

Je t'adore, courroux des vierges, ô délice
Farouche du sacré fardeau nu qui se glisse
Pour fuir ma lèvre en feu buvant, comme un éclair
Tressaille! la frayeur secrète de la chair:
Des pieds de l'inhumaine au cœur de la timide
Que délaisse à la fois une innocence, humide
De larmes folles ou de moins tristes vapeurs.

This strange passage dividing the narration is well summarized in the opening word, *je t'adore*. What he worships is the terror, both feigned and real of the nymphs. The myth of love is recapitulated in the two reactions which the faun feels in the bodies he holds: the passion of the experienced nymph and the opposition of the inexperienced one. The faun almost philosophizes about love, even as the struggle is going on, but it is the very struggle in its two parts of fear and capitulation that he worships. It was necessary for him to hold the two nymphs at once, in order to realize and experience the complete unfolding of a conquest. And yet there was not perhaps in all this adventure a completed experience. How had he failed? He resumes the narration with a theory on his error which he pompously calls a 'crime.'

'*Mon crime, c'est d'avoir, gai de vaincre ces peurs*
'*Traîtresses, divisé la touffe échevelée*
'*De baisers que les dieux gardaient si bien mêlée:*
'*Car, à peine j'allais cacher un rire ardent*
'*Sous les replis heureux d'une seule (gardant*
'*Par un doigt simple, afin que sa candeur de plume*
'*Se teignît à l'émoi de sa sœur qui s'allume,*
'*La petite, naïve et ne rougissant pas:)*
'*Que de mes bras, défaits par de vagues trépas,*
'*Cette proie, à jamais ingrate se délivre*
'*Sans pitié du sanglot dont j'étais encore ivre.*'

The crime was simply a defect in stratagem, for after all, this faun has not had much traffic with nymphs. He forgot for an instant that he was holding two nymphs, and as he concentrated his passion on one, the more experienced, by plunging his face in her hair, his grasp on the timid nymph lessened. He was even hopeful that she would be attracted by this picture of love-making and learn by observation, while the whiteness of her skin would be coloured by the first blushes of sensuality. At the same time, his own passion mounting affected the tenseness of his arms enfolding the nymph he was kissing, and easily, with the quickness of animals, the two creatures slipped out of his grasp at the very moment of climax. The triumph was a sob because the faun was suddenly alone. He was drunk with the expense of his feelings and the emptiness of the space within his arms. The sculpturesque group he describes is that of fabulous half-animal creatures, and yet the feelings are human: the frustration and sobbing of the faun, and the heartless cunning ingratitude of the nymphs. Duplication or doubling is everywhere: in the faun, who is animal and artist, vicious and romantic; in his prey, who is timid and bold, blond and brunette. To explain his failure, the faun may well have invented, even for himself, the existence of two nymphs, in order to heighten the sense of combat as well as to increase the physical desire. The element of dream is still strong in the over-elaborate and over-idealized picture of realism.

The monologue is resumed with a boyish exclamation: *Tant pis!*

> *Tant pis! vers le bonheur d'autres m'entraîneront*
> *Par leur tresse nouée aux cornes de mon front:*

In a flash he not only renounces the realization of his desire, but with a well known male assurance he announces many conquests to come, desired by other nymphs who will weave their hair on his horns. Instantly, in the very wake of defeat, the image of success forms again in the same pattern. Imaginatively the faun sees himself as the prisoner of those he desires. His passion becomes so real that he addresses it as if it were a person.

> *Tu sais, ma passion, que, pourpre et déjà mûre,*
> *Chaque grenade éclate et d'abeilles murmure;*
> *Et notre sang, épris de qui le va saisir,*
> *Coule pour tout l'essaim éternel du désir.*

The symbol of the pomegranate has been preceded by that of the grapes, and before that, by the crimson of the flesh (*Leur incarnat léger*). In all three cases the faun talks about the various symbols (which are really one) as if they are the justifications of his desire. The pink flesh of the nymphs is the deliberate and classical allegory, the pure dream vision of the adolescent. The bunch of grapes almost

resembles a toy on which the faun expends his passion by trans-
forming it into intoxication and then deriding it. There is more calm
and a deeper acceptance of desire in the image of the pomegranate.
The fruit has matured and burst, attracting to it a swarm of bees.
The juice of the pomegranate, which has burst its limits, is like the
blood of the faun filled with desire, eternally offered to desire.
There is less boasting in this image of the opened pomegranate.
Passion is endless and is serious. He who contains it is its victim.

But the time of day is passing. With the alteration of light,
comes, not a disappearance of passion, but a shift in its intensity.
Each man desires all women. Passion is clothed in many legends.

> *A l'heure où ce bois d'or et de cendres se teinte*
> *Une fête s'exalte en la feuillée éteinte:*
> *Etna! c'est parmi toi visité de Vénus*
> *Sur ta lave posant ses talons ingénus,*
> *Quand tonne un somme triste ou s'épuise la flamme.*
> *Je tiens la reine!*

In the reckless imagination of the faun, the image of the bursting
pomegranate is replaced by the more impressive volcanic mountain
of Etna. But the principle is the same because the desire remains the
same and unsatisfied. In their duration, the images grow and the
fictional appeasement grows. The nymphs are forgotten now because in their place the faun sees the goddess Venus walking on the
lava of Etna. The late afternoon is descending over the forest, and
with it, the fires of the noon sun are diminishing and the sleep of
noon is now a sad slumber. But the faun is still able to transport
himself to the site of his dream and he sees himself clasping the
queen-goddess. The dream is becoming more fitful. Its accomplishment is more rapidly stated, and the immediate acknowledgement
that what has been described has been dreamed proves that the faun
is wearying of his everlasting pretence.

The element of time undergoes throughout the poem a curious
and significant modification. It has at first the expansiveness and
eternal dilation of time in a dream where there is time both for
meditation and action. But by the end of the eclogue the faun has
wearied of this game with time. The Etna episode, which is
essentially the same kind of dream as that of the nymphs, is told
rapidly in five lines and a half, and its conclusion is reduced to
three words:

O sûr châtiment . . .

To achieve in his dream the embracing of Venus (*Je tiens la reine!*) is to realize immediately that it is only a dream, that the apparition has vanished and that he is again alone with his desire. A dream of conquest is always followed by the reality of its loss.

And once again is felt the drama of three emotions, one rapidly succeeding the other. First, the dreamed conquest: *Je tiens la reine!;* the frustration of awakening of reality: *O sûr châtiment . . .;* and then the mock indifference to it all, dream and reality: *non.* This time, the faun is weary of the drama and there is no bunch of grapes at hand with which to invite oblivion.

> *Non, mais l'âme*
> *De paroles vacante et ce corps alourdi*
> *Tard succombent au fier silence de midi:*
> *Sans plus il faut dormir en l'oubli du blasphème,*
> *Sur le sable altéré gisant et comme j'aime*
> *Ouvrir ma bouche à l'astre efficace des vins!*

He first speaks of himself as the musician who has nothing more to play (or the poet who is emptied of words), and then of the creature whose body is tired. When he first awoke at noon, he was surrounded by a deep silence (*l'air/Assoupi de sommeils touffus*). What has transpired since has taken almost no time. This line, *Tard succombent,* might well be the proof of the faun's immobility during the entire monologue. In a few condensed minutes he relived his dreams and now wants to resume his sleep. But he wants a dreamless sleep, one that will contain no erotic picture of ravishment and conquest. Without moving from his initial place, he stretches out again on the sand, which is as thirsty as he, because they are both dried up by the sun. He opens his mouth to the sun, whose fire is maturing the grapes and preparing the wine. The faun is alone, but he has the physical comforts of the sun and the sand. He is about to succumb to silence and immobility and sleep. One final thought lazily floats through his mind. One final reminiscence of the dream he had had and the dream he had recalled. He thinks again of the two nymphs who loved each other and not him, and not without a tinge of irony, he bids them farewell: *Couple, adieu;* and announces that in his new sleep he is going to behold the shadow or the pure emptiness which they have become: *je vais voir l'ombre que tu devins.*

The term 'pure poetry' is far from being precise or determinable, but if it has any meaning at all, it might well apply to *L'Après-Midi d'un Faune*, whose beauty is without any didactic pretext, whose form seems to grow out of the spell-binding virtue and power of language. The classical Alexandrine line, unit of such regularity and tradition in the history of French poetry, appears almost transformed in the poem. It transcribes all the various moods and adjusts to each variation of temperament: action, song, interruption, and always within the same context of continuous grace and freedom of reverie. Marcel Proust, in a letter to Mme E. Strauss, refers to three poems of Mallarmé, one of which is *L'Après-Midi*, and speaks of their particular kind of clarity which doesn't expell all mysteriousness.[14] Mme Paul Valéry has in her possession a black moleskin notebook, dating from 1888, in which Paul Valéry, still in his last year at the lycée, inscribed his favourite poems. *L'Après-Midi d'un Faune*, as well as Rimbaud's *Bateau Ivre*, are completely copied in it. Many friends of Valéry remember his reciting from memory the Mallarmé poem.

It is difficult to separate *L'Après-Midi* from its companion piece, *Hérodiade*. Both poems were begun at the same time and both were worked over during a long period. They represent two complementary sides of Mallarmé, or rather two studies of complementary problems of adolescence. *Hérodiade* celebrates what might almost be considered a mystical interpretation of adolescence in which the rite of chastity conceals all desire of love. *L'Après-Midi*, on the other hand, is closer to a Pagan song dedicated to the voluptuousness of the senses. Mallarmé's preoccupation in *Hérodiade* is philosophical, in that he is facing the mystery of being itself and the profound problem of life and death. His preoccupation in *L'Après-Midi* seems at first more limited in that it concerns mainly the mystery of the senses, but deep in the poem is the problem of the relationship between the life of the senses and the life of the creative artist.

Mallarmé's faun, despite its narrative of abduction, is essentially the adolescent artist whose principal action is dream and meditation. The theme of the awakened senses is very real in *L'Après-Midi d'un Faune*, but it is constantly being expressed in the form of introspection. The adolescent wants to see himself as lover, but he is more permanently poet and to that role he returned in order to justify and acclaim his amorous dream. What is purely instinct in most adolescents cannot be realized except as it is converted into

Two Nymphs

song or some other form of art. It must always be remembered that the art itself, Mallarmé's poem in this case, not only reproduces a primal instinct, but celebrates it and exalts it. Art inevitably magnifies instinct, and gives it an importance and an amplitude that it doesn't possess in its normal accomplishment. Behind every work of art is the metaphysical need of the artist to understand himself as a man and to discover in his childhood and adolescence what secret forces contributed most to his formation.

When the faun awakens at noon and sees the sunlight streaming through the leaves of the forest, he asks himself two questions which are closely related with one another. The first question concerns the nymphs: how can he accomplish union with them? The second question is that which always follows hard upon the first: how can he accomplish himself? how can he create and re-create himself? The presence of the sun awakens this desire and these questions. The faun wants to see, and he accedes to the reign and the power of the sun. His blood is stirred by the warmth and grows exuberant. He has faith in life and the simple demands of living. He even believes in art and the intercommunication between life and art. He is the ingenuous poet. He is even virginal.

The faun's condition of virginity is his great bond with Hérodiade. Whereas the faun wants to see and live in the sunlight and feel with all his senses, the princess chooses the night, when she cannot see and when she will be able to dominate her senses. Her state of virginity permits her to walk unharmed among the lions, whereas the faun's similar state permits him to have dreams of conquest so strong that they are confused with reality and that they even leave physical traces on his body. Together, the faun and Hérodiade form one adolescent tormented by the desire to accomplish something and by the belief that he is destined to accomplish nothing. Day and night are the two settings for action and reverie, for accomplishment and frustration, for animal-like agility and hieratic immobility.

In the two poems on youth, neither the sun-inspired faun seeking an exaltation of his senses, nor the night-princess seeking an extinction of her being, knows any satisfaction. They both learn from their first dream and their tower meditation that what is true about the world is what is said about it. It would be difficult to discover poems of greater subjectivity, or poems whose unique subject matter is subjectivism. Hérodiade's mirror in which she sees herself as she wants to (*Je m'apparus en toi comme une ombre lointaine*) is equivalent to the faun's flute by means of which he transcribes his adventure in the form which would have given him pleasure (*Moi, de ma rumeur, je vais parler longtemps/Des déesses*). To the mirror and the flute, symbols of vision and sound, vision replacing the sun and sound replacing the night, synonyms of the female world contained and mirrored in itself and of the male world objectified in some creative accomplishment outside of the self, are entrusted the beauty and the significance of the poems.

The faun is predominantly the male in his willingness to forget a failure, to make light of it, and to begin again on a similar pre-destined failure. Four times, the brief negative of irritation and failure is heard: *Que non!* (v. 14); *mais bast!* (v. 42); *Tant pis!* (v. 93); *Non, mais l'âme* . . . (v. 104), even when the dream seemed real, even when teeth marks on his chest seemed to prove the realness of a struggle. But he renounces the image abruptly, and in each case turns to the surer reality of his song. He is more intoxicated by his art than by his adventure. If the male principle lives by inter-ruptions, failures and recommencements, Hérodiade is its counter-part in her determined solitude and self-sufficiency, in her self-imposed chastity and coldness where there is no chance of failure, but where on the contrary there is every chance for extinction. She is the phantom which the faun evokes in the final line of his mono-logue (*je vais voir l'ombre que tu devins*). When she first appears, the nurse asks if she is a ghost: *vois-je ici l'ombre d'une princesse?* Hérodiade's desire, so different from the faun's, is to see herself live in the midst of creation, to watch herself live eternally there. The mirror is the symbol of eternity because it is the reflection of the real world. It is the perfect intimation of the unreal. What the faun wants is a minute's satisfaction, and then a return to indolence and flute-playing. What Hérodiade wants is totally unknown (*J'attends une chose inconnue*) because it is eternal in a world of time and change. The female principle is permanence and continuance. Hérodiade adorns herself with hard everlasting jewels, and spurns the offer of perfume, symbol of transitory satisfaction. In her mirror she is the eternal princess and different from the girl existing in the illusion of matter. By looking into the mirror, she transforms herself into the idol, into the appearance of purity and inaccessible Beauty. The faun's dream might be his mirror, but in it he sees not himself but what is different from himself.

Reverie, by its very nature, is impotency. Hérodiade, by principle, and the faun, by indolence, are dreamers. The vainness of solitary beauty and the frustrations of sexual desire are leit-motifs in the two poems. Dreams however are composed of bestiaries and metamorphoses. As Hérodiade wills to become her reflection in the mirror and hence exempt from the contingencies of living, so the poet Mallarmé becomes the faun of his dream and lives the myth of a metamorphosis, even as Rimbaud became the drunken boat and Lautréamont the projection of a very pronounced animalism. Throughout *L'Après-Midi* there is an important confusion between the animal and the musician, which is the myth of the dreamer and the metamorphosis in his dreams. But 'confusion' in this case is not so precise a term as 'fusion'. The two forms are fused in the poem as they are in certain scenes of Ovid and Dante.

Dreams of children are often biological in nature, reflecting animal stories and pictures.[15] Mallarmé's faun is a more classical or mythological treatment than *Les Chants de Maldoror* which contain biological secrets that have hardly yet been studied.[16] But *L'Après-Midi* illustrates admirably to what close degree a poetic metaphor is related to a biological metamorphosis. The dream of a faun playing a flute in order to compensate an amorous defeat reveals the deep-seated human instinct to be something other than what one is. When such a familiar complex is cast into language, and highly poetic and difficult language at that, it reaches the possibility, for poet (as well as reader, to some extent), of being exorcised. The essential freedom of a poet lies in his capacity of being someone else. In each new poem he is always thinking of something else.

NOTES TO CHAPTER V

1. In collection of H. Mondor. 'Mais pourquoi te parler d'un Rêve qui ne verra jamais son accomplissement, et d'une œuvre que je déchirerai peut-être un jour, parce qu'elle aura été bien au-delà de mes propres moyens.' (Quoted by Mondor, *Vie*, p. 161.)

2. 'J'ai laissé *Hérodiade* pour les cruels hivers: cette œuvre solitaire m'avait stérilisé et, dans l'intervalle, je rime un intermède héroïque, dont le héros est un Faune. Ce poème renferme une très haute et belle idée, mais les vers sont terriblement difficiles à faire, car je le fais absolument scénique, non possible au théâtre, mais exigeant le théâtre.' June, 1865 (coll. H. Mondor).

3. This first version of the poem, *Monologue d'un Faune*, has been printed in the Pléiade edition (pp. 1448-51) and in Mme Noulet's important work, *L'Oeuvre Poétique de S. Mallarmé*, where there is a detailed study of the differences between the early and the definitive versions (pp. 229-247).

4. '... et je commence *Hérodiade*, non plus tragedie, mais poème.' Letter to Cazalis, Nov. 1865 (coll. Mondor).

5. 'Je me remets le 1er mai à mon *Faune*, tel que je l'ai conçu, vrai travail estival . . .'

6. Mondor, *Histoire d'un Faune*, Gallimard, 1948.

7. In 1887, in the edition of the *Revue Indépendante*, under the direction of Edouard Dujardin, the text of the poem appeared with only one change, in the 45th line:

> Rêve en un long solo que nous amusions (1876)
> Rêve dans un solo long que nous amusions (1887)

8. (1) I had two nymphs.
   (2) I want to dazzle these nymphs.
   (3) I want to perpetuate these nymphs.

9. (1) There undulates the scattered whiteness of a flock.
   (2) There undulates an animated whiteness at rest.
   (3) There undulates an animal whiteness at rest.

10. (1) Farewell, nymphs: duo of virgins when I came.
    (2) Couple, farewell, I am going to see the shadow which you became.

11. cf. H. Mondor, *Sur 'L'Après-Midi d'un Faune de Stéphane Mallarmé', L'Illustration*, Sept. 1948, and his book, *Histoire d'un Faune*.

12. A. Schinz, *D'Où sort 'L'Après-Midi d'un Faune'*, Modern Language Notes, Nov. 1937.

13. I want to perpetuate these nymphs.
> So clear,
> Their light rose colour, that it floats into the air
> Heavy with the sleep of the woods.
>
> Did I love a dream?
> My doubt, accretion of ageing night, ends
> On their branches, which, remaining the real
> Woods prove, alas, that alone I offered to myself
> As a triumph the ideal fault of roses.
> Let me reflect . . .
>
> or whether the women whom you explain
> Figure a desire of your fabulous senses!
> Faun, the illusion escapes from the blue cold
> Eyes, like a spring weeping, of the more chaste girl:
> But, the other one all sighs, would you say that she contrasts
> Like the warm breath of day in your fleece?

But no! in the motionless and tired faint
Suffocating with heat, the cool morning, if it struggles,
Does not murmur with any water which my flute doesn't pour
Over the wood sprinkled with chords; and only the wind
Out of the two pipes to exhale before
Dispersing the sound in an arid rain,
It is, on the horizon, not disturbed by a line,
The visible and serene artificial breath
Of inspiration returning to the sky.

O Sicilian edges of a calm swamp
Which to the envy of suns my vanity destroys,
Tacit under flowers of sparks, TELL
'That here I cut empty reeds conquered
'By talent; when, on the green gold of distant
'Verdure dedicating its vines to fountains,
'Floats an animal whiteness at rest:
'And that at the slow prelude where the pipes are born
'That flight of swans, no! of nymphs escapes
'Or plunges . . .'

                Inert, everything burns in the dark hour
Without showing with what art together scampered off
Too much marriage desired by him who looks for A:
Then I shall awake to the first fervour
Upright and alone, in an ancient flood of light,
Lilies! and one of you for ingenuousness.

Other than that soft nothing scarcely sounded by their lips,
The kiss, which low assures perfidiousness,
My chest, virginal of proof, shows a mysterious
Bite, due to some august tooth;
But enough! Such a secret chose for confident
The vast and twin reed we play on under the sky:
Which reed, turning back to oneself the emotion of the cheek,
Dreams, in a long solo, that we amused
The beauty of this place by false
Confusion between itself and our credulous song;
And [dreams] of performing so high that love will modulate for itself
—As vanishing from the ordinary dreams of a back
Or a pure flank followed by my closed eyes,—
A sonorous vain and monotonous line.

Try then, instrument of flights, O cunning
Flute, to reflower at the lake where you await me!
I, proud of my noise, am going to speak at length
Of goddesses; and by idolatrous paintings,
Continue to remove belts from their shadows:
Thus, when I have sucked the light from the grapes,
To banish a regret dispelled by my pretence,
Laughing, I raise to the summer sky the empty bunch
And blowing into their luminous skins, avid
With drunkenness, until evening I look through them.

O nymphs, let us inflate diverse memories.
'My eye, piercing the reeds, looked at each immortal
'Neck, which dips in the water its burning
'With a cry of rage toward the forest's sky;
'And the splendid bath of hair disappears
'In the myriad lights and shimmerings, O precious stones!

'I hasten; when, at my feet, are embraced (bruised
'With the languor coming from the pain of being two)
'The sleeping girls amid their relaxed arms;
'I seize them, without separating them, and fly
'To that mound, hated by the frivolous shade,
'Of roses drying all perfume in the sun,
'Where our struggle is similar to the consumed day.'
I worship you, anger of virgins, O terrified
Delight of the sacred nude burden which escapes
To avoid my burning lips, like a flash
Trembles! the secret terror of the flesh:
From the feet of the inhuman one to the heart of the timid
Whom an innocence abandons at the same time, humid
With mad tears or with less sad humours.
'My crime, was to have, happy at calming those treacherous
'Fears, divided the loosened hair
'Of kisses which the gods so well combined:
'For, scarcely had I hidden my passionate laughter
'Under the happy folds of one of them (holding
'With a single finger, so that her feather whiteness
'Should be tinted at the emotion of her sister growing excited,
'The smaller one, naive and not blushing:
'When from my arms, relaxed by vague deaths,
'That prey, for ever ungrateful, liberates itself
'Without pity for the sob with which I was still drunk.'

I don't care! toward happiness others will lead me
By their tresses entwined about the horns of my brow.
You know, my passion, that, red and ripe already,
Each pomegranate bursts and murmurs with bees;
And our blood, in love with whom is going to seize it,
Flows for the eternal swarm of desire.
At the moment when the wood is tinted with gold and ashes
A celebration resounds in the extinguished foliage:
Etna! it is on you visited by Venus
On your lava placing her innocent feet,
When a sad sleep thunders or the flame itself dies.
I hold the queen!

O sure punishment . . .

No, but my soul
Empty of words and my heavy body
Succumb late to the proud silence of noon:
Without more I must sleep in forgetting the blasphemy,
Lying on the thirsty sand and how I love
To open my mouth to the potent star of wines!

14. 'S'ils sont nouveaux pour vous, confessez, encore qu'ils soient de M. Mallarmé, qu'ils sont clairs et que la clarté n'en dissipe pas le mystere.' (This letter belongs to Mme S. Mante-Proust).

15. cf. Rimbaud's *Sonnet des voyelles.*

16. The best psychological study so far seems to be that of Gaston Bachelard, *Lautréamont*, Paris, José Corti, 1939.

CHAPTER VI

TOAST FUNÈBRE

In the literal sense, *Toast Funèbre* is the only long poem of Mallarmé, which beyond any doubt was provoked by an event. The death of Théophile Gautier occurred on October 23, 1872. The writers particularly close to him conceived the idea of a literary 'tomb', a *tombeau* which would contain a series of poetic homages to the deceased master. Mallarmé, who had been in Paris for a year, was among those solicited for a contribution. He accepted the invitation to compose a poem in honour of Gautier, who had been one of the poets of his youth and whom he had continued to esteem. But Mallarmé was to use the occasion not only to celebrate the disappearance of a distinguished poet. *Toast Funèbre* far exceeds a testimonial of homage and affection. It became a meditation, almost philosophical in its profundity, on the poet's vocation. It is not only one of Mallarmé's most important statements about the meaning of poetry, it is one of his most elaborately developed poems in terms of metaphor and rhetoric. It has, in the meagre and closely unified work of Mallarmé, its own particular vibrancy and poetic individualization.

The large collection of pieces, *Tombeau*, addressed to Gautier and his memory, appeared on the first anniversary of his death, in October 1873. It was published by Lemeere. *Toast Funèbre* figured in it, and fixed to a certain degree the position of Mallarmé in French letters, that of a difficult poet, whose poetic expression was infinitely demanding of a reader. Mallarmé was only thirty years old at the death of Gautier, but he had evolved already into the kind of poet he was to remain henceforth. Baudelaire had died before Gautier, in 1867, and he had been closer as a poet to Mallarmé, but the passing of Gautier had been turned into an occasion for poetic composition. *Toast funèbre* was a *pièce de circonstance*, a species of command performance, and the first opportunity Mallarmé had to testify publicly, in his artist's capacity, to the memory of one of the poets of his youth. This exercise of writing about an artist of the past and of discovering in him an eternal meaning of art, was to be performed many times afterwards in Mallarmé's life. In 1872 he found both a theme and a pretext which never failed to precipitate important examples of his poetic work.

The first line of *Toast Funèbre*, isolated typographically from the rest of the poem, stands apart also in its strong tone of apostrophe and in its only partially veiled dogmatism or even didacticism.

> *O de notre bonheur, toi, le fatal emblème!*[1]

Initially it is announced that Gautier is representative of all poets. Mallarmé speaks to the dead poet as if he were the emblem, that is, the sign or the symbol of a poet's happiness, which in this particular context seems to be fairly close to the meaning of 'life'. The adjective 'fatal' applied to 'emblem' adds the all important aspect of predestined vocation against which there can be no successful striving. *Emblème*, the first long sound which is heard in the poem and which terminates the first line, is the statement of death. Emblem, synonym of poem in Mallarmé's conception, is that which represents or symbolizes what was once life.

The first part of *Toast Funèbre* (v. 2-15) is the stanza on death, on the toast (*salut*) which is held out to the void. The lines slowly and patiently elaborate the idea of nothingness. The man who is sought is absent. His tomb possesses him entirely, but he lives no longer. Already we realize that what was intended to be homage is not really that, or rather it is much more than that. What was conceived of as panegyric is being executed as drama. Strong verbs of action and struggle (*souffre, éteindre, enferme, allume, retourne*) infuse the stanza with a meaning far different from that of the usual funeral encomium. Gautier himself has ceased struggling against death, but that struggle is being re-enacted and perpetuated by those who follow him and who, living, are enduring a premonition of the void which awaits them. The struggle is fated. Man is a fatal emblem.

The toast itself,

> *Salut de la démence et libation blême,*
> *Ne crois pas qu'au magique espoir du corridor*
> *J'offre ma coupe vide où souffre un monstre d'or!*

is a sign made to the void. It is dementia and not wisdom. It is a pale colourless libation. At the bottom of the goblet a gold monster struggles against the toast, against the magic which might call it up into view, as Faust once summoned Mephistopheles by drinking a secret potion. The corridor, magical if Mallarmé could walk down it, would be the means of communication between the living and the dead, between the outer world where the living poet stands and the still centre of the tomb where the dead poet lies, the very communication between speech and silence. The word 'magic' is justly attached to this 'hope of the corridor', but its force is especially felt in the verse of the 'empty goblet'. The magic would be performed if the goblet were filled when held aloft in the poet's hand, if the sparkling crystal were suddenly flooded by the literal champagne and the monster of intoxication and genius released.

But even if the magic were carried out, even if the deceased poet were to rise up from his ashes, the living poet would not be satisfied.

> *Ton apparition ne va pas me suffire:*
> *Car je t'ai mis, moi-même, en un lieu de porphyre.*

Mallarmé again recalls the role of Faust. A magical apparition, an effect of witchcraft or demonization, would only be that for Mallarmé who was present at the funeral ceremony of his master and knows that the once-living body is now encased in marble. The body of a poet, when placed in its tomb, symbolizes the foreordained separation of a man from his work. The simple verse, in which Mallarmé states that he was one of the mourners at the service, *Car je t'ai mis, moi-même, en un lieu de porphyre*, contains the germ of the entire *Toast:* a belief in the resurrection of the pure poet after his death. The ritual which has to be performed is the separation of the living from the dead:

> *Le rite est pour les mains d'éteindre le flambeau*
> *Contre le fer épais des portes du tombeau:*

The line describes a symbolic gesture of death, the extinguishing of a torch against the iron door of the tomb, whereby the hands of the living re-enact what has already occurred: the extinction of a life. Ritual is the microcosmic act of living and is close in its significance to the art of poetry which condenses life into imagery in order to deepen the meaning of life. Yet ritual and poetry also stand by themselves in their new formalized communication. So, the extinguishing of a torch is closer in its form to the poetry of Gautier than the death of the poet.

The following three verses, introduced by an unusual phrase which almost needs a translation, make an absolute statement about the tomb and hence the ceremony of the grave.

Et l'on ignore mal, élu pour notre fête
Très simple de chanter l'absence du poëte,
Que ce beau monument l'enferme tout entier.

We would be wrong not to believe, Mallarmé insists, that the poet is now completely within the marble tomb. Another 'monument' is simultaneously implied, that of the present poem, the 'toast' which Mallarmé is composing, and within these verses, in another way, the poet also exists integrally. *Toast Funèbre* is the most elaborate of the 'tombs' which Mallarmé erected in honour of artists: Baudelaire, Poe, Verlaine, Puvis de Chavannes, Wagner. Death is the celebration of the work of the artist. Whatever event in life we feel deeply, we are called upon to celebrate, and celebration means ritual, symbol, poetry. Life, if it is to be protracted, ends by becoming art.

Verses 12-15 complete the first section of the poem.

Si ce n'est que la gloire ardente du métier,
Jusqu'à l'heure commune et vile de la cendre,
Par le carreau qu'allume un soir fier d'y descendre,
Retourne vers les feux du pur soleil mortel!

If it is only the popular glory of the writer which is sought, then Mallarmé counsels (with no little bitterness in his voice) a return to the mortal sun, as temporary and fragile as renown and acclaim. Evening descends into the fires of the sun as a human life disappears into death at the moment of its greatest brilliance, but this brilliance is reflected in a pane of glass. The artist who insists upon worldly fame will know first the levelling power of death, the common change of flames into ashes. 'An evening' (*un soir*) in this passage alludes to Gautier's death, comparable to the sinking of the sun into the darkness of ashes. The true vocation of a poet is not life but poetry, and this particular meaning of vocation will be the subject matter of the second part of the poem, indicated in the typography, as verses 16 to 31.

The introductory line, solemn and slow, dominates the entire passage which gradually grows into the form of a drama, ending with a question and an answer. The opening lines recapitulate the solitude of death and the emptiness of the tomb. There the dead poet is seen in contrast with the living who surround his remains and provide a strange life within the tomb. By the attitude of the living poet toward the deceased, the passage broadens out into phrases almost resembling those of an encomium where Gautier is seen as a hero. The words, *vierge héros*, mark the culmination of this passage which announces a drama. In violence and swiftness the drama then is stated: the poet is seen as the hero opposing nothingness.

The sixteen lines fall into the three movements of ritual or preparation, or definition where the protagonist is named, and finally of drama, reduced and poignant, transcribed by means of a question and an answer.

> *Magnifique, total et solitaire, tel*
> *Tremble de s'exhaler le faux orgueil des hommes.*

The two opening lines praise death, and oppose it to life, paraphrased in the words, 'false pride'. True pride, which is death, appears. 1. 'magnificent' (the beauty of ritual and the unknown); 2. 'total' (the absolute quality of death); 3. 'solitary' (each one in death is unique and alone). These three words represent three human strivings, never realized in life, but which death consecrates. Three aspects of the foolish pride of man become finally real when they are recapitulated and revindicated in death.

> *Cette foule hagarde! elle annonce: nous sommes*
> *La triste opacité de nos spectres futurs.*

Mention of the crowd brings us back once again to the funeral ceremony and the mourners, who by now are looked upon much more as spectators incapable of fully realizing the experience of death. The mourners appear 'wild'[2] when contrasted with the resolved and magnified state of death (*magnifique, total et solitaire*). They announce, without having to speak, that they now are the opaqueness of the spirits they are to become. They signify this simply by being in the presence of the magnified one. The meaning of death is studied by Mallarmé (it is the occasion of the poem, after all) before it is subsumed into the meaning of poetry.

Then follows a single verse, typically Mallarmean in its role of interruption or pause.

> *Mais le blason des deuils épars sur de vains murs*

The two preceding statements on death and life had been brief and oppressively absolute, each encased in two verses, each narrated in highly stylized language. The opening phrase of the fifth line, *Mais le blason*, is almost an explosion of relief, almost a turning away from the meditation. After intensely considering the dead poet and the living mourners, Mallarmé turns to what is left: the walls of the tomb. They are *vain* walls because they actually contain nothing and also because they are disguised by the funeral draperies bearing the coat of arms. All the attachments to life and to genealogy are as vain as the solid walls which embrace nothingness.

After the single unpunctuated line, Mallarmé returns to himself, to his feelings and to his connection with the poet he is celebrating.

> *J'ai méprisé l'horreur lucide d'une larme,*
> *Quand, sourd même à mon vers sacré qui ne l'alarme,*
> *Quelqu'un de ces passants, fier, aveugle et muet,*
> *Hôte de son linceul vague, se transmuait*
> *En le vierge héros de l'attente posthume.*

He feels he must disdain tearfulness and any simple sentimentality, when he realizes that the poet to whom he is addressing his ceremonial piece—the present poem—is not moved by it. The reference to Gautier is no longer precise; Mallarmé is speaking of any poet: *quelqu'un de ces passants,* and uses another phrase of three adjectives to designate the posthumous poet: 'proud', 'blind' and 'mute'. When the body of the poet, the 'vague shroud', has been cast off, he is then transmuted into the 'virgin hero' of another period. The poet at death ceases being man and becomes a hero, virginal and invulnerable in that new state where action or struggle is a waiting. The erratic and harassing action of life then becomes the life of the poet's work which awaits a comprehending public. The poet is then assured of ultimately conquering, of ultimately deserving the title of 'hero'.

The final part of this section, lines 26-31, is one of Mallarmé's earliest appraisals of his belief about poetry.

> *Vaste gouffre apporté dans l'amas de la brume*
> *Par l'irascible vent des mots qu'il n'a pas dits,*
> *Le néant à cet Homme aboli de jadis:*
> *'Souvenirs d'horizons, qu'est-ce, ô toi, que la Terre?'*
> *Hurle ce songe; et, voix dont la clarté s'altère,*
> *L'espace a pour jouet le cri: 'Je ne sais pas!'*

It is a passage on the void and on cancellations, no longer related to death, but to the unwritten work of the poet. The uncreated words, those formed and articulated by the poet, fill the formlessness of the fog and the wind. The limitless extent of nothingness speaks to the man who has now been abolished from his former state of manhood and who therefore participates in the formlessness of the air. His spirit is still close enough to form and matter, still sufficiently un-dissolved, so that he hears within him, as if nothingness itself were speaking, the question about the reality of the world: 'what is the earth?' It is the central question for all artists who must necessarily depict matter. But time is passing and rapidly converting the essence of man into the elements. The answer, already fading, comes back as if the space containing the earth were tossing it about like a toy. And the answer resembles the final answer made by all men to all philosophical inquiries: 'I do not know!'

No matter what has been said about the earth in a poetic work, nothing really has been said because man does not know. He dreams and thinks of knowing, and those very dreams and thoughts fill the vast space above the earth. They are bolder and truer than the written work whose profound role is to testify to their existence. Death and void meet here and equate one another. Therefore the ghost, in his new state of ghostliness, asks the question about matter, *Qu'est-ce que la Terre?* and its answer, in the diminishing negative, underlines the irony of all art: its unreality, its approxi-mation, its game. Mallarmé stands not only before the tomb of Gautier which is emptying itself, but before the earth over which the wind is rushing. That is another void comparable to the un-spoken work of the poet. Gautier is seen as a hero in death because he has reached the superior state of silence. Mallarmé who succeeds him as a poet, is able to sing of that very silence, of the words not said. His emotion arises from the experience of the void. After the image of the tomb, *ce beau monument*, comes the image of air and space, of exhalation and fog, which is a second kind of tomb to which Mallarmé offers his toast. The drama, implicit in the question and the negative answer, leaves the protagonist, *le vierge héros de l'attente posthume*, immaculate and invulnerable in his final essence.

The third section of the poem, lines 32-56, is in a different tempo, as if the piece were a musical composition. The rapidity of the drama is over. The theme of reminiscence or of peaceful theoriz-ing begins. The poem, almost as if to justify itself, is going to end on a theory of poetry, on a passage of subtle but precise didacticism. This would seem paradoxical after the preceding passage on the hero-poet of death and words not uttered. Despite the greater

vocation of silence, Gautier and every other poet have known the
vocation of poetry. It too has to be defined, as well as the void, and
in relation to the void. The great originality of *Toast Funèbre* is the
relationship it studies between the void and poetry, between the
hero of silence and the master of speech, between the work as it
exists in the mind and the work consigned to the printed page, between life and the life created by the writer.

In the four opening verses the poet and his vocation are defined
in terms of an elaborate conceit.

> *Le Maître, par un œil profond, a, sur ses pas,*
> *Apaisé de l'éden l'inquiète merveille*
> *Dont le frisson final, dans sa voix seule, éveille*
> *Pour la Rose et le Lys le mystère d'un nom.*

Le Maître is a title in French designating not only the teacher but
the master-artist, the writer whom the young follow as guide.
Baudelaire had used it in dedicating to Gautier his *Fleurs du Mal:
au maître impeccable* . . . It sets the tone of the entire passage: the
poet seen as spiritual guide, as the exponent of a tender familiar
didacticism. He is the man who sees profoundly (*par un œil profond*)
and whose vision will be the point of departure for the work of the
next generation. In one sense, each great poet cancels the work of
preceding poets. Today, for example, the work of Mallarmé has, for
young practising poets, pushed into oblivion the work of Gautier.
But in another sense, each poet contains and prolongs the work of
preceding poets. Poetry is a continuous process. Its newest vision
always retains some reflections from older visions. Eden, the first
garden to be seen by man, is also the contemporary garden for the
most recent poet who wonders by what name he can call the flower
growing there. The poet first literally walks through the garden, and
then re-creates it in his verse (*sur ses pas*). What first trembled in the
real sunlight finds in the composed lines of the poet a composure, an
appeasement, an immobilization. What was first seen by the eyes of
a living man can be remembered only by the sound of words. What
the poet says confers a mysterious life on such an object as a rose or a
lily. To name a rose is to cause it to live differently than by its first
botanical existence. The symbol of the garden and its flowers is
used by Mallarmé in *Toast Funèbre*, as well as in the more elaborate
ars poetica of *Prose pour des Esseintes* to depict the poem and the specific
words or images in the poem. To read a poet's work is to walk

through a kind of universe where we recognize objects and where we try to understand patterns and figures and the use of the various parts. Poetry is a tranquillized universe as compared to the real world, and yet something of the trembling of light, of shadows and obscurities, continues to exist in the mystery of words. Each word is familiar, but its particular place in a verse or a phrase is like a rose in a garden which appears different in the changing light of every hour.

The poet, in his mysterious naming of objects, is seen to be a kind of consecrator, comparable to the priest who, by words, confers on a wafer a supernatural quality. The three lines which follow the introductory four touch on the religious problem of immortality.

> *Est-il de ce destin rien qui demeure, non?*
> *O vous tous, oubliez une croyance sombre.*
> *Le splendide génie éternel n'a pas d'ombre.*

The question seems to concern the mortal destiny of Gautier, and Mallarmé's answer to it is in the form of a command to forget the conventional and morbid belief in immortality. Man disappears in death. The poet will not be survived by a spirit or a ghost, for the change is absolute. The word itself of 'genius' dispels whatever 'shade' might grow around death. Valéry will be more insistent and more bitter in *Le Cimetière Marin* where he mocks funeral ceremonies and practices aimed at restoring a belief in personal immortality.

The long passage which follows (v. 39-47) is a single sentence describing Mallarmé's desire, which reflects the desire of all those present at Gautier's funeral, to see the surviving flowers which are the poems.

> *Moi, de votre désir soucieux, je veux voir,*
> *A qui s'évanouit, hier, dans le devoir*
> *Idéal que nous font les jardins de cet astre,*
> *Survivre pour l'honneur du tranquille désastre*
> *Une agitation solennelle par l'air*
> *De paroles, pourpre ivre et grand calice clair,*
> *Que, pluie et diamant, le regard diaphane*
> *Resté là sur ces fleurs dont nulle ne se fane,*
> *Isole parmi l'heure et le rayon du jour!*

Whatever Mallarmé is celebrating in this poem, is being carried out in the name of all those present, and especially of the poets present.

He is preoccupied with their desire for survival (*de votre désir soucieux*), with their poetic immortality. The passage is about the vanishing gardens of the real world, so closely allied with the disappearance of a simple human life, and the survival of words, the solemn sound of verses which like a chalice of red wine or an opened erect flower containing the dew and the rain, is isolated in time and space by each reader who considers it. The planet and its physical composition are transitory. When death comes to a poet, when he falls from his star (*du tranquille désastre*) in the silent event of death, his work is his survival. His words are like chalices and blossoms, containing the intoxication of wine and the freshness of rain, and illumined by their own light. Poems are a species of life separated from life. They are the physical survival of the spirit which has been received back into the air.

The end of the poem is a second long sentence of nine lines (v. 48-56) which was separated typographically from the rest of the poem in the first publication of 1873. It is, however, the continuation of the garden metaphor which is now joined with the earlier tomb image.

> *C'est de nos vrais bosquets déjà tout le séjour,*
> *Où le poëte pur a pour geste humble et large*
> *De l'interdire au rêve, ennemi de sa charge:*
> *Afin que le matin de son repos altier,*
> *Quand la mort ancienne est comme pour Gautier*
> *De n'ouvrir pas les yeux sacrés et de se taire,*
> *Surgisse, de l'allée ornement tributaire,*
> *Le sépulcre solide où gît tout ce qui nuit,*
> *Et l'avare silence et la massive nuit.*

Much of the particular vocabulary of the poem is here repeated, almost as if the lesson were learned and the images now familiar. The gardens reappear as groves, and the composition of poetry the sojourn in the groves. 'Pure' has already the sense of 'absolute' which Valéry will give to the word. The pure poet is the one who writes and who therefore abandons the dream of the poem. The dream about reality constitutes for the poetic temperament the temptation and the trap of indolence. Poetry is the subjugation of the dream to words. It is almost the betrayal of the dream by words, but it is the necessary arduous labour which will permit the poet, at death, to know all that Mallarmé puts into the final six verses of his *Toast*.

'The morning of his proud rest' is both the first morning for

Gautier after his death when his sleep has the lofty duration of death, and the same morning for his friends who consider him now not as a man, but as a poet, as a 'pure' poet. Death has tracked down mankind for so long that it is called 'ancient', and its mark has always been the closing of the eyes and the silencing of the voice. The morning commences the new state of death and reveals in its new light the tomb. The adventure of death is so extraordinary that the world, from this perspective, may be conceived of as being a 'corridor' (v. 3) or as a 'path' (*allée*, v. 54) through which the living seek to communicate with the dead. Poetry is the reverse: the communication of the dead, who have formed an absolute 'voice' in their silence, with the living who will never cease wondering what the absolute meaning of poetry is. The path, or the way between the living and the dead (the toast extended by Mallarmé to Gautier), contains, because it belongs more to the land of the living than to the land of the dead, a tomb, a solid sepulchre of marble in which everything that was purely human, everything that was opposed or harmful to the pure spirit of man, now lies. The tomb is that marble on which one engraves the words, *ci-gît* (*hic jacet*). It is the appendage, the 'tributary ornament' of the world because it holds what was once life, and now resembles a simulacrum, even a mimicry of life.

In the two substantives of the final line, 'silence' and 'night', Mallarmé condenses his entire poem. The silence of the tomb is avaricious and as protective of the death of Gautier as is the silence of all the words never said by him in his poet's existence. The bequeathed work in words takes much of its force and beauty from the unwritten and the omitted work, from the white of the margins and the speech unarticulated. The contour of each real poem exists because of the many poems which were not written. Initially there was a wildness in the words not said (*mots qu'il n'a pas dits*), and now it is a ceremonial silence surrounding the created work and protecting it jealously. The work transmitted to posterity exists because there was a work not transmitted. The silence is vaster than the work, and eternally bent upon preserving itself. The final word of the poem, 'night', with its accompaning adjective, 'massive', summarizes the tomb of porphyry, the extinction of the earth and the very darkness of the poet's work. All the themes of the *Toast* are recapitulated in the single syllable of *nuit*: the literal night when he dies, and the obscurity of the poems which is their native state, resembling the shadows of groves or of gardens.

Thus, *Toast Funèbre* seems to present itself in its three parts, joined and interrelated with one another, forming a drama on death and on poetry, a uniquely Mallarmean poem on the antithesis absence-presence. In the first part (v. 1-15) the funeral toast or farewell is given directly to the man who has disappeared and to the emptiness of his poet's vocation. As the torch is extinguished against the gate of the tomb, so is the spark of a man's life put out and so is the goblet of wine emptied in the ceremony of the disciples' farewell. Man exists mortally, as the sun appears and disappears in its physical circuit. The dream of vocation and whatever accomplishment is made in a vocation are mortal too and allied with the course of the sun. The absolute is elsewhere. The absolute is something else.

And so, the second part of the *Toast* (v. 16-31) celebrates the poet as hero, as the seeker of the absolute. The heroic line is the first: *Magnifique, total et solitaire,* but we realize immediately that it designates the poet in death, the man who in life is always less than a hero. The silence brought by death consecrates the other silence, that of the unwritten work. As the traditional hero often appears solitary and silent when opposing the force destined to crush him, so the new poet, created by death, waits invincibly in the midst of the winds whirling about him. Whatever his literal work is, it is made real and audible by the confused wind of his unsaid poems. These latter are perhaps saying more about the horizons of the earth from which they arise, than the completed poems which transcribe only approximately what their living author has imperfectly understood. A work of art exists thanks to the silence and the space surrounding it. Its very form implies separation and distance. Its very uniqueness implies obscurity. A poem which continues to exist as a poem testifies to a poet turned hero participating in an absolute state. As the poem becomes known and real for the living spectators, so the poet becomes unknown and unreal for them. When the poet hero is finally able to answer the ultimate questions concerning the earth: *Qu'est-ce, ô toi, que la terre?* he has entered his final and absolute silence.

After the funeral which celebrates the disappearance of the man and the void of a human life, after the hero's portrait which celebrates the disappearance of the world and the void of the unwritten work, Mallarmé extends his toast to the poetry of the poet, by means of which he celebrates the coming to life of the poems, a magical resurrection capable of being performed only after the two acts of disappearance, the dual initiation to the void. The most delicate and evanescent kind of mystery surrounds this passage on the creation of poetry. First, the key verb, *éveille* ('awakens'), describes the role of the poet's voice. By his speech the poet awakens the mystery of the name of such an object as a rose or a lily. The second key verb, *s'évanouit* ('vanishes'), describes the opposite action and applies to the existence of the poet. A man may disappear from the real gardens of the world, after which the words consecrated by him, as if they were the physical containers of wine and light, begin their own isolated poetic existences. Our contemplation of art (*le regard diaphane*) never permits a total vision. What we see is not in itself diminished (*ces fleurs dont nulle ne se fane*), but we never see perfectly. The work rises up (*afin que . . . surgisse*) before us in the same way as the tomb in its cemetery site. It is visible and palpable, but its contents are invisible since they have been absorbed back into silence and night. The shape of the tomb and the form of the poems bear a curious analogy. They are both pledged to duration and secrecy. They both testify to a principle of the void. The image of ashes encased in marble equates and supports the image of human experience committed to words. *Toast Funèbre* celebrates the essential paradox of poetry and of all art: the transitoriness of human experience fixed in a form of permanency.

The element of aesthetics in this poem and of elegant didacticism will not completely disappear from Mallarmé's future poems. Countless times the lesson will be repeated evasively and mysteriously. The meaning of a poem for Mallarmé is so closely related to the idea of the poem, to that part which is not capable of being transcribed into words, that the image of absence is everywhere. A poem is even comparable to a dead person from whom the full meaning of life has disappeared. Hence, Mallarmé's constant preoccupation with tombs and death. *Toast Funèbre*, of 1873, is in itself a complete expression and a complete theory. But the image of a tomb, allied with the meaning of poetry, will persist throughout the poet's career. Mallarmé's method is not so much the creation of a poetic work, the putting into words of a rich and powerful imagination, such as that of Rimbaud, as it is the refurbishing, the prolongation, the ever deepening understanding of a very few poetic images. Almost all that Mallarmé has to say about poetry is contained in each one of his major poems and is lucidly reflected in the less important poems.

A sonnet of 1877, which remained unpublished until the collection *Poésies* of 1913 (*Nouvelle Revue Française*) is reminiscent of *Toast Funèbre* and yet is cast in a form closer to that of Poe and Baudelaire. It is inscribed to a deceased woman about whom nothing is yet known.[3] The entire sonnet, which begins, *Sur les bois oubliés quand passe l'hiver sombre*,[4] is spoken by her. It is winter and her lover, to whom she addresses her words, he who is the *captif solitaire du seuil*,[5] laments because the tomb is not covered with flowers. This line describing the tomb,

> *Hélas! du manque seul des lourds bouquets s'encombre*[6]

as the critic, Charles Mauron, has pointed out, is purely Mallarmean. The absence of flowers in winter becomes for the surviving lover a reality. In the rest of the sonnet one thinks instinctively of Baudelaire's *La Servante au grand cœur*. Almost the same scene is evoked: the firelight and the ghost seated in the familiar armchair. Mallarmé's ghost says that not too many flowers should weigh down the tombstones so that she may raise it. What she needs most in order to return for this nightly visit is the reciting of her name by her lover as he waits for her. The Poesque and Baudelairian elements are obvious in the sonnet. Only the line on the absence of flowers distinguishes it and yet that is sufficiently central to characterize the poem. It is constructed around the idea of the absence of flowers which on the one hand causes the grief of the lover and on the other hand permits the spirit to return to the hearthside. What happens in the poem is due to the disappearance of the woman. Her speech is heard because she is not there. The creation of a poem inevitably reflects a dissolution, a vanishing.

A more important sonnet, composed probably later than *Sur les bois oubliés*, bears an even more marked relationship with *Toast Funèbre*.[7] It belongs to the group of major sonnets, especially to those on the various tombs. Whereas *Toast Funèbre* illustrates the poetic expansiveness which Mallarmé permitted himself so seldom in his career, the sonnet, *Quand l'ombre menaça de la fatale loi*, is one of the poet's most ardent meditations on night and on its related subjects: the life of the genius, his death, his future. With these themes—its first title was *Cette nuit*—it attaches itself to *Toast Funèbre* and assumes responsibility for one more lesson on the ever present dilemma of the poetic creation.

Three substantives and their resolution in an image construct the first quatrain.

Quand l'ombre menaça de la fatale loi
Tel vieux Rêve, désir et mal de mes vertèbres,
Affligé de périr sous les plafonds funèbres
Il a ployé son aile indubitable en moi.[8]

The three main words: *ombre, loi, Rêve,* might be considered in reverse order for explication. The dream (*Rêve*), printed with a capital letter in Baudelairian fashion, is the ancient and inevitable preliminary vocation of the poet. It is the dream of the creator, the primal urge to create and the actual vision of what is to be created. It is the surging upwards of desire and because of its harassing restlessness, it causes pain in the very bones of the poet. 'The fatal law' (*la fatale loi*) is signalled by the word, 'shadow' (*ombre*), because the law is the disappearance of the dream without its realization, and because it disappears in some act of obscuring. These words, all central in Mallarmé's vocabulary and creed, are also limitless in their meaning. They all converge on the word, 'night', *cette nuit*, which is both the literal night and the darkness of vision, that absence of light into which dissipates the poet's dream. At every mention of night, Mallarmé has a literal image for its designation, and in this instance it is the 'funereal ceilings' (*les plafonds funèbres*), source of the elaborate conceit in the second quatrain. The symbolic night, this time, is the darkness within the poet. The image of the quatrain, exactly contained in the fourth line, is that of a bird folding its wing inside the poet.

As the dream (*Tel vieux Rêve*) is the surging upwards and the desire to create, closely allied with the sexual dream, its collapse is a sinking backwards, a dissolving within, where the dream continues to exist somnolent in a diminished form. The resurgent desire is the bird rising in the air and the quiescent desire is the same bird folding its wing for repose. The curious adjective, qualifying 'wing', *indubitable*, a brittle prosaic word, may well accentuate the thought that the desire is always within the poet, that its existence cannot be doubted. Almost the same vocabulary occurs in Baudelaire's poem, *Spleen, Quand le ciel bas et lourd*. The sky which is a ceiling (*plafonds pourris*) and Hope (rather than Dream) which is a bat (*une chauve-souris*) form the setting for the violent poem on frustration. Whereas Baudelaire translates the despotism and cruelty of hope, Mallarmé moves beyond the personal anguish of the creating artist and the living man, into the cosmic drama, into an almost abstract and depersonalized image of the poetic psychology. Baudelaire's bat beating its wings against the walls of its cell,

> *une chauve souris,*
> *S'en va battant les murs de son aile timide*

becomes in Mallarmé's sonnet the bird, unnamed, which aware of its limitations and its endless desire, folds its wings and accepts its fate. The disproportion between dream and its realization may induce insanity and delirium, as it did in Baudelaire (the final stanza of Spleen is the actual image of insanity) or it may, as in the case of Mallarmé, induce a meditative, a more philosophically-motivated poetry. The natural image for Baudelaire is the closed-in space, the sky becoming a cover, the earth a prison, the rain prison bars. His cry is that of a man trapped by the night. But the natural image for Mallarmé is the night seen as a luxury of space, as a void well suited to the endlessness of the poet's dream.

This is the conceit of the second quatrain.

> *Luxe, ô salle d'ébène où, pour séduire un roi*
> *Se tordent dans leur mort des guirlandes célèbres,*
> *Vous n'êtes qu'un orgueil menti par les ténèbres*
> *Aux yeux du solitaire ébloui de sa foi.*[9]

This poetry is far from Baudelaire's art. The lines are uniquely Mallarmé's expression and inspiration. It is the example of an image, visible even at first reading, but whose relationship with the rest of the sonnet is difficult to determine. Once determined, however, it appears clear and irrefutable. Again, three words justify the general form of the image and the final line resolves and reaffirms the entire stanza. *Salle, guirlandes* and *ténèbres* compose the setting, anticipated by the first stanza phrase, *plafonds funèbres*. If the anticipation was one of funereal gloom, the realization is one of magnificence. The 'garlands' celebrate and charm a king in a 'hall' of ebony. The 'darkness' cannot obscure the vast pride which the garlands extol. Not until the fourth verse where the poet (*le solitaire*) is described as being dazzled by his faith (*ébloui de sa foi*) do we sense the familiar pose of Pascal (*le silence éternel de ces espaces infinis m'effraie*), indicated in M. Charles Mauron's commentary. From this intuition, the *salle* becomes the universe, the *guirlandes célèbres* become the stars in the sky, and the *ténèbres* the literal night by means of which the garlands are illuminated. The faith of the poet (*sa foi*), recalling its distant rhyme of the first verse (*la fatale loi*), would seem to be his power of thought, of wonderment, of imagination, the ancient dream which never abandons him. His faith would not be precisely faith in the absolute, but in the survival of his dream, in his power of evocation, in his very power of seeing the stars as garlands charming and celebrating a king. Into the single syllable *foi* are poured the two meanings of *Rêve*: the poet's mental image of his poem; and of *loi:* the fatal vanishing of the mental image into the void of night.

The movement of the two tercets, with their strong introductory affirmation: *Oui, je sais* . . . is outward into the cosmos, into the garlanded spaces from which may be seen the light of the earth itself. The material fires of the earth give testimony to the celebration of a genius. The poet is the man capable of thinking space, night, illuminated stars. His work is cast into time and space, and ends by filling them and signifying them.

Thus the leading question of *Toast Funèbre:* 'What is the earth?' is repeated in the sonnet, *Quand l'ombre menaça.* The vision of the earth peculiar to Mallarmé is that of the earth plunged into night. It is the absence of colour and contour when the poet imagines a celebration. Poetry resembles this earth covered in darkness where everything is seen from within, where, if flowers are seen, not one will fade (*ces fleurs dont nulle ne se fane*). The two earths, or the two domains, are mutually necessary: the earth of real gardens and the flowers seen when one's eyes are closed. The latter are the poems which Mallarmé is defining, by this pattern of images, as relics of the void. They are pure things rescued from the temporality of matter. 'The genius of an illuminated star' in the sonnet is as diaphanous and spiritual as the 'virgin hero of the posthumous waiting' in *Toast Funèbre.*

Pascal in the cosmos listened to a silence which terrified him. Baudelaire felt the cosmos changing into a dungeon and experienced its weight. Mallarmé saw the cosmos as a void. In his imagination and in his poetic theory, everything became this void or became lost in the void. First, the night, its permanent symbol and its complete expression. Secondly, man. And this is the central subject of *Toast Funèbre,* a poem which celebrates the nothingness of man. Everything is contained in the phrase of the opening line, *le fatal emblème.* An 'emblem' represents. It is therefore in itself empty. 'Fatal' qualifies a force which cannot be resisted. Man fatally becomes an emblem; that is, a signification and not a being. The sonnet, *Quand l'ombre menaça,* likewise has at the conclusion of its first line the word 'fatal': *la fatale loi,* which slightly helps to clarify the meaning of *fatal emblème,* by making it more abstract. The 'fatal law', referred to in the sonnet, is attached to the Dream. 'Fatal' therefore applies both to the poet and the poem. The law of the void involves the creator and his creation. The initial word, 'emblem', signifies both the poet after his death and the poem after its creation. The meaning of the word is difficult to grasp because of its dual function: it is a word of alliance, of connivance.

This lesson in theory, woven into the very texture of *Toast Funèbre,* is applicable to the history of Mallarmé as poet and to his particular kind of poetry. There are many testimonials to Mallarmé's existence as a poet and to his life as a man. But these testimonials, when added together, give us very little information about what he was, who he was, what his secret was, what the mysterious work he planned and referred to, actually would have been. In posing the leading questions about Mallarmé as a man and poet, one instinctively answers with the words he uses in *Toast Funèbre* when asking about the nature of the earth: 'I do not know!' The language of Mallarmé's poetry has always its own distinct form, a clarity and precision based upon an ever-painstaking avoidance of the cliché, and yet its meaning deepens and changes with each reading until one realizes that its total or its absolute meaning is not attainable. In the last analysis, it must be considered as poetry whose meaning is endless and evanescent, so closely related is it to the void it speaks of, to the limitless space filling the void. Ultimately the same answer given to the question: who was Mallarmé? will have to be given to the question: what is his poetry? The irascible wind of the words not uttered whirls around all those so parsimoniously bequeathed to us and protects them through time. *Survivre,* 'to survive', is one of the leading verbs in *Toast Funèbre.* The survival of the poetic word alone is assured in the ever-forming void of the world. The verb *survivre* is not in the sonnet, but it is paraphrased in the description of the light which the earth casts at a tremendous distance and after a long period of time: *d'un grand éclat l'insolite mystère.* The poem is the surviving mystery.

Mallarmé, after Pascal and Baudelaire, is another poet of the abyss, but without the expression of anguish associated with that theme. Mallarmé had unquestionably felt that anguish during his early years of teaching at Tournon, Besançon and Avignon. His letters of that period testify to a constant depression and mental suffering. Extracts from these letters have been published by Henri Mondor in his *Vie de Mallarmé*. But Mallarmé's poetry, that which follows the early Baudelairian pieces, rid itself of any trace of the anguish. This is stated succinctly in the final line of *Toast Funébre: Et l'avare silence et la massive nuit*. After *Igitur*, of 1869, Mallarmé becomes what he will remain for the rest of his life, the hero of the void and the posthumous waiting. His poetry grows progressively purified until it attains in its greatest utterances the music of absence, night, the void, nothingness.

Poetry is always a transformation and never an explanation. It creates enigmas and makes no pretence at solving them. In poetry the universe and all its problems are revealed once again. The heroes of the void succeed one another. Mallarmé follows Gautier in asking the same questions and in finding in language the only absolute possible for a poet.

NOTES FOR CHAPTER VI

1. You, the fatal emblem of our happiness!

Toast of madness and pale libation,
Do not believe that to the magic hope of the corridor
I offer my empty glass where suffers a golden monster!
Your apparition will not suffice me:
For I myself have put you into a place of porphyry.
The rite is for the hands to extinguish the torch
Against the thick iron of the doors of the tomb:
And we are beginning to understand that, chosen for our very simple
Celebration of singing the absence of the poet,
This handsome monument contains him entirely.
If it is only the blazing glory of the profession,
Return to the fires of the pure mortal sun
Through the glass which an evening proud of descending there illumines,
Until the common low hour of ashes!

Magnificent, total and solitary, such
That the false pride of men trembles at being expelled.
This savage crowd! announcing: we are
The sad opaqueness of our future ghosts.
But the escutcheon of scattered mournings on vain walls
I scorned the lucid horror of a tear,
When, deaf even to my sacred verse which does not alarm him,
One of these men, proud, blind and mute,
Host of his vague shroud, was transformed
Into the virgin hero of the posthumous waiting.
Vast hollow carried in the mass of fog
By the angry wind of the words he didn't say,
Nothingness to this abolished Man of yesterday:
'Memories of horizons, O you, what is the earth?'
Shouts this dream; and, like a voice whose clarity fades,
Space takes for a toy the cry: 'I do not know!'

The Master, with his piercing eye, has, on his way,
Appeased the restless marvel of Eden
Whose final trembling, in his voice alone, awakens
For the Rose and the Lily, the mystery of a name.
Does nothing remain of this destiny, nothing?
You must forget such a dark belief.
The glorious eternal genius has no ghost.
Worried over your desire, I want to see,
After the man who vanished yesterday in the ideal
Duty which the gardens of this star perform for us,
For the honour of the tranquil disaster
Survive a solemn agitation in the air
Of words, drunken red and large clear chalice
Which, rain and diamond, the diaphanous glance
Remaining there on those flowers not one of which fades,
Isolates in the hour and the light of the day!

Already this is the entire sojourn of our true groves,
Where the pure poet has the humble and broad gesture
Of forbidding it from the dream, enemy of his charge:
So that, on the morning of his proud sleep
When ancient death is for Gautier
Not to open his consecrated eyes and to keep silence,
May rise up, a tributary ornament of the path,
The solid tomb where rests all that brings harm,
The miserly silence and the massive night.

2. The adjective, *hagarde*, applied to the crowd, bears its full French meaning of 'wild-eyed', 'terrified', 'savage'. Its origin is in the Germanic word, *haga*, or '*hedge*' (Fr. *haie*). In mediaeval falconry, the bird, pursued by the falcon, took cover in the hedge, where, 'terrified', it tried to escape.

3. A manuscript of this poem exists in the collection of Henri Mondor. Dr Bonniot and his wife (Geneviève Mallarmé), when they released the poem for publication in 1913, revealed nothing about the circumstances surrounding its composition.

4. Over the forgotten woods, when dark winter passes.

5. Lonely captive of the threshold.

6. Alas! is encumbered only with the absence of heavy bouquets.

7. Both Mme Noulet and Charles Mauron have discussed this filiation. cf. the discussion of the tercets in chapter II of this study.

8. When the shadow threatened with the fatal law
   The old dream, desire and pain of my vertebrae,
   Grieved at perishing under funereal ceilings
   It folded its certain wing within me.

9. Luxuriousness, O room of ebony where, to charm a king
   Are twisted in their death celebrated garlands,
   You are only pride travestied by the darkness
   In the eyes of the solitary man dazzled by his faith.

CHAPTER VII

PROSE POUR DES ESSEINTES

In 1884, eleven years after *Toast Funèbre*, Mallarmé wrote *Prose pour des Esseintes*,[1] one of his longest and one of his most often and variously interpreted poems. If one excepts *Le Guignon*, an early piece of sixty-four lines, and the two long works: *Hérodiade* and *L'Après-Midi d'un Faune*, the only remaining poems of any considerable length are *Toast Funèbre* and *Prose pour des Esseintes*, each of which has fifty-six lines, although *Toast* is in alexandrines and *Prose* in octosyllabic verses. *Un coup de dés* is, of course, a poem, but it stands apart from the regular poems by the marked originality of its form.

One of the purest poetic expressions of Mallarmé, *Prose pour des Esseintes*, has preserved throughout countless efforts of explication, a mysteriousness still quite intact which is actually its principal beauty. It is first a poem of narration. There are characters and some action transpires within it. It almost begins like a fairy story, 'Once upon a time.' The setting could be that of a fairy story: a magical garden and an island. But each commentator wants to go beyond the story as if the literal voyage undertaken in the poem were a concealment. One senses that the work has been allegorically devised, that the characters must signify something, that the action bears some relationship to poetic creation. Since Mallarmé is always concerned with the meaning of poetry and the functioning of the poetic process, this supremely mysterious voyage, dedicated to des Esseintes and entitled *Prose*, must be his supreme expression in poetics. It is highly probable that the poem is Mallarmé's most complete and hence most difficult *ars poetica*.

The title is also the poem's dedication. Or rather the character for whom the poem is composed appears so important to the poet that he is the title and hence, to some degree, elucidates the meaning and the occasion of the poem. Des Esseintes is the aesthete-hero of the novel by Joris Karl Huysmans, *A Rebours*, published in 1884. Huysmans met Mallarmé not much earlier than 1882. In a letter of that year to Mallarmé, Huysmans indicated the plan of what was to become *A Rebours* and asked to see poems and prose poems.[2] *A Rebours*

Drawing for *Prose*

played an important part in calling attention to the new poets, such as Corbière, Mallarmé, Verlaine, in appraising such writers as Baudelaire, Barbey d'Aurevilly, Poe, Villiers de l'Isle-Adam. Des Esseintes is the type of symbolist or 'decadent' hero, scornful of humanity, bored, impotent, hypocondriacal. He is the seeker of rare sensations, the reader of Lucan, Petronius and the modern writers of prose poems. In the 14th chapter of the novel, where des Esseintes describes his preferred readings, approximately eight pages are given over to a discussion of Mallarmé's art, all the more remarkable at that time because of the infrequent appearances of Mallarmé's prose and poetry. The comments on the early poems and on *Hérodiade* and *L'Après-Midi* are among the first attempts to explicate Mallarmé and characterize his art. Something of Mallarmé's sensitivity and aloofness was doubtless carried over into the character of des Esseintes. At any rate, he is one of the ideal readers of Mallarmé, whose life is a cult of art, a devotion to aestheticism, a constant awareness of beauty as artifice. He could easily apprehend Mallarmé's imagined voyage of the poem and enjoy its deliberate secrecy.

But far more than the proper name composing the title, its first word, *Prose,* has elicited much speculation. If the word bears its customary and banal meaning, it might signify that what would be poetry and therefore hermetic communication to the ordinary reader, is for des Esseintes, trained in mysteries and symbolisms, lucid and prose-like. More likely than this elementary interpretation, Mallarmé, always conscious of precise and original meanings, had in mind the ecclesiastical use of the word, *prose,* signifying a Latin hymn composed of verses without meter, but rhymed. In the Catholic liturgy, the Pentacostal hymn, *Veni, sancte spiritus,* would be an example of a *prose.* A subtitle to one of Mallarmé's very early poems, *Mysticis Umbraculis,*[3] of 1862, is the phrase *Prose des Fous,* which indicates that the liturgical meaning of the word was known to him long before the period of *Prose pour des Esseintes.* As the Latin of the Church *Proses* is comprehensible only to the priests and the initiated, so the *Prose* of Mallarmé is apprehended by the lineage of des Esseintes, those readers who possess patience and science, who understand that poetry is a kind of liturgical mystery.

The literary scandal, for so long associated with this poem and others of Mallarmé, already belongs to another period. Long acquaintanceship with exceptional works of art always ends by converting them into familiar objects. A great poem is like a friend, unknowable in any real sense, but recognizable, who both changes through the years and remains the same. We learn to love the mystery of a human being, his secrets uncommunicated because they are incommunicable. It is enough that *Prose pour des Esseintes* has persisted through the fifty years since the death of Mallarmé. Longevity of a poem is our knowledge of it. The verses once ridiculed become proverbs. Almost every one of the fifty-six lines in *Prose* has its own beauty of language, familiar now, which has converted the line into something we say and therefore feel. The entire poem is something else, a work of complexity, so multiple in its possible meanings that we still read it with the proper sense of wonderment. A friend who reappears before us, after any amount of absence, still bears the traits we love and recognize, but the completeness of his being and the full story of his life we will never know. A great principle of love is applicable to the poetic art: our attraction to the unknown and the indecipherable, to an experience and a sex that are not ours. To love is to be attracted to that which we cannot know. To love a work of art is to discover in it traits of resemblance with our own experience and shadows which we cannot penetrate.

The legend of Mallarmé's life was the great work dreamed by him, the unique work destined to subsume all other works. But it was never composed, *Prose pour des Esseintes* might well be its prefiguration, one of the purest of the completed and hence minor works where every word is miraculously situated and illuminated, where a sense of communication and a sense of mystery seem equally proportioned. The poem bears a strong relationship with the tradition of preciosity in French literature. From the very first word, *Hyperbole,* to the very last, *glaïeul,* a synonym perhaps of the first, the language is extreme in its symbolic power, in its evasion of the ordinary, in the veiled amorous courtship it seems to depict.

The first two stanzas are prelude to the narrative. In the first publication of the work (*La Revue Indépendante*), they were separated from the other stanzas by a line. They are explicit and authoritative. The poet, assured of his vocation and genius, calls upon his highest ambition and the very poem itself which is to arise from his memory.

> *Hyperbole! de ma mémoire*
> *Triomphalement ne sais-tu*
> *Te lever, aujourd'hui grimoire*
> *Dans un livre de fer vêtu:*[4]

All poetry, all art is exaggeration and hyperbole. In the first word, a vocative, of the poem, is contained the concept that poetry is composed far away from the original subject. It is language superior to the original expression. In the lower and obscurer part of the poet's memory, from which the poem will have to emerge (throughout *Prose* there is constant reference to the movement of rising up and resurgence), it exists locked up as in a book of black magic, couched in a formula resembling some algebraic condensation. Poetry is the expression in words and rhythm of an experience which lies dormant and wordless in the subconscious. The shock which will give it form is poetic ambition, precisely the theme of these opening stanzas. The triumph to be realized is the will to give to a quiescent experience a hyperbolic expression. Language is a dangerous mode, capable of so losing itself in hyperbole that what it originally set out to transcribe is dimmed. And yet to articulate any experience, it has to undergo some modification, it has to approach some degree of hyperbole.

The second stanza changes from the vocative case to the statement of poetic ambition.

> *Car j'installe, par la science,*
> *L'hymne des cœurs spirituels*
> *En l'œuvre de ma patience,*
> *Atlas, herbiers et rituels.*

Here Mallarmé gives the reason, deliberately and almost pedantically expressed, for his bold apostrophe of the beginning. He is the creator of hymns, poems which will be apprehended by those who pay attention to the spiritual meaning of the universe. The science, by which these hymns are composed, is the sum of all the problems concerning man and the world. Everything relating to these two key mysteries is the subject matter of poetry. The total work of the poet is aptly characterized by Mallarmé as that of patience, which is the long waiting for the poem to find its form. No one was more meticulous, painstaking and patient than Mallarmé in the slow creating and perfecting of his poems.

In apposition with 'the work of his patience' are the three final words of the stanza, three brief words in French, which in English almost necessitate paraphrases. The 'atlasses', first, are the books of geography, the names and the places of the poetic action. In the narrative part of the poem we will read of a landscape, an iris garden, an island and a river bank. The *herbiers* are collections of dried flowers used in study. The irises and the final flower of the poem are going to explain the meaning of *hyperbole*. The *rituels* are books which contain detailed explanations of ritual and ceremony. They are guide books for priests and for the present poet about to embark on a voyage-ceremony of initiation. The three objects, *atlas*, *herbiers et rituels*, are therefore explicitly described in the poem which is about to begin. But beyond their immediate reference and use in *Prose pour des Esseintes*, the three words bear possible meanings applicable to every poem. There has to be a site, a position (*atlas*) for the poetic experience whether it be a garden or the heart or the conscience, almost as if a poem, as well as a tragedy, demanded unity of place. The flowers of the *herbiers* are the symbols with which the poem is concerned. Like the hero of a tragedy, the dominant symbol of a poem is that object on which the action is to be felt and the object belonging to the particular place of the poem. In every poem, the language, which is the action, is unfolded ritualistically according to rules and traditions (*rituels*). These three elements of place, symbol and action are clearly discernible in the other poems of Mallarmé. They are elements which give form and precision to a poem, elements which have to be applied, almost as remedies, to the first idea of a poem, characterized in this case by the word, *grimoire*. In the magician's book, as in the poet's mind, the trick exists in the state of formula, of recipe, which has to be expanded and performed. The initial word, *hyperbole*, resembles a magical word of incantation. Once it is said, as in the poem, something will happen. The poem follows it and seems to grow out of it, as if it possessed the power of infinite extension. The use of the word, *grimoire*, accentuates Mallarmé's belief in the absence of chance in the creation of poetry. It is the art of control, no matter how mysterious the control. A short phrase in *Igitur* unites *grimoire* and *hasard: le hasard était nié par le grimoire.*[5]

The final word of the introduction, *patience*, which opens up into its three divisions of place, symbol and ritual, succeeds the first stanza word, *grimoire*. The poet slowly builds up his poem from a magical incantation, almost as an ascetic awaits during a lifetime the experience of grace. Mallarmé's poetic asceticism cannot be over-emphasized. His initial Baudelairian anguish, discussed in his letters to Cazalis, Coppée and Lefébure between 1866 and 1868, changed into a more serene, and precisely more ascetic, preoccupation with the unrealizable dream of his work. His conscience learned to fill his ever-increasing poet's solitude, necessary to widen and deepen for the extraordinary project he meditated.

After two introductory stanzas, the narrative of the poem begins and occupies ten stanzas. It is the voyage to the island, as mysterious as all voyages, which are penetrations into the unknown, as unreal as all islands, which are lands severed from reality. There on the island, the huge flowers are separated from the gardens and the two voyagers, the poet and his sister, experience some kind of ecstasy.

The first of the ten stanzas maintains the tone of slight pedantry.

> *Nous promenions notre visage*
> *(Nous fûmes deux, je le maintiens)*
> *Sur maints charmes de paysage,*
> *O sœur, y comparant les tiens.*

The unusual insistence on the pronoun 'we' and the fact that the voyagers are two in number is the main characteristic of the stanza. The familiar poetic 'I' has broken down into two, and the second is actually given the name of 'sister' whose beauty is likened to the bewitching charms of the landscape. The story or fable of the poem is rendered all the more believable by the existence of two characters, but the poet is always one and poetry is the most relentlessly subjective of all arts. The accompanying 'sister' has been given various interpretations by commentators. Soula calls her the ideal sister or the consciousness of the poet; Thibaudet sees her as the ideal reader of the poet or his mistress; Mme Noulet names her the poet's patience. There are possible justifications for all these meanings. The poem illustrates, in the form of a tantalyzing allegory, a schizoid moment, a splitting into two of the poet's ego. But this is a classical necessary moment, and not the result of a neurotic state unless one denotes as neurotic any state of excessive awareness and sensitivity. A doubling of the conscience is indispensable for the artist. The first and more permanent ego is the analysing conscience of the poet. He is the *je* of the second stanza. The second ego is the conscience which experiences life directly, which learns and feels and loves. This second would correspond to the 'sister'. The actual splitting of the poet's conscience is, I believe, the profound subject of the poem, as it is, to some degree, of every poem. We might even call it the activity of the poetic conscience which is always multiple. Opposed to the logical conscience in us which knows, it seizes upon the multiple in the universe and divides itself in its eagerness to apprehend the multiple.

Prose pour des Esseintes is a poem on Mallarmé's androgynous nature. In it he appears first as the man who 'establishes' (*car j'installe*), through knowledge and patience, a hymn of spiritual import, and then as the being of feminine sensitivity who receives the experiences of the world, who learns them as a pupil does, but who finally is unable to convert them into a work of art because he (she) lacks the objectivity, the patience and the analytical power of the teacher.

Stanzas 4 and 5 form one sentence in which we learn quite explicitly that the poem is about a fictional voyage but which is going to maintain all the appearances of a real voyage.

> *L'ère d'autorité se trouble*
> *Lorsque, sans nul motif, on dit*
> *De ce midi que notre double*
> *Inconscience approfondit*
>
> *Que, sol des cent iris, son site,*
> *Ils savent s'il a bien été,*
> *Ne porte pas de nom que cite*
> *L'or de la trompette d'Eté.*

The ego who directs with authority suddenly and unpredictably loses his authority. The analytical ego no longer is able to analyse because the second ego has been moved sensuously. The verb, *troubler*, very often in French bears the connotation of awakened eroticism. It almost belongs to the language of preciosity, and the entire line, *L'ère d'autorité se trouble*, might well define some precise moment on Mlle de Scudéry's *carte de Tendre*. From this line on, the atmosphere of allegory penetrates the poem. What is happening has no motivation or no reason (*sans nul motif*) and it is being apprehended and recorded by the double subconsciousness (*notre double inconscience*). Supported by such expressions, the kind of experience in the allegory would seem to be that of love. The ego of analysis, or the teacher, is bereft of his power when the sentient ego, the pupil, feels in herself the unaccountable beginning of love. It has come without solicitation and one is abruptly changed by its invasion. The self becomes different. The sudden use of the pronoun *on* helps to indicate this: *on dit / De ce midi*.

The word, *ce midi*, can hardly be translated by one meaning only. It is first the south or the exotic country that is being visited. Unmistakably it has some relationship with *atlas*. But it is also the time of noon, when the sun is at the zenith and casts its most direct rays which burn everything. It is therefore a facile symbol for love which arrives fatally in the cycle of a lifetime, as the sun mounts the heavens each day without fail. This *midi* is perceived not by the consciousness of the poet but by his subconsciousness in its double capacity of male and female, of analytical and sentient ego, and contains finally, according to this still broader interpretation, the entire situation of allegory and meaning in *Prose pour des Esseintes*.

After the stanza of the double subconsciousness, comes the stanza of proof and reality, as a reaffirmation that the experience which is being related is not solely psychological. There is an earth here covered with one hundred irises, *sol des cent iris*. The *sol* repeats the notion of real landscape (*paysage*) and the irises are that which rises up from the earth, as the extreme expression of the soil's fertility. A flower testifies to the existence of soil and place and warm southland (*ils savent s'il a bien été*), as the sensation of hyperbole, of the expanding flower in its sexual meaning, testifies to the experience of love. This land has no name because it is not purely geographical. In the last two lines, the poet explains that he has not stopped at some well-known summer resort, blatantly advertised by signs and attractions (*L'or de la trompette d'Eté*). The place of the site of his experience is more personal, more subconscious. It is not even an experience shared by two people (*notre double inconscience*). It is a double experience felt by one person. But the allegory of the brother and sister, of the teacher and pupil has been formed, and the female part will not disappear from the rest of the poem.

The experience is going to be related through the symbolism of the flowers, and the next two stanzas are concerned with them.

> *Oui, dans une île que l'air charge*
> *De vue et non de visions*
> *Toute fleur s'étalait plus large*
> *Sans que nous en devisions.*

> *Telles, immenses, que chacune*
> *Ordinairement se para*
> *D'un lucide contour, lacune*
> *Qui des jardins la sépara.*

The opening *oui* is the narrator's emphasis. The assurance he wishes to give of the realness of his experience. 'On an island' (*dans une île*) marks the beginning of the theme of separation. Even if the poet appears as two characters on this voyage, the image of the island is that of his fundamental loneliness and oneness. It relates not only to the *atlas* of the second stanza, but also to the uniqueness of the poet and the uniqueness of his experience. This island has a supernatural quality, like Prospero's, because its air permits one to see. What we think we see in the real world is only visionary, but here one is endowed with sight and not vision (*De vue et non de visions*). What the poet sees with this new power of sight is a mysterious event. Each flower grows and enlarges without the two travellers being especially aware of them or referring to them. Again, the role of the analytical teacher, of the conscious and calculating artist is reduced. The poet has become his femaleness. He exists and feels and experiences directly, and the world has been so changed that it is an island where he sees flowers grow magically.

The flower, the object seen and not merely imagined, grows to a gigantic size. Around each flower, as adornment, is a clear circle or a kind of halo, which Mallarmé calls a lacuna or emptiness, but which is more a circle of light separating each flower from the garden. We have returned to the prosaic word, *herbiers*, of the second stanza, and the poetic word, *hyperbole*, of the opening. What has just been described as the strange growing of the flower is both the magical incantation of a word (*hyperbole*) which grows by its own power, once it is said, and the sensuous, even sexual experience of dilatation and will to power, which comes from mental images of extraordinary sight. When two lovers are together and separated from the world, the mounting of the sexual desire is more rapid in the male and, despite his necessary closeness to the woman, the urgency of his desire separates him from her.

After the word of 'separation', so precisely stated, we read its paradoxical synonym, 'desire', which fills the following stanza.

> Gloire du long désir, Idées
> Tout en moi s'exaltait de voir
> La famille des iridées
> Surgir à ce nouveau devoir,

This is the boldest stanza of the narrative and marks its apogee in many senses. The flower symbol here becomes what it symbolizes:

the secret desire of creation. The voyager sees the irises (*iridées*) rise up to their duty of testimonial, beauty, achievement, to their goal of supreme growth and expansion, at which moment the cycle of fertilization and flowering will begin again. The unusual juxtaposition in the first line of *désir* and *Idées* is not understood until it recurs in the third line as a joining of the two words within one: *des iridées*. On the narrative level of interpretation, this is the moment when the ideas of the teacher have impregnated the girl, when the lesson has finally been understood, and when for the teacher the ideas he taught have turned into his desire to know and perhaps to love the pupil. He is now the exalted one (*Tout en moi s'exaltait*). What he sees on the island: the rising up of the flowers, is now being enacted within him, without his control. He has become the mirror of his own sight. The teacher has found a new exercise (*nouveau devoir*).

But (*Mais*) as soon as the apogee is reached, everything collapses.

> *Mais cette sœur sensée et tendre*
> *Ne porta son regard plus loin*
> *Que sourire et, comme à l'entendre*
> *J'occupe mon antique soin.*

The sister is just the opposite of what she should be at such a moment: 'sensible and tender' (*sensée et tendre*) rather than 'sensitive and passionate' (*sensible et amoureuse*). The new exercise of the teacher will not be performed, since the girl of the legend does not respond. She even smiles, a sign sufficient to dissipate any mounting passion, and when she speaks, the teacher-poet is thrown back into his original role of analytical guide, of passionless expositor.

In the next three stanzas of the poem, which complete the narration, we are curiously thrown back in time to the moment before the collapse when the girl failed to respond to the teacher turning lover. As if in retrospect, the poet returns to the crucial moment of the experience in a final effort to understand and describe it.

> *Oh! sache l'Esprit de litige,*
> *A cette heure où nous nous taisons,*
> *Que de lis multiples la tige*
> *Grandissait trop pour nos raisons*
>
> *Et non comme pleure la rive,*
> *Quand son jeu monotone ment*

A vouloir que l'ampleur arrive
Parmi mon jeune étonnement

D'ouïr tout le ciel et la carte
Sans fin attestés sur mes pas,
Par le flot même qui s'écarte,
Que ce pays n'exista pas.

In order to explain the 'spirit of litigation' and discussion, it doesn't seem necessary to invoke the possible detractors of the poem, as Camille Soula does in his *Gloses sur Mallarmé,* but simply the spirit of pedagogy which had once existed between the two characters of the narrative. The moment of silence is precisely the change from pedagogue to lover which was symbolized by the intense amplification of the flower. The stalk of the multiple lilies (once they were called *cent iris*) grew to such an extent that analysis and reason were unable to comprehend the miracle. The stanza recapitulates the opening stanza on the island theme: *Oui, dans une île.* At that time also, there had been an absence of speech (*Sans que nous en devisions*) accompanying the apparition of the hyperbolic flower.

After this reiteration of the principal event or miracle taking place on the island, the two stanzas which follow unfold as the most diffi-cult linguistic expression in the poem. I believe that they still con-cern the miracle of the island, but no longer the miraculous flower. What the voyager sees on the shore (*la rive*) of the island is not com-parable to what transpired for him in the garden of irises. The syn-tax of the opening line, *Et non comme pleure la rive,* is in violent con-trast with the preceding stanza. The poet seems to be saying that the single extraordinary growth of the flower which had taken place in the garden is not comparable to the weeping of the bank, to the monotonous exercise of the tide in its rising and falling. That too is an action of growth and amplitude, but its exceptional appearance, say, of an inrushing wave, was not destined to create a youthful astonishment in the poet. That astonishment was the numbing of his reason and the failure of his pedagogical devices. On the very word, *étonnement,* depends the twelfth stanza. The exceptional experi-ence he underwent was illuminated by the sky of the island under which he walked (*tout le ciel et la carte / Sans fin attestés sur mes pas*). Its poetic reality is proved (*attestés*) as the words (*sur mes pas*) which relate it are said. Once the wave had withdrawn (*Par le flot même qui s'écarte*)

to reveal the island, and yet now that the experience is over and collapsed as in a dream, the monotony of the real waves (*son jeu mono-
tone*) is trying vainly to prove (*ment à vouloir*) that the miraculous
island did not exist (*Que ce pays n'exista pas*).

The final two stanzas form a conclusion both to the narration of
the island miracle and to the opening stanzas which concerned the
poet's work. In fact, they help to demonstrate how intimately the
introduction is joined to the narrative and how completely the literary theory is fused with the symbolism.

> *L'enfant abdique son extase*
> *Et docte déjà par chemins*
> *Elle dit le mot: Anastase!*
> *Né pour d'éternels parchemins,*
>
> *Avant qu'un sépulcre ne rie*
> *Sous aucun climat, son aïeul,*
> *De porter ce nom: Pulchérie!*
> *Caché par le trop grand glaïeul.*

These lines complete the allegorical adventure and at the same time
force the reader's attention to the lesson on poetry which the poem
contains. The poem, as it moves toward its conclusion, stated in sym-
metrical fashion in the two groups of stanza-concluding substantives:
1. Anastase—parchemins; 2. Pulchérie—glaïeul, becomes everything
at once: story, theory, parable, even psychology. The 'sister' is now
named the 'child', since she is younger than her guide. Her 'ecstasy'
has been her increased knowledge during this walk with her teacher,
as in answer to his mute supplication (that which he is unable to say
after having said so much), she uses a word of great age, Anastase,
associated with a period of ancient learning. The teacher has been
hidden from her by his rich lessons. Only the past, which he has explicated, has counted for her and he has become confused for her
with the very parchments to which he referred. But behind the
faintly-suggested papal lineage of Anastasius, there is its original
meaning of 'rise up'. Erudition was promulgated during the island
peripetetics (the *science* of the poem was announced initially), but the
central experience was the unaccountable growth of the flower
which came about as in response to the first word of the poem, *hyperbole*. The pupil has observed ecstatically the magic hyperbole of the
garden, and now in her new knowledge she says to her teacher,

Anastase, which is both a name and a verb of command. By this one word, she is saying to him 'Remain the teacher' and 'Produce the work'. By it, she prevents his becoming the lover and insists that he celebrate the glory of words, the resurrection of poetry.

The final stanza of the poem seems to depend on this second meaning of *Anastase*, its ancient etymological meaning of 'Rise up!' It is curious that the last words, of a serious rational nature, are said by the girl, almost as if she has learned the lesson so thoroughly that she replaces the teacher. She urges him to rise up (as he had once initiated the rising up of the flower by speaking the word, *Hyperbole*) before the tomb bearing her name, *Pulchérie*, will join her with her ancestors. The tomb would contain the void of human experience, the nullification of life and love and even the inscription on the tomb, the designation of her name Pulchérie, would be hidden by the oversized gladiolus. If the teacher realizes himself as a poet, the miraculous experience will not be forgotten. At least the name of *Beauty* will persist, and the words of the poem which are the hyperbole of the experience, will narrate the allegory of what transpired. The literal tomb contains a literal emptiness, whereas a poem is a fictional tomb containing that which may be perpetuated of human experience: its hyperbole, its symbol, its scene as observed under a very special sky (*sous aucun climat*), that of the poetic imagination.

So the story ends when the poet and his pupil reach the tomb on the island walk. The parable ends when the characters are named: *Anastase*, the spirit of knowledge; *Pulchérie*, the symbol of beauty. The poetic theory ends when the magic word, *Anastase*, is said, and the artistic work begins to grow into its existence. The lesson of psychology ends when the girl refuses the experience of love, too ephemeral and transitory, and insists upon the experience of art, which alone will assure the survival of human experience.

The obvious subjective element in *Prose pour des Esseintes* is the poet's role of peripetetic master, the subtle symbol-creating expositor who is able to initiate the listener or the pupil into an exceptional world. Mallarmé defines himself accurately enough in the two opening stanzas, although he doesn't employ the word itself of *Maître*, as he does in *Toast Funèbre*: *Le Maître, par un œil profond,* and in the sonnet, *Ses purs ongles: Car le Maître est allé*. Mallarmé literally played the role in all its forms during his lifetime: in the classroom where he was often enough *le professeur à chahut* or the jeered at teacher; in his salon on Tuesday evening, where he was respected and even revered and where he imparted his knowledge without interference; in his letters and lectures where he was always the gracious pedagogue, explaining himself and encouraging others; in his poems which are all lessons on the meaning of words and the symbolism of objects in the universe. Even in his disguise of a faun, Mallarmé remains very delicately but recognizably the pedagogue. The teacher is always to some degree the seducer. *Le Maître* in *Toast Funèbre* discovers for the Rose and the Lily the mystery of a name, as the poet-teacher in *Prose* indoctrinates in order to love.

In each of these instances, Mallarmé, in his role of master, undertakes a voyage: to an island, in *Prose pour des Esseintes;* to Eden, in *Toast Funèbre;* to the Styx, in the sonnet, *Ses purs ongles;* to a Sicilian swamp, in *L'Après-Midi d'un Faune.* The analogy with Mallarmé going to his classroom and into his salon, is not without meaning. The teacher needs a virginal setting for his exposition. If his words are to contain the necessary magic and transform the habitual world, they must be spoken in a place where he is solely the magician-teacher. The island is a strong enough symbol to illustrate the perpetual need of separation from the familiar. In its ultimate meaning the island is the poem which comes into being magically, as the result of incantation (*Hyperbole*), and which, despite its multiple analogies with life, is totally abstracted from life. Man has to go there in order to be a poet, in order to fulfil his vocation of poet, as another man requires a stage and artificial lighting in order to be an actor.

After assuming the role of master and after going to some exceptional geographical site, a third act is necessary for the completion of this particular adventure, which is in its deepest sense the poetic creation. This third act unquestionably concerns the word, *Hyperbole*, in *Prose*, and what *Hyperbole* engenders: *iris* and *glaïeul*. One remembers the allusion to the rose and the lily in *Toast Funèbre.* Familiarly with Mallarmé, the ultimate expression of the enigma or the poetic symbol is a flower. In *L'Après-Midi d'un Faune*, the lily, symbol of fervour, is upright and alone: *Droit et seul, Lys* ... And the hollow reeds, destined to become the pipes for the musical faun, are described as being vanquished by talent (*domptés par le talent*). The hyperbole of the flower (in the sonnet, *Ses purs ongles*, it is the mysterious object, *le ptyx*) represents the poetic enigma in its most miraculous aspect.

These three elements of master, island and flower bear an obvious

analogy with the priest, the altar and the miracle of transubstantia-
tion. They are all implied in the specific words: *atlas* (island-altar),
herbiers (irises-wafer), *rituels* (poet-priest). Art is a ceremony capable
of 'representing' in many ways, of bearing simultaneously multiple
meanings. The mediaeval four-fold method of interpreting a work
of art, described by Dante in his letter to Can Grande and by St.
Thomas Aquinas in his *Summa Theologica*, might be applied to *Prose
pour des Esseintes*. Only the first of the four levels, the literal, seems
impossible to ascertain. The poem itself contains no clue to a literal
or autobiographical or historical event which is being celebrated.
Modern symbolism is limited to the three purely symbolic levels of
interpretation: the allegory, the trope and the anagoge.

If the literalness of the voyage undertaken in *Prose* has been lost,
its allegorical meaning seems to concern love, and as opposed to the
usual mediaeval allegory (cf. *The Divine Comedy*) it is love not triumphant, not realized, not prolonged. In fact, it is so faintly suggested
as to be almost non-existent. The allegory of love, in modern art,
appears often as a kind of adumbration of love. The modern hero
is too timorous to state his case forcibly, too awkward to bring about
a conclusion. This psychosis is as evident in the teacher-poet of *Prose*
when he resumes with no struggle his ancient pose (*J'occupe mon
antique soin*) as it is in Mr Eliot's Prufrock (*Do I dare?*) and in Charlie
Chaplin's choreographic expression of the modern hero. In each of
these cases, the girl is unaware of the fact that the man beside her
loves her and is undergoing, because of her indifference, a particular
kind of anguish. Introversion is the modern myth of love. In the two
poems of Mallarmé and Eliot, and in the films of Chaplin, the hero
appears fundamentally alone, walking in a garden or down a street.
The episode of the girl might well be invented in order to substantiate an inner monologue, a parody of question and answer between
the maleness and femaleness of the artist.

The tropological or moral voyage of *Prose pour des Esseintes* is apparent throughout the poem. In fact, the work is based upon a moral
duty or command, heard by the poet, to create his poem. Out of the
obscure markings in the book of magic (*grimoire*), the poem (*Hyperbole*) must arise. The series of words: *science, autorité, ils savent, soin,
attestés*, culminate in the name, *Anastase*, the name which celebrates
the marriage of discipline and magic. As the modern love allegory
differs from the mediaeval in being strongly narcissistic and impotent,
so the modern morality differs from the mediaeval orthodoxy in

stressing the supremacy of the work of art, the moral urgency in the artist to create the art, rather than the private morals of the man who is artist. In the allegorical voyage the lover is transformed into the poet, and in the tropological voyage moral man is transformed into *Anastase*.

Finally, the anagoge of the voyage, which would be for the mediaeval mind glorification, the supernatural appearance of heaven in the form of an opened yellow rose, is for the modern mind sublimation, the magical appearance of the poem in the form of a growing gladiolus, *le trop grand glaïeul*, appropriately the final word. Dante's rose is the ultimate symbol of life triumphant in God, and Mallarmé's iris is the perfection of the poem, symbol and expression of life. As the poem itself contains what has vanished from life, so the iris in the poem conceals the emptiness of the tomb.

In the history of French poetry, the mediaeval fourfold method of interpretation is fairly unusual, and a poem like *Prose pour des Esseintes* may be explained more satisfactorily by its place in a permanent tradition and style of French poetry, that of preciosity. Mallarmé and his principal successor, Paul Valéry, are among the most recent of the masters of preciosity in France. It is a tradition much older than that of the court poets of the 17th century, with whom the word is usually associated. Because of such pieces as Oronte's sonnet in the first act of Molière's *Le Misanthrope*, and of Trissotin's sonnet in *Les Femmes Savantes*, the term preciosity developed a pejorative meaning, but it belongs rightfully to a noble tradition of poetry, the 12th century, when, in a Thibaut de Champagne,[6] for example, the 'precious' elements are apparent. An entire aspect of the poetry of Maurice Scève of the 16th century, which has recently been studied by Verdun Saulnier in a thesis published in 1949, belongs to the tradition of preciosity. The work of Jean Giraudoux, of the 20th century, is perhaps best explained by its relationship to preciosity.[7]

In a very fundamental sense, preciosity is concerned with the role of a special kind of woman who demands that man go against his nature and pay homage to her without receiving any of the physical recompenses of that homage. The 'précieuse' appears at times as a 'coquette' who insists upon a prolonged and elaborate courtship or as a 'prude' who is shocked by the carnal implications of love. The 'précieuse' relentlessly refuses love. In the Mallarmé poem, then, the female role of the *sœur sensée et tendre* is reminiscent of the *précieuse* (who in Molière's time grew into *la femme savante*). The entire action of *Prose pour des Esseintes* resembles the painful and intricate courtship demanded by some heroine of Mlle de Scudéry or of d'Urfé.

Courtesy and gallantry characterize the attitudes of the world of preciosity. Violence and passion are ostracized from its society. The court is its locale, the ceremonious court and the salon, where the relationships between the poet and his lady are of the most delicate and tenuous nature. In *Prose*, the court of Champagne or the salon of Mme de Rambouillet have been transformed into the island, another setting cut off from the ordinary world, and propitious for the unfolding of the strange drama between poet and lady whose real feelings are veiled and transformed.

In Mallarmé's poem, as in the full tradition of preciosity, the amorous role is closely associated with the creation of poetry. One might even say, without exaggeration, that the poetic act is the same as the gesture of the precious lover. The two are so perfectly fused in *Prose* that the reader is unable to perceive which illustrates the other, which precedes the other: love or the poetic celebration of love. In preciosity, love, because of its constant confusion with poetry, is always an intellectual activity, a *jeu d'esprit*. The role therefore of language is pre-eminent, so much so, in fact, that 'to make love' seems to equate 'to make poetry'. The homage of the precious lover is not so much that of his heart as that of his mind. The first lovers in the tradition of preciosity were the *troubadours* of the south and the *trouvères* of the north. Mallarmé's approach to love also is through its abstraction and symbolism in language. The tent and the castle of Thibaut de Champagne where he wrote his poems became the small study of Mallarmé where he laboured over his verses and combined the experience of love with the experience of language. A prolonged metaphor ends by becoming an allegory. The metaphor of Mallarmé's irises becomes a story of desire and of irises (the rhyme of *désir, Idées* and *des iridées* is an admirable example of precious language), and one almost forgets at the end that it is a love story because one learns to accept it as a story of poetry. Preciosity has always been a secretive mysterious code, an art for the initiate, the noble caste of a court or the habitués of a salon. The characters of the 13th century precious poem, *Le Roman de la Rose* (first part), lose all particularized and personalized traits. We follow, in the work of Guillaume de Lorris, not so much his characters as their sentiments. And in the poem of Mallarmé, we follow, not the psychological developments of the characters which are of the most rudimentary nature, but the growth and expansion of the flowers.

In his work, *Littérature*, Paul Valéry has given a bold and arresting definition of poetry when he calls it the effort to represent by means of language what tears, cries, caresses, kisses attempt to express.[8] The prestige of poetic language and the familiar, although diminished, means of allegory, dominate *Prose pour des Esseintes* and whatever experience initially the poet set out to express. In the tradition of precious poetry, experience becomes interpretation, action becomes metaphor, and the poem in its final form bears the appearance of an intellectual game or exercise. In the same work just referred to, Valéry says that a poem should be a celebration of the intellect.[9] But it is a sanctified ceremonious game, with meaning. It is the picture of man in an unusual pose and setting. Mallarmé as traveller, on his island. Each time that a poet looks into himself, as did Narcissus bending down over the still water of the fountain, he sees something which no one else can. He sees first a reflected self and then a second self (*Nous fûmes deux, je le maintiens*) between whom the drama of self-knowledge is going to be engaged. Such a poem as *Prose* has the solemnity of a drama as well as the aftermath of a drama when the stage appears as a stage, and when the garlands strung across it are seen to be made of paper.

1. The poem was first published in *La Revue Indépendante*, January 1885. Later versions contain only slight changes in punctuation.

2. The letter, dated 27 October 1882, is still unpublished. Its existence is revealed in the Pléiade edition, p. 1467.

3. cf. p. 1389, of the Pléiade edition, where the editors have quoted a line from the prose poem, *Plainte d'automne*: *le latin enfantin des premières proses chrétiennes*.

4. Hyperbole! from my memory
   Triumphantly can't you
   Rise up, today a conjuror's recipe
   In a book clothed with iron.

   For I establish, by science,
   The hymn of spiritual hearts
   In the work of my patience,
   Atlases, flowers and ritual books.

   We cast our glances
   (I insist we were two)
   Over many beauties of the landscape,
   O sister, comparing with them your beauty.

   The era of authority is troubled
   When, with no motivation, they say
   Concerning this south which our double
   Subconscious perceives deeply

   That, earth of a hundred irises, its site,
   They know whether it really was,
   Does not bear any name cited
   By the gold trumpet of Summer.

   Yes, on an island which the air charges
   With sight and not with visions
   Each flower grew wider
   Without our talking of it.

   So large that each one
   Was usually adorned
   With a clear outer circle, an emptiness
   Which separated it from the gardens.

   Glory of the long desire, Ideas
   Everything in me rejoiced at seeing
   The family of irises
   Rise up to this new duty.

   But this sensible and tender sister
   Did not go farther
   Than smile, and as I heard her
   I capture my ancient care.

   Oh! may the Spirit of litigation know,
   In this hour when we are silent,
   That the stalk of multiple lilies
   Grew too much for our reason

And not as the bank weeps
When its monotonous game lies
In wishing for the fullness to come
To my young amazement

Through hearing all the sky and the map
Endlessly attested on my walk,
By the very wave which withdraws,
That this country did not exist.

The child abdicates her ecstasy
And already learned by her walks
She says the word: Anastase!
Born for eternal parchments,

Before a sepulchre rejoices
Under some sky, her ancestor,
At bearing this name: Pulchérie!
Hidden by the too large flower.

5. Chance was denied by the conjuror's book. (Pléiade edition, p. 445).

6. cf. René Bray, *La Préciosité et les Précieux,* Paris, Albin Michel, 1948, pp. 19-33.

7. cf. the excellent study of Claude-Edmonde Magny, *Précieux Giraudoux,* Paris, Le Seuil, 1945.

8. 'La poésie est l'essai de représenter, ou de restituer, par les moyens du langage articulé, ces choses ou cette chose, que tentent obscurément d'exprimer les cris, les larmes, les caresses, les baisers, les soupirs, etc. . . .

9. 'Un poème doit être une fête de l'Intellect.'

CHAPTER VIII

UN COUP DE DÉS

THE FINAL poetic work of Mallarmé, *Un coup de dés*, was first published in the magazine, *Cosmopolis*, of May 1897. It was published separately long after the poet's death, in 1914, by *La Nouvelle Revue Française*, under the editorship of Dr Bonniot. Its strangeness and originality have been especially stressed in the critical statements about it. Mallarmé's genius was at all times that of an innovator, but in *Un coup de dés* he seems to have attempted the impossible. It represents his supreme effort to break with the conventional and the arbitrary in poetic creation. But this supreme effort was prepared in almost all the great poems of his career. Each major poem had been the discovery of a strangeness and the attempt to compose a rigorous symbol out of the fundamental chaos of the poet's inner life. Each work of Mallarmé is a new way of seeing and apprehending certain matters or themes which remain fairly constant throughout his life. The central images in *Un coup de dés* of the sea and the sky, of a ship and of its particular adventure occurred previously on many occasions.

At the seventh banquet of *La Plume*, presided over by Mallarmé in January 1893, he recited a sonnet as a toast to his fellow poets and the younger poets, which was published the next month (15 February) in *La Plume* as the inital text, and which he chose for the opening poem of the edition of his own poetry he was working on at the moment of his death and which was published posthumously.[1] The foam of the champagne in his glass calls up the image of the sea and of sirens diving into the water. The foam, like a line of poetry, designates only the surface: the reality is underneath.

> *Rien, cette écume, vierge vers*
> *A ne désigner que la coupe;*
> *Telle loin se noie une troupe*
> *De sirènes mainte à l'envers.*[2]

The image of the banquet room of poets becomes a ship where Mallarmé stands alone at the far end and his younger friends forward where the boat cuts through the waves. Mallarmé's toast to his companions contains the elements of the poetic adventure, words which relate also a sea voyage: the 'solitude' of poetic labour, the 'reef' of danger and suffering, the 'star' of guidance and inspiration. The sail has the whiteness of the page. One registers the wind of the elements and the other, the words of the mind.

> *Nous naviguons, ô mes divers*
> *Amis, moi déjà sur la poupe*
> *Vous l'avant fastueux qui coupe*
> *Le flot de foudres et d'hivers;*
>
> *Une ivresse belle m'engage*
> *Sans craindre même son tangage*
> *De porter debout ce salut*
>
> *Solitude, récif, étoile*
> *A n'importe ce qui valut*
> *Le blanc souci de notre toile.*

A much earlier poem, written in Tournon probably in May 1865, *Brise Marine*,[3] is Mallarmé's most direct contribution to the romantic-Baudelairian theme of flight and voyage. In Baudelaire's *Parfum Exotique*, the presence of his mistress incites in the mind of the poet the image of an island and the sea and all the exoticism of a tropical climate. But in *Brise Marine* the incitement comes from physical and mental fatigue.

> *La chair est triste, hélas! et j'ai lu tous les livres.*[4]

The poet wants to leave what he loves the most: his garden, his night labours of a poet, his wife and child.[5] What he imagines the most acutely is the intoxication of birds suspended between the ocean foam and the sky. Even the vessel he needs for the voyage, to take him away from all that is familiar and safe, he willingly imagines wrecked near a fertile island. The song of the sailors he hears in his heart has the echo of vast spaces, of a willed freedom that has no bonds of civilization. The image of the sea is the desire to depart. It resembles a manipulation of fate because it signifies the leaving of all that is most precious and intimate in a man's life. And the wreck of the ship substantiates this need of total separation. Desire is as absolute as the sea, as the void of the sea. The symbol of foam, both the champagne foam of *Salut* and the sea foam of *Brise Marine* leads to the most private and the most abiding of man's adventures.

The water image of *Petit Air* I, a poem dating from Paris, late in Mallarmé's life, 1894, seems to be that of a river in a city, quite possibly Bruges. The scene is one of solitude for the poet beside the quai in the midst of a sunset. As he turns his glance down from the sky, he sees three things at once which explain his reverie and his loneliness: a white garment on the bank, a bird gliding along the surface of the river and the quai, and the nude body of a woman, the poet's companion plunging exultantly into the water.

> *Mais langoureusement longe*
> *Comme de blanc linge ôté*
> *Tel fugace oiseau si plonge*
> *Exultatrice à côté*
> *Dans l'onde toi devenue*
> *Ta jubilation nue.*[6]

Water, especially river water, is a female symbol. It is simple and simplifying. It conceals great human forces of constancy and intimacy. Water is also the symbol of metamorphosis and change, a Heraclitean sign. In this sonnet, *Quelconque une solitude*, the water becomes the woman (*Dans l'onde toi devenue*). She merges with the element joyously and admits the metamorphosis, as if her human destiny were comparable to that of the water in its flowing and changing quality. The man's pose in the sonnet is more similar to that of Narcissus, the observer. His fate is solitude and sadness. He renounces his glance at the sky, covered with the brilliant sunset, in order to watch in the water beside him the jubilant body of his mistress and the flight of a white bird. Water incites vertigo in the man who watches it, whereas it invites the woman to participate in the vertigo by becoming it exultantly.

Many of the water themes occur in the sonnet, *Au seul souci de voyager*, which was published nowhere before its appearance in the posthumous collection, *Poésies*, of 1899. It evokes the ocean voyage of exploration of Vasco da Gamo, but the poem is dominated by the bird of annunciation shrieking monotonously over the mast of the ship as it dips into the ocean foam. The course of the boat is maintained (*Sans que la barre ne varie*). The bird's song is as constant as the night of the voyage, the despair of the navigator and the precious stones he sees beyond the horizon: *Nuit, désespoir et pierrerie*. The three words of the line narrate all the aspects of the voyage in the same way as the line in *Salut: Solitude, récif, étoile,* occurring in the same place in the sonnet, relates in three words the imagined voyage of the toast poem. The sonnet ends dramatically with the entire scene reflected in the pale smile of the navigator.

> *Par son chant reflété jusqu'au*
> *Sourire du pâle Vasco.*

It would seem that the first whiteness of dawn is dispelling the night (*Nuit—pâle Vasco*) and that da Gamo, facing the east, is experiencing the mixed feelings of despair at never reaching the goal, and of hope of finding the Indian riches (*pierrerie*). His position of solitude on the boat is not unlike that of the poet-navigator in *Salut*. The proximity of water, especially the vast stretches of the ocean, caused the dream to assume universal cosmic proportions. The extent of the ocean is sufficient to contain all the secrets of a man. Whereas the contemplation of a fountain or a pool stimulates the narcissistic reverie involving an individual, the contemplation of the sea, infinite, leads out from the individual to the problems and the manifestations of the cosmos.

The water of a lake or of a pond occurs more often in Mallarmé's poetry than the ocean. In *Le Pitre Châtié*, the lake is the symbol of the false liberation in which the clown loses the sacredness of his calling. In this case the reverie became so real that a tragedy ensued. In *Ouverture Ancienne* the water described is that of a pool reflecting autumn desolation. In *Scène* of *Hérodiade*, however, the image of water is that of the princess's hair (*le blond torrent de mes cheveux*) or the mirror before which her hair is combed and into which she looks deeply as into the past (*Miroir | Eau froide*). A similar transposition takes place in *L'Après-Midi d'un Faune* where the notes of the faun's flute are compared to drops of water (*au bosquet arrosé d'accords*). The literal water in the eclogue is a swamp which comes to life when the white bodies of the nymphs plunge into it causing a sparkling shower (*pierreries*). Although the central image of *Prose pour des Esseintes* is an island, there is little mention of the water surrounding it except for the monotony of the waves. The swan sonnet (*Le vierge, le vivace*) is built around the nightmare experience of the water of a lake freezing and immobilizing a bird (*ce lac dur oublié*), as if the aquatic world contemplated by Narcissus ends by becoming his prison. The night sonnet in -yx, *Ses purs ongles*, contains a descent, lower than night it-self, when the Master goes to the river Styx in the underworld.

It is not difficult, therefore, to prove that water is one of Mal-larmé's obsessions and is used by him as a principal symbol of sig-nificance. But no single poem announces as succinctly as the sonnet, *A la nue accablante tu*, his major work on the sea and a shipwreck, *Un coup de dés*. In the metaphysical-cosmological sense, *Un coup de dés* is closely related to *Igitur*, but in the more metaphorical poetic sense, it is closer to *A la nue accablante tu*. The sonnet dates[7] quite certainly from a period when Mallarmé was in full possession of his power of condensation and brilliant ellipsis. It is a purely Mallarmean piece in tone, symbol and syntax. As a poetic expression it is perhaps more successful in its own form as sonnet, than *Un coup de dés* is in its form.

The two quatrains are joined and produce one expression. The subject of the poem, the shipwreck, isn't stated until the fifth line, but it is carefully prepared in each verse of the opening quatrain. The principal verb, a familiar one with Mallarmé and which recalls the ever-present theme of absence, doesn't occur until the eighth line where it completes the entire scene of the ocean, so miracul-ously composed in seven lines, each one of which describes one trait.

> *A la nue accablante tu*
> *Basse de basalte et de laves*
> *A même les échos esclaves*
> *Par une trompe sans vertu*
>
> *Quel sépulcral naufrage (tu*
> *Le sais, écume, mais y baves)*
> *Suprême une entre les épaves*
> *Abolit le mât dévêtu*[8]

A low cloud, resembling heaps of rock and lava, marks the initial note of catastrophe. In its midst, the single syllable *tu* (pronoun or past participle?) provokes a mystery. Its meaning becomes clearly that of the verb *taire*, in its relation with *échos* and *trompe* and finally with the subject itself of the sonnet, *Quel sépulcral naufrage*. The ship-wreck has been silenced and the trumpet, which might have created a warning, was powerless, even in the slavish echoes which would have followed the sound. But the subject is preceded by the inter-rogative adjective, *Quel*. It is not certain that a shipwreck occurred, therefore. Only the foam remaining on the surface knows what happened and the poet addresses it familiarly all the while deploring that it is only foam and incapable of revealing its cause. The belief that it was a shipwreck persists, and the poet imagines the highest mast, stripped of its sail, sinking last into the water. Something has been abolished. The word itself, *abolit*, contains the poetic power of evoking what might have transpired and left in its wake a surface of foam. The threatening cloud, pressing low against the water, has followed a storm which has left its mark in some unaccountable way.[9]

The opening of the tercets indicates, by its syntactic violence, a marked shift in expression. The tercets, despite all lack of punctuation, represent another sentence and another hypothesis. The same tempest is referred to but it is now given a moral significance. To warrant such calamity, such disturbance of the elements, some crime or high treason must have been committed.

> *Ou cela que furibond faute*
> *De quelque perdition haute*
> *Tout l'abîme vain éployé*
>
> *Dans le si blanc cheveu qui traîne*
> *Avarement aura noyé*
> *Le flanc enfant d'une sirène*

If it was not a ship that sank, might it have been a child siren, drowned ironically because the ocean could find no lofty reason for its lashing fury? Indeed the thin hair of foam floating on the surface would bear a closer relationship to the meagre body of a young siren.

The sonnet begins and ends with a question. Some act which is just over must have been tremendous in its spectacle and in its meaning. Almost nothing of it remains: a low cloud and a bit of foam. The act has descended into its own secret. Water is that element which changes constantly and swallows up whatever tries to live in it. For Mallarmé each poem is quite comparable to the foam in *A la nue accablante tu*. A poem, in its reduction and apparent verbal tranquillity, is an absence, a separation from an experience or an object of a tragedy that can only be guessed at. In the shipwreck sonnet, some violence of chance or fatality had been perpetrated on the ocean. What remains of it, a fringe of foam and a dark cloud, is similar to the poem in the Mallarmé sense which is always the result of a tireless effort. The struggle of the artist to create out of the chaos of experience is not unlike a tempest of nature. The mystery of all art is the seeming chance, a throw of dice, for example—out of which an order of logic and construction is achieved. *A la nue* is a sonnet, like so many other poems of Mallarmé, on the abyss that exists between the final manifestation of art and the initial experience that has been abolished by the constant change of time.

The poems of Mallarmé, however, testify, not only to the making of a poem, but to some aspect of the poet's experience and sensitivity. Poetic symbols are keys to a world that is both personal and universal. A poet chooses his symbols because of some identification between himself and them. At certain moments in his work, Mallarmé identifies himself with Hamlet and Hérodiade, for example. Such a close identification is difficult to establish in such a poem as *A la nue accablante tu*, although Charles Mauron[10] believes that the *enfant sirène* of the sonnet may well be Ophelia whose death by drowning, as described by the Queen in Shakespeare's tragedy (act IV, scene 7) is not unlike the scene suggested by the tercets of the sonnet. Hamlet calls Ophelia a 'nymph' and asks her to remember his sins:

> *Nymph, in thy orisons*
> *Be all my sins remember'd*
>
> (act III, scene 1).

Ophelia has become a symbol of a woman's suicide. She is merged with the river. Her hair floats on it, and the water in its flowing brings about a change. In many passages of Jules Laforgue[11] there is a synthetic image of water, woman and death. The element of water has always described an experience of sadness, if not of danger and disaster: 'By the waters of Babylon we sat down and wept.' It is closely related to the idea of death, but of death as an elementary, simple and inauspicious event.

Paul Valéry has described in some detail[12] his visit to the apartment on the rue de Rome, in 1897, when Mallarmé read to him in a low even voice the text of *Un coup de dés*. Valéry believed that he was the first to hear the work. As soon as the reading was over, Mallarmé showed his young friend the manuscript which constituted the real surprise. Valéry had the impression of looking for the first time at the figuration of a thought occupying space.[13] The physical extent or extension of the poem seemed to be speaking and creating temporal forms. Later, at Valvins, when Mallarmé showed Valéry the corrected proof prepared for *Cosmopolis*, he said, 'Ne trouvez-vous pas que c'est un acte de démence?'[14]

The very typography and disposition of the large pages translated the work. Each page bore its own particularized graphic physiognomy. On the evening of the day at Valvins when Mallarmé accompanied Valéry to the station, the younger poet relates how he was conscious of the vast July sky and how the universe had taken on for him the appearance of a *text*. During the walk. Valéry continued to marvel at the courage and inventive genius which *Un coup de dés* represented. With the example of the night scene around him, he summarized his impression of Mallarmé's extraordinary attempt by saying that he had tried to raise a page to the power of the starry sky[15].

This final work of Mallarmé testifies to his lifelong antipathy toward the current use of words and the habitual typography of modern books. One aspect of his so-called hermeticism is in the meticulous care he always brought to the physical appearance of his poems, to the silences of the margins and the white pages. *Un coup de dés* is the extreme example of the effect which the actual typography and pagination of a work should produce on a reader. In a lecture which André Gide gave at the Vieux-Colombier, on November 22, 1913,[16] he quoted a letter from Mallarmé concerning *Un coup de dés* in which this theory is explained. Mallarmé talks of such and such a word demanding large print and a whole page for itself. He says that the constellation in the work will actually take on the form of a constellation as far as a printed page will allow, and that the vessel in the poem will appear to be pitching from the top of one page to the bottom of the opposite page. He wants the rhythm of a sentence to correspond to the subject of an act.

The page itself constitutes a unity, as, in another sense, a perfect verse constitutes a unity. In the brief preface which Mallarmé wrote for *Un coup de dés*, he elaborates this theory, and speaks of the intervention of the paper each time an image is completed. The moment of appearance on a page is very important, as well as the duration of the image. By the appearance of the poem, the thought reveals its very life; its hesitations, prolongations, designs, disappearances. A page is comparable to a musical score. *Un coup de dés* has indeed a leading motif and secondary motifs which may be followed by their typography. Mallarmé ends his preface by acknowledging that his work participates in the modern poetic movement, and especially in the attempts to create new literary forms by means of *vers libre* and prose poems.

For the edition of the poem which Mallarmé was so carefully preparing, Odilon Redon made four lithographs. But the edition never appeared. Thibaudet believed[17] that the publisher may have sold the proofs and the four lithographs through fear of scandal and derision. The poem appears today in the Pléiade edition, on pages of ordinary format, but the disposition of the phrases and the various sizes of the letters are rigorously observed. It is still obvious that, in order to read it, one has to heed more elements than usual. It is the boldest and most exacting of Mallarmé's poems. Each word, each space, each silence has to be apprehended. The most careful reading leaves in the reader only a vague approximation to the poem as a whole. Roulet's[18] lengthy and detailed analysis is doubtless only the first of many treatises to come,[19] on the exegesis of *Un coup de dés*, which is still a work that is unique in modern literature.

Its difficulty may well come from the fact that the inner life of the poet has, in this work, preserved more of its purity and directness than is usual in literary composition. The rhythm of the phrases is perhaps closer to the rhythm of passion and feeling and thinking. Each of the great poets brings a new way of seeing the world and of manifesting the poetic sensitivity. *Un coup de dés* seems to come from some region and time preceding poetic sensitivity which is necessarily a conscious sensitivity. The final statement in the work: *Une pensée émet un coup de dés*,[20] is perhaps the clue. The work is about a thought in its genesis and life. It is seized at its very birth and then followed without any restrictions being imposed on it. It is the game of thought, given its freedom of expression. It unfolds in its real and native plenitude, as if it grows by its own purely intuitive power. No rules and prepared logical recipes intervene between its initial appearance and its final completed manifestation. If it appears chaotic, that is because the words of man's inner life don't possess the organizing rhetoric and devices that permit us to follow most of his utterances.

The thought is a familiar one with Mallarmé and as it unfolds, as it 'emits its throw of dice', one recognizes themes and images of a life-long work. The problem of human destiny and freedom is contained within the principal image, which many years previously had been propounded and examined in *Igitur*. The character, Igitur, had once asked the question which *Un coup de dés* is going to answer: is the mind of a man ruled by chance, or is he able to overcome the force of chance? The very title, with its strong negative, gives the answer. The title announces a failure, and the entire poem is going to elaborate a cosmic elemental tragedy. The absolute is inaccessible because chance bears at least a close relationship, if not an identification, with Mallarmé's familiar image of the void.

The poem begins with the phrase, 'A throw of dice—never—even if it is cast into eternal events—from the depths of a shipwreck.' From the title the reader knows that 'never' is to be followed eventually by 'will abolish chance' and the large type of the word holds its meaning in suspense. 'A throw of dice' is a kind of act and at the end of the poem it is more closely defined as the act of thinking, as a thought. Even if the dice are thrown into those spaces that seem infinite and governed by abiding laws, they may be lost as in some shipwreck catastrophe, which the science of navigators, of numbers and accuracy, was unable to prevent.

The word 'shipwreck' introduces a subordinate clause, *Soit que*, and the ocean scene is evoked. The 'eternal circumstances' of the heavens are abandoned for the more immediate consideration of the 'abyss' which is the sea covered with white foam and angry. The waves are described as wings which are unable to fly (cf. *les vols qui n'ont pas fui*, of the swan sonnet). Deep in between two waves, a boat rocks from side to side as if it were about to be engulfed.

Gradually the thought (*coup de dés*) is unfolding. From the sky (1. *circonstances éternelles*) we have come down to the sea (2. *l'Abîme blanchi*) and within two waves of the sea, to a boat (3. *la coque d'un bâtiment*) that is about to be submerged. And now on the boat itself we see a captain (4. *le Maître*). He appears abruptly (*surgi*) as if he might be the Dutchman on the Phantom Ship, aged. Once he directed the ship (*jadis il empoignait la barre*), but now the whole ocean at his feet threatens and a successor must rise up (*l'unique Nombre*) who will not be different from the aged pilot. The difference between the old man (*le vieillard*) and the young man (*celui son ombre puérile*), son and yet the same, is established in this intricate passage where an actual drowning is described (*Naufrage cela direct de l'homme*). What is attempted by the ancestor (*par l'aïeul tentant*) is a marriage with the sea (*Fiançailles*) out of which will rise up a Son (*son ombre puérile caressée et polie et lavée*). As the one sinks into the ocean, the other, immemorially protected by all forms of nature, arises. The heavily-stressed word, *N'Abolira*, concludes the passage. Someone is abolished and is not abolished. Out of the strange coupling (*une chance oiseuse*) of the Master with the ocean, the result of chance, is born the continuator. Beneath the image of the shipwreck scene, one continues to follow the adventure of a thought. A thought succeeds itself in time, in its constant renewal, as the ocean engulfs one captain, to give birth to a younger one. *L'unique Nombre* is the Son, but he is also the Father. A disappearance (*la disparition*) is followed by an ambiguous appearance (*quelqu'un ambigu*), but there is no real break in the continuity. Thought grows and joins with its probability.

Then, as if (*Comme si*) the thought wanted to review and recapitulate, the words depict again the ocean. All is silence and foam, but that is irony. Soon the abyss will open again. The supposition closes with a repetition of *Comme si*, and the poem continues with the foam described as a feather isolated on the surface: *plume solitaire éperdue*. As in the sonnet, *A la nue accablante tu,* where the foam calls up the image of a child siren, here in the longer work, the foam calls up to mind the image of a plume and of a young lord's velvet toque. When the young lord is called the 'bitter prince of the reef' (*prince amer de l'écueil*), the name of Hamlet is fixed, as if he were the Son or the Number, successor to the Master (or King). The thought is derisive (as all thought eventually appears) in that it contrasts a single figure with the entire sky. Hamlet's reasoning was that of a man, but all his uncertainties of youth and expiation appear ridiculous in the presence of the absolute.

A long pause (or white space) follows the mention of the plume and also follows the associated image of the young prince who questions by silence and by laughter. A final image of Hamlet is struck off before the theme vanishes completely. A pale figure of a siren seems to be standing in his shadow, and a wave in the form of a manor or castle is sketched in before disappearing into the fog.

With the vanishing of the ocean scene begins the passage on the *Number* (or the Son, the continuator) about whom four questions or four hypotheses are asked. 1. Even if he existed . . .2. Even if he had a beginning or an end . . . 3. Even if he were known by some number or symbolic sign . . . 4. Even if he cast some light on the universe . . . These are the suppositions, and the answer comes immediately: 'It would be worse' (*Ce Serait pire*). The law of *chance* would follow and surpass the rule of *Number*. The feather which had just now (*naguères*) appeared on the crest of a wave, sinks into the one neutrality of the ocean. What had been planned and ordered, has been given over to chance, which is perhaps only another word for man's ignorance . . .

The final passage, covering two of the double pages, begins appropriately with the word, *Rien* (as in the sonnet, *Salut*, of a sea image). 'Nothing' remains of the great crisis (or catastrophe) on the sea (a further reminiscence of *A la nue accablante tu*). Whatever happened, in the course of events, didn't happen. The waves that rose once have descended and left no trace of their eruption (*une élévation ordinaire verse l'absence*). Only the Place (*Que le Lieu*) remains, which is the ocean, a monotonous low lapping of water (*inférieur clapotis quelconque*) which has dispersed all action. Whatever was destined to perdition is now dissolved (again, as in *A la nue*). 'Nothing' is the first impression, but perhaps there is an exception. The final word in large type is *Une Constellation*, the north star rising obliquely (as described in the sonnet, *Ses purs ongles*). It rises in the sky to its position, shining over the vast scene which has emptied itself of its catastrophe, and stops there as if it were the figuration of a thought propelled through space like a throw of dice.

The history of a thought is like the history of a speculation imperilled at every moment and at every place. Like an upheaval in nature, it reaches its climax and then descends into absence and oblivion. All forms vanish except the ocean which is formless. A thought is a living irony, formed by successive births and finally lost in the pure absence of death. The language of a thought can have no absolute precision, no absolute meaning because of the chance it encounters in its expression. Poetry is a game of risk, of magic and incantation. Its meaning is always hidden under the brilliance of its images and the unusualness of its analogies.

After the initial announcement of *Un coup de dés* thrown up into the sky, an act which is the very image of chance, comes the immediate picture of the ocean storm and the shipwreck. The same impulse of hurling continues. Successively the waves try to fly up like wings and the boat tries to keep from sinking. Chance rules a throw of dice and a ship in distress. The adventure occurs in a vast space, in an ocean abyss as if the entire world were needed for the testing of the word, for the unfolding of a thought. The opening of the poem is a gigantic upheaval. Air and water are bent upon destroying what has been made by man to withstand air and water.

The appearance of the Master (*Le Maître*) explains the first two themes: the throw of dice and the navigation. The Master is the Poet, the man of calculation, who was to annihilate the law of chance and create the perfect work of control. He will disappear only when his reign of control is over. In *Salut* he stood on the stern of the deck in a pose not unlike that of *Le Maître* in *Un coup de dés*. In *Au seul souci* he was apparent in the traits of pale Vasco. The absent Master of *Ses purs ongles* had gone to the Styx. The distance between the yawl of Mallarmé on the Seine at Valvins and the phantom ship of his final poem is tremendous, but the meaning of the navigator is clear. The dangers of a boat in its course are comparable to the dangers of a poem in its composition. For the first time, Mallarmé accentuates the age of the navigator. His time is over and the storm has come, to bring about a succession. The work of poet and navigator is immemorial. When the work is achieved, the poet becomes a phantom and another takes its place. The catastrophe is therefore not tragic, because it is necessary for the history of the world. The many tombs of poets which Mallarmé built have little trace of funeral solemnity. The principal thought of *Un coup de dés* grows in all its ramifications and complexities. Everything is successive and simultaneous: the sky, the sea, the boat, the captain, and the sky again adorned with its constellation. The style is narrative, but the effect is that of a picture in which everything is seen at once.

Each motif is dependent on the principal theme. The foam on the surface of the water takes the form of a feather, and the young successor, the Number, is Hamlet, by the shape of a foam-designed toque. But Hamlet is also the Master in all his need for certainty, in all his viril reasoning. But this 'prince of the reef' is the foam or what remains of some secret catastrophe, some sepulchral shipwreck (as in *A la nue*). Something has been abolished, some predecessor to Hamlet, and Hamlet himself, because there is only foam and one doesn't even know what crime is being punished by the will of the gods (cf. *Quelque perdition haute* in *A la nue*). What has disappeared is not only the crime (*la perdition* in *Un coup de dés*), but the result of the crime. In previous poems Mallarmé had said: *Rien, cette écume* (*Salut*), and *Rien, ni les vieux jardins* (*Brise Marine*), and now he says: *Rien de la mémorable crise*. A crisis is nothing because it is over and lost and only its site remains, because the world continues to remain after all conflagrations and woes.

The final page designates physically the sky with a shining *Constellation* in the centre. The poet's vision is traced on the page where the words are counted out in hierarchical formation. As if it were manifesting the end of the world, where the air is purified and the place of all disasters has been voided, the poem ends on the thought (*Toute Pensée*) which transcribes and transforms reality. All is cleared and levelled. The word has not only translated an idea and an occurrence; it has occupied a physical space on paper.

Despite the familiarity of most of the images of *Un coup de dés*, they multiply and disperse themselves more rapidly and abundantly than in other works of Mallarmé. The architecture of the work, as Roulet and other critics have pointed out, is contrapuntal and symphonic. A powerful movement, similar to that of a maelstrom, drags the images down as soon as they appear. The fate of the ship, announced at the beginning, presides over all the analogies and metaphors. In many ways the poem repeats the action of a storm creating its turbulence and effecting a final calm. Always, the analogy with the develpment and culmination of a thought is maintained. From chaos it takes its start and moves toward the final clarity of a star around which order and tranquillity will reign.

The drama of a thought is transcribed in terms of a human drama whose protagonist is the pilot. He is the man who directs the ship, who knows the calculations and the scientific laws necessary for the success of his voyage. His struggle is waged against the unpredictable, the unheralded storm which sinks the ship and drowns him. The sea in fury had been precisely that hazard that could not be known in advance. Once a thought is engaged, it encounters oppositions which risk turning it aside from its original path. Each human life is endangered by the mysteriousness of nature and natural upheavals. Man never possesses enough scientific knowledge concerning the natural universe to combat it successfully when it is unleashed against him. Chance in the universe can never be totally abolished.

But each poem of Mallarmé bears some relationship to the persistent problem of poetics. His protagonist is always, to some degree, the poet. The pilot, in *Un coup de dés*, who is a successful navigator until an overpowering storm causes his destruction, is the poet Mallarmé, meticulous worker for whom poetry is a science of calculation and law, but whose science cannot account for the final extraordinary beauty of his poems. The secret of each poem rises outside of and in spite of all the calculations. A poem is written to contradict chance, and yet if it is a great poem, the part which came about unexpectedly (as a storm in the ship's voyage) constitutes its principal achievement. At some point or other in the fabrication of his poem, the poet is helpless and useless before the gift of chance. After Mallarmé, both Valéry and Gide will speak of this part given gratuitously to the artist, the part of God in a work of man. It would seem that to the science of art, the passion of existence has to be added. Little wonder that the surrealists found in *Un coup de dés* a theory of art compatible with their own and a work of art whose beauty is surreal.

Un coup de dés corresponds more exactly than Mallarmé's other works to his greatest poetic ambition, to his definition of the poet's duty as he defined it for Verlaine:[21] namely, an orphic explanation of the Earth. In it one comes close to understanding something of the persistent theme of absence. More than what absence means currently, it seems to imply in this poem ultimately the power of a single being to expand into the universal, to exceed oneself perhaps by means of the word or the poem. This may be the loftiest meaning of the 'suicide' in *Victorieusement fui*, and of the shipwreck and the drowning in *Un coup de dés*. On the scene of the visible world, a drama takes place which is the confronting of the poet with nature. We pass through two stages of dramatic action. First, the reflection of the universal in a single individual: the appearance of the pilot on his ship at the moment of disaster. Second, the extension of the individual in the universal, when at the end the solitary number rises in the sky in the form of a constellation. Man and the universe intermingle in *Un coup de dés* as a compromise forms between time and eternity. On the one hand, the fury of the ocean is Dionysian, and on the other hand, the stoicism of the pilot, finally reflected in the constellation, is Apollonian. Order is established over chaos, and the poem, supreme and ultimate among the works of Mallarmé, remains his most infinitely suggestive in its attempted mirroring of infinity.

NOTES FOR CHAPTER VIII

1. *Poésies,* Deman, Bruxelles, 1899.

2. Nothing, this foam, virginal verse
   Designating only the goblet;
   Thus, far off, many a group of sirens
   Drown plunging backwards.

   We are sailing, O my various
   Friends, I already on the stern
   You on the glorious bow which cuts
   The wave of lightening and winters;

   A beautiful intoxication urges me
   Without fearing its pitching
   To bear standing up this greeting

   Solitude, reef, star
   To whatever was worth
   The white care of our sail.

3. First published in *Le Parnasse Contemporain,* of May 12, 1866.

4. The flesh is sad, alas! and I have read all the books.

5. Mallarmé's daughter, Geneviève, was born in Tournon, in November 1864.

6. But languorously moves along [the quai]
   Like white linen removed
   A bird in flight if plunges
   Exultant beside

   In the water become you
   Your naked joy.

7. First published in the German magazine, *Pan,* in April-May, 1895 (Berlin), where it was reproduced in facsimile. In France it was not published until the edition of *Poésies Complètes* of 1913. The manuscript, in the collection of Henri Mondor, is identical to the printed text of 1913.

8. Under the massive cloud silenced
   Base of basalt and lava
   Even with the slavish echoes
   By a powerless trumpet

   What sepulchral shipwreck (you
   Know, foam, but drool there)
   Supreme among the débris
   Abolishes the stripped mast

   Or perhaps, furious for lack
   Of some high perdition
   The entire vain ocean spread out

   In the very white hair which lingers
   May have drowned avariciously
   The child torso of a siren.

9. The actual meaning of the quatrains is therefore clear, despite the editorial or typographical errors which occur in certain publications, such as *As* instead of *A* in the third line, which would alter the meaning of *tu;* and of the sixth line: *Le sais écume mais y braves.* cf. F. Calmettes, *Leconte de Lisle et ses amis* (Paris, 1902) and the extended commentary on these errors in Noulet's *Dix Poèmes de Stéphane Mallarmé,* Genève, Droz, 1948.

10. Charles Mauron, *Le 'Coup de Dés,' Les Lettres,* 1948, p. 155-177.

11. cf. especially the opening page of *Hamlet* in *Moralités Légendaires.*

12. *Variété II,* Gallimard, 1929, pp. 169-175.

13. 'Il me semble de voir la figure d'une pensée, pour la première fois placée dans notre espace.'

14. Don't you consider it an act of madness?

15. 'Il a essayé, pensai-je, d'élever enfin une page à la puissance du ciel étoilé.'

16. Subsequently printed in *La Vie des Lettres,* April 1914.

17. Thibaudet, *Poésie de Mallarmé,* p. 417.

18. Claude Roulet, *Elucidation du poème de Stéphane Mallarmé: Un coup de dés, Aux Ides et Calendes,* Neuchatel, 1943.

19. A doctoral dissertation on the poem has been presented at Yale University by Robert Cohn.

20. A thought emits a throw of dice.

21. *Autobiographie,* 10 November 1885. 'L'explication orphique de la Terre, qui est le seul devoir du poëte et le jeu littéraire par excellence.'

PART III

BEYOND THE WORK

Woman with Fan

CHAPTER IX

THE POET AS RITUALIST

APPROXIMATELY FROM the beginning of the Second World War the work of Mallarmé has attracted a large number of fervent admirers. Before the publication of Mondor's *Vie de Mallarmé* (1941-42) and the Pléiade edition of the *Oeuvres Complètes* (1945), relatively little was known about him and especially about the relationship between the poet and his work. Mondor's generous extracts from his letters (which still remain to be published in their complete form and which will, beyond all doubt, establish Mallarmé as one of the great letter-writers of France) revealed in part the theorist and helped to confirm the traits of the priest-like character. His cult of poetry and his belief in the poet emphasized the sacredness of his vocation. His life, his style, his themes all make him into an extraordinary figure, composite of poet, professor, magician. Ritualist is perhaps the word which includes all the aspects of his character. The book or the poem is for Mallarmé the book of magic, the *grimoire*. By his language, he reveals himself as a kind of contemplative, a man who watches the mysteries of the universe as if he were watching the absolute. The greatness of his work raises the man himself to a kind of greatness. He disappears behind his masterpieces, but because of them, because of their content and their magic, the figure of Mallarmé the ritualist becomes clear.

There is something very strong and permanent about his resolution to be a poet and his belief that nothing higher exists for man. His life was a refusal of everything else. He represented the stubbornness of a man convinced. His work never satisfied him. It was a ritual which had to be performed daily. The repetition is what counts the most. His patience was inexhaustible because his goal was so high. Even when Mallarmé was approved by a small circle of friends and surrounded by younger poets who accepted him as a master, he never relinquished his struggle, he never believed he had accomplished anything. When he showed the manuscript of *Un coup de dés* to Valéry, he asked the younger man whether it didn't seem to be an act of madness. In his final note to his daughter, in which he asks her to burn all remaining papers, he says that the work which he hadn't been able to accomplish would have been beautiful. Of all that he wrote, which now appears to be far more extensive than was originally believed, he preserved only that which he judged most nearly perfect.

Poetry was never an indulgence or an escape or an antidote for Mallarmé, and never a mode of dreaming. Yet it is certain that the Dream (*le Rêve*) meant something quite particular to him which his readers and critics may never know with exactness. His conception of the dream enveloped his life. There is the mysterious dream of *Igitur*, dating from Mallarmé's early career as a poet, and there is the dream, unspecified, but centrally dominant, in one of his final poems, *Mes bouquins refermés*.

His life was dedicated to the sufficiency and the life of the word. His aim was always to reach a degree of meaning whereby an object is changed, whereby a moment is prolonged. Mallarmé seemed always to be teaching that a symbol has its own sanctity. The familiar objects with which he lived: a console-table, a Venetian mirror; and the far-away objects he evoked: the ocean, the island of Paphos, he raised to a power of meaning and reality. He resembles a priest surrounded by an invisible theatre for his operations. The presence of Mallarmé is in all the objects he named, but he is yet more invisible than they. We see his clown in the lake, his swan in the ice, Igitur on the stairs, Hérodiade before her mirror, the faun on the bed of roses, more steadfastly than we see the poet Mallarmé in his classroom, in his salon, in his yawl on the Seine. Each poem is like a protective shelter for an event or an object which Mallarmé favoured with his priest-like craft.

In his autobiographical letter written to Verlaine, who had requested it, the facts about his existence are few. The central paragraph concerns the works he will not write, the ideal work. He speaks of his alchemist's patience and of the book in several volumes, the work which he capitalizes, *le Livre*, and which would provide, if he were able to compose it, the Orphic explanation of the earth. This religious interpretation he concedes to be the sole duty of a poet. He is willingly consecrating his life to the execution of one fragment of it.

Throughout his writings, the word 'book' is always pronounced reverently. In one instance at least, he revindicates the celebrated proposition, so often ascribed to him, that 'everything in the world exists to end in a book. [1] If in his poetry the solemn word, *Maître*, is used on several occasions by Mallarmé to designate the poet, he appropriates on other occasions in prose the word, *histrion* (mediocre actor), which maintains the idea of performance. 'The writer', says Mallarmé, 'must present himself in the text as the spiritual actor of his evils, dragons which he had coddled, or of a joy.'[2] This striking definition is almost a psychoanalytic approach to the writer who 'performs' his complexes in his work and thereby seemingly transcends them. The exercise of art is the public exploitation of the neuroses of the artist, and this histrionic use of the neuroses takes the place of psychoanalytic treatment or cure.

The most often repeated criticism levelled at Mallarmé is his 'obscurity'. But a man, trained to see the world ritualistically, accepts mystery as the norm. Ritual, precisely, embraces and transcends mystery. When questioned by Jules Huret[3] about the obscurity of his poetry, Mallarmé replied that often a poem is termed obscure because of the insufficiency of the reader. 'A poem', he concludes, 'must always contain some enigma. The purpose of literature is to evoke objects.'[4] Here, again, the poet appears as ritualist, in his belief that poetry should evoke or suggest or symbolize rather than describe or narrate. A ritual is a fixed form and so is a poem, in Mallarmé's sense. The meaning of a poetic work is inseparable from its structure. The language of a poem, which cannot be changed or paraphrased, is its meaning. The words of a poem, their sequence and their rhythm, are absolute. To modify them or to substitute other words for them, is to break their spell. A ritual is valid only when it is performed exactly and integrally.

An article on the mysteriousness of poetry, written at the very beginning of his career,[5] states in vigorous terms Mallarmé's belief. Later, the terms and the exuberance of the essay will be modified but the ideas it expresses remain central in the poet's creed. The general attitude of the youthful Mallarmé is not unlike that of Vigny and of Baudelaire's dilettante. Everything sacred, he says, is enveloped in mystery. Poetry, like religion, has its own secrets which it should protect. Mallarmé laments the fact that a page of poetry (he cites *Les Fleurs du Mal* as example) is not like a page of music, incomprehensible to those who are not competent, who are not trained in the art of deciphering. Since poetry is the greatest of the arts, Mallarmé wants to claim for it the deepest secrecy. He regrets it hasn't found that 'immaculate language' which will render it inexplicable to all those who are not poets or those few fervent readers of poetry. Missals, he reminds us, have their gold clasps (*O fermoirs d'or des vieux missels!*) and ancient languages are protected by their hieroglyphics.

The main result of this lack of mystery in poetic works is the vulgarization to which they are subjected. Poetry is taught and analysed in schools to students of all tastes and abilities. The ordinary man feels therefore that he can judge Homer and Hugo, and doesn't hesitate to do so! He is less bold with painting and music because they have been able to preserve something of their mystery. But poetry is communicated by the printed page, and since everyone in the modern world learns to read and memorize poetry, no one feels timid at pronouncing approval or disapproval about a given poem. A new education is necessary which will dispense the ordinary man from the obligation to study poetry and to pretend that he understands it. Mallarmé points out to the poet the danger of reaching a large audience. The artist must remain an aristocrat. If they must read, let the masses read treatises on morals and not poetry! In this final proud sentence, Mallarmé clearly aligns himself with Baudelaire as denying any didactic purpose to poetry.

Even more than in this early essay, Mallarmé revealed his conception of poetry in his letters to Cazalis and Aubanel. They were often direct commentaries on the poems he was writing at the time (*L'Azur, Hérodiade,* etc.) and faithfully transcribed his state of feelings, his creative anguish and creative aim. These letters, not yet published in their complete form, show, in their fragments, commented on by Mondor, Mallarmé's fervent unity of purpose and sense of the intransigency of the poetic act. He felt the need of expelling all other preoccupations from his mind and of remaining resolutely within his subject. *J'ai voulu rester implacablement dans mon sujet,* he wrote to Cazalis in 1864. The letter concerns the agonies experienced over the composition of *L'Azur,*[6] agonies which prove that the writing of a poem was for Mallarmé a deeply spiritual exercise as well as linguistic and aesthetic exploration. A certain *agonie* is described in the poem itself, the anguish of the artist before the absolute of the work he wants to create, an inner torment exasperated by the serene blue of the sky, and another *agonie* within the poet. This latter seems to be a fear of sterility (*ma navrante impuissance*), a psychological block which has to be removed before the poet can work. Before understanding the actual writing, a first victory had to be won over himself: the attainment to a moment of perfect lucidity. These phases of struggle and advance all have their equivalents in the life of a religious. The moment of grace in the experience of a religious might equate the writing of the poem itself. At that moment another kind of anguish begins. A state of grace is usually of short duration. And in the same way, the exhilaration from a poetic discovery is followed by discouragement at the impossibility of translating the discovery. Because the universe is a mystery and is revealed analogically to the poet, the poem has to become a comparably solid whole, clothed with a mysterious language.

When, in 1864, Mallarmé wrote to Cazalis[7] that he had finally begun work on *Hérodiade*, he spoke of the 'terror' the new writing created in him, since he was trying to invent a new language worthy of his poetic belief whose aim was to describe not the thing itself but the effect it produces. The words of a poem, he goes on to explain, must contain 'intentions', and the words themselves should be so powerfully suggestive that they disappear in the wake of the sensations they generate. As work proceeds on *Hérodiade*, Mallarmé writes in further letters to Cazalis[8] on his continuing terror as the impressions and visions multiply when he is engaged in poetic labour. He anguished at that time over the appropriate impression to fix on paper and spent days wondering which to choose. Already, he considered the poem as a jewel which could be extracted from his thought, but in order to succeed in the operation, he needed intense solitude and silence. He knew the value of a very silent solitude, when no distraction would intervene, in order to hear more audibly the poem that was being composed.[9] To his friend Aubanel he confides his need of isolation and solitude in order to feel 'other-worldly impressions' (*les impressions extra-terrestres*) and to study himself during those moments.

No one single text of Mallarmé gives a complete statement of his poetics. For something comparable to Shelley's *Defence of Poetry* or Poe's *Poetic Principle* or Rimbaud's *Lettre du Voyant*, one would have to draw on all of Mallarmé's writings and probably his conversations. Paragraphs from his *Autobiographie*, from his early article, *L'Art pour Tous*, and from his early correspondence would furnish a logical and profound statement of belief of this poet-priest.

The experience of religion for Mallarmé seems to have been completely merged with that of art, and particularly joined with the experience of the theatre and of music. On certain of his pages of prose, he has left traces of deep reflection on the Church: its nave, its darkness, the freedom of entrance; on the liturgy of the Roman Church, whose meaning, in its mythic and universal sense, he understood. The liturgy, like a poem, is to be experienced solemnly because it points the way to or stands for an absolute. Religion Mallarmé sees as a state function, by which the state takes care of the individual. The pomp of the Church protects and unites the individual members in it. Men of today, he believes, are in closer relationship with the absolute than they appear to be. Our secret desires and impulses have an orthodoxy which, because it is confided in the priesthood, is diminishing. We go into a church today with the conviction that we are going to participate in an experience of art, but an old joy is rediscovered in the ancient canticles and hymns. The place itself of a church is a mystery. If the Church's doctrine has lost its forcefulness and literalness, there still remains for the 'faithful' the liturgy, the brilliance and *éclat* of orthodox ritual. The bare voice of a boy or a man singing the chant and responses (or the unison singing of plainchant) translates for Mallarmé the idea of human existence both multiple and one. Totally different from the music of opera, it serves to proclaim the multiplicity of the worshippers, the oneness of the worshipped, the regular and prolonged development of man throughout time.

Mallarmé shows an extraordinarily lucid observation of religion in his own day, of what might loosely be called the aesthetic approach to religion. At a time when the reality of the religious experience seemed dimmed and insipid, he saw the power of religion maintaining itself, especially in three ways.[10] First by the exaltation that comes from singing in a nave, from the 'response' sung in incomprehensible Latin by a choir, whose members project themselves as high as their voices rise. Secondly, by the role of the priest, hero of the Divine Drama, who is not so much an actor as he is the officiant in that he simply outlines the spiritual presence with which the people wish to confuse him. Thirdly, the organ, which, although placed near the door of the church, expresses the vastness of the dark and the attempt to understand the universe. Its music affords a sense of security and pride to the listeners. Thus Mallarmé summarizes the dramatic presentation (*la mise en scène*) of the state religion. The singing is an invitation to participate in the Divine Presence. But the figure of Christ (whose role the officiating priest adumbrates) is invisible. The infinity of the Presence is, however, translated by the sonorous vibrations of the organ music.

The theme of absence, which Mallarmé made so predominantly his in his vision of an analogical universe, is the central term for his threefold significance of religion. No literal religiosity penetrates the poetry of Mallarmé, but this theme of absence or invisibility, by its insistence and subtlety, translates an addiction to a religious feeling, an awareness of mysteries and analogies which poetry and music are able to create. One of his early poems, *Sainte*, comes closest perhaps to being a liturgical statement. The poem builds up to a remarkably organized picture—of absence and silence—without ever deviating from its original tone. Like plainchant, it continues almost expressionless,[11] but in its own total simplicity it announces and terminates within its brief measures a poetic paradox.[12]

The lyric divides neatly into two parts of two quatrains each. The first part shows the saint at a window. We learn about what the window conceals and what is manifested there with the figure of the saint.

> *A la fenêtre recélant*
> *Le santal vieux qui se dédore*
> *De sa viole étincelant*
> *Jadis avec flûte ou mandore,*
>
> *Est la Sainte pâle, étalant*
> *Le livre vieux qui se déplie*
> *Du Magnificat ruisselant*
> *Jadis selon vêpre et complie:*[13]

With the simplicity of a ballad, the saint is described as standing by the window. But such simplicity is deceptive. The symmetry is too studied to designate just what it says. The window conceals an object that is old and worn out, the viola or emblem of Saint Cecilia, martyr and patroness of music. We are reminded that the wood of the instrument, if we could see it, would appear old and faded, but we are also reminded of its former brilliance in combination with other instruments. The saint appears at the window with her book of canticles and psalms. But the book or missal is old also. The hymn of the Magnificat, highly illuminated on the page, appears still fresh as it was once long ago sung at Vespers and the night office of Compline.

The second part of the poem elaborates the time paradox of past and present, so deftly stated in the first part.

> *A ce vitrage d'ostensoir*
> *Que frôle une harpe par l'Ange*
> *Formée avec son vol du soir*
> *Pour la délicate phalange*
>
> *Du doigt que, sans le vieux santal*
> *Ni le vieux livre, elle balance*
> *Sur le plumage instrumental,*
> *Musicienne du silence.*

The window, referred to in the opening of the poem (*A la fenêtre*) turns out to be one depicted in a stained-glass window which is shining luminously as if it were a monstrance (*A ce vitrage d'ostensoir*). There is no visible instrument, but the angel's wing is spread open as if she were going to fly into the evening (*son vol du soir*). Her finger, which might have plucked the string of an instrument, had it been there, or followed the words of the Magnificat, had she been holding a real book, touches her wing resembling the shape of a harp. The sun setting in the sky gives such life and glow to the picture in the stained-glass that the angel appears to be a musician: her wing is a harp, and the accompanying instruments are invisible behind her. Her music is silence. The psalter or missal which is figured as opened before her is emblematic of the inaudible music.

All the arts are evoked in this poem: graphic, musical, literary. They are related to the past: *jadis* is twice repeated, and the angel, as musician of silence, presides over this power of the past so mysteriously guarded by the arts of the past which permit the present to know them. The life and martyrdom of the saint are preserved in the stained-glass which comes to life thanks to the actual rays of the sun. The pose of the saint is one of waiting and expectancy and potentiality. The final word of *silence* is expounded throughout the piece: the unplayed instruments, the unsung words, the harp that is really a wing, the musical saint who figures in a stained-glass window.

Poe's poem, *To Helen*, which Mallarmé translated, contains a similar passage.

> *Lo! in yon brilliant window niche,*
> *How statue-like I see thee stand,*
> *The agate lamp within thy hand!*[16]

But Keats' *Ode on a Grecian Urn* bears a much closer parallel to *Sainte*. A poem, like a ritual, is a performance of much that is not seen and not heard. The figuration on the urn,

> *Thou still unravish'd bride of quietness,*
> *Thou foster-child of Silence and slow Time*

and the saint's portrait in the window,

> *Musicienne du silence*

testify to sounds that are not audible: the pipes and timbrels of the Greek scene,

> *Heard melodies are sweet, but those unheard*
> *Are sweeter*

and the instruments of Saint Cecilia, both concealed and silent,

> *sa viole étincelant*
> *Jadis avec flûte ou mandore.*

From what is depicted on the urn and the glass, another complementary world is imagined:

> *What little town . . .*
> *Is emptied of this folk . . .*
>
> *Du Magnificat ruisselant*
> *Jadis selon vêpre et complie.*

The paradox of Keats is in the phrase, *Cold Pastoral!* and that of Mallarmé in *Musicienne du silence*. The same paradox, in its ritualistic sense, is admirably expounded in Wallace Stevens' poem, *Peter Quince at the Clavier*. As the poet plays, the sounds make another music on his spirit which translates what he feels for the woman he loves:

> *Music is feeling then, not sound . . .*
> *It is like the strain*
> *Waked in the elders by Susanna . . .*

Within the experience of waiting and contemplation, everything is formed, everything finds its source.

The attendance at a concert is for Mallarmé's interpretation of modern society a sign or substitution for ritual. It represents even a seasoned return of worship. The opening of a symphony series in autumn unites those who, unconscious of the deepest significance of their will, are celebrating the autumnal desert and the disappearance of the leaves. The orchestra leader, in raising his baton for the opening measures of the music, is initiating, in a setting of worldliness and multi-lighted munificence, a ritual not so much of aesthetics as of religiosity. Music is the last human cult, the final vestige of celebration and mystery. The vast public, united around this cult, comes from its daily political journalistic preoccupations, to experience the purity of music, which Mallarmé calls wordless poetry (*la poésie sans les mots*).[15]

The mystification of a modern concert is the relationship existing between the sober dignified assembly and the orgiastic form of the music it hears. An immemorial human trait is maintained in the obscure celebration still enacted at the performance of music. Mallarmé calls the concert a religious service (*un office*) at which deep passions are expended. Despite the conventional poses maintained by the listeners, they participate in something divine. On such occasions, the assembly (*la foule*) is the guardian of sacred mysteries (*gardienne du mystère*) in much the same way that Saint Cecilia in the poem is the 'musician of silence'. From the symphony performed on Sundays, the Frenchman, despite the seeming conventionality and bourgeois banality of the audience, has preserved the form of a sacred initiation. A kind of excitement is propagated throughout the crowd when the orchestra leader raises his baton. His gesture is almost sacred and is recognized as such.

Mallarmé's meditation on Catholic ritual, *Catholicisme*, appropriately follows his essay on the symphony, in the Pléiade edition of his works (pp. 390-395). In the darkness of a church nave, to the accompaniment of an organ, men today can feel something about their nothingness and the absolute of death. The idea of eternity is one of our heritages, although we seem to experience it infrequently. The beginnings of our period go back to the Middle Ages,[16] even if much of mediaeval belief has been relegated to the deepest most obscure part of us. Mallarmé refuses any real meaning to the word, 'laicity' (*laïcité*) which seemingly renounces 'higher aspirations'. Whatever is daily practice becomes a rite in some sense, even if its original practice has simply been transported or adapted to some contemporary mania. The reading of Huysmans has taught Mallarmé this, he testifies.

The miracle of music opens up an abyss which modern man refuses to define or acknowledge. Abyss or emptiness, it is a kind of 'absence' which no one of the spectators can traverse but which remains there before him. We encircle this great vacancy (or metaphysical abyss) like heroes who cannot reach to the centre of themselves because that space is forbidden. Music opens up the abyss and protects any entrance to it. Greek tragedy was more objective, even if the Athenian spectators of Prometheus and Orestes felt terror at the representation. The modern 'Passion', celebrated with all the pomp of the Church, represents humanity assimilated with the festival of the year. The theatre has become the temple. That is, it has become what it came from originally.

The tragic actor represents a 'real presence', and in the theatre a modern kind of 'communion' takes place (even if nothing is literally consumed, such as the host at mass) which is always a participation of the one with the many, or the many with the one. As the individual actor mimes a character, that character, like a god, becomes diffused throughout the audience. Nothing new in the world is ever born except from its source. Mallarmé pursued, with the tenacity of a scholar as well as with the intuition of a genius, his liturgical memory which he considered a national legacy.[17]

In Catholic liturgy he observed especially what has happened to the earliest myths of man. He marvelled at the crowd's capacity to identify themselves with the officiating priest. More than in the priest, he is interested in the crowd, in the collective spirit and fervour of the crowd. He expresses almost a fondness for the instincts of the crowd, for its childlike simplicity and unwavering attention. For the theological term of 'transcendency', Mallarmé would probably substitute that of 'initiation' whereby a man's soul understands what reaches it and welcomes what communicates with it. A sorcerer's spell or witchcraft (*sortilège*) is a term preferred by Mallarmé to 'religious experience'.[18] Our experience in a crowd, which is a cult, reveals a pure part of ourselves which is rarely felt in the ordinary episodes of our existence and outside of all aesthetic experiences.[19] Each man has an inner need of festivity and celebration which makes itself felt when he participates in a crowd. To give a name to the celebration would be, for modern man, to betray it, and yet he secretly or unavowedly hopes for some organizing power or some leader to give form to the celebration. Every modern assembly of people, whether it be for tragedy or music or politics, reveals a nostalgia for a religion or a religious celebration which might fill the emptiness of daily life.

The cult for Wagner during the last ten years of Mallarmé's life constituted for the poet the possible beginning of a new religion. The orchestra leader he saw occupying the celebrant's place at mass. Wagnerian opera was a new rite, as combination of drama and music, and yet it perpetuated elements of ancient rites by confering upon its listeners a sacrament of sound. The music transforms the listeners into a worshipful community. Mallarmé's remarkably profound definition of the effect of music enunciates this belief and this interpretation. 'The miracle of music', he writes, 'is that penetration, by reciprocity, of the myth and the spectators.'[20] Yet, natively pessimistic, Mallarmé believed in this doctrine of the religious character of the theatre wherein a people might be unified and made conscious of their common aims, and at the same time he despaired that the century which was ending had any understanding of such a doctrine or would care about it, if it did comprehend.[21] But in many passages where he elaborates his doctrine,[22] he forgets his pessimism in the ardour of his conviction. The purpose of the new religion will not be to rediscover God, but to recognize what is divine in each man, both what is greater than himself and identical to himself. This is quite evident in Mallarmé's essay on *Catholicisme* where he describes the rapid mystical awareness in a great theatre of the 'abyss' between the music performed and the listener.[23] Mallarmé stresses the importance of the *poem* in this new cult, and hence the new function of the poet. He ends an important essay, *Solennité*, with this exact phrase, *le ministère du Poëte*. This quasi-ritualistic role of poet is reminiscent of Victor Hugo. In a certain sense, Mallarmé saw even farther than the romantic vision, into a future era of collectivism where the state would participate mystically in its own ardour governed and magnified by the Poet-Priest.

The art of the theatre was one of Mallarmé's constant preoccupations. From the original version of *Hérodiade* (1864), destined for stage performance, and the unfinished metaphysical play of *Igitur* (1869), to the late prose writings on the theatre (such as, *Crayonné au Théâtre* of 1887), Mallarmé never interrupted for long his meditations on the meaning of the theatre and on the sacredness of drama. Increasingly it appears to be the central theme of his life, involving and elucidating the other themes of absence, analogy, symbolism. It is inextricably allied with Mallarmé's teaching on the poet: his character, his mission, his art.

Centrally within this greater theme of the theatre stands the figure of Hamlet, appropriated by Mallarmé in a personal and hence almost secretive way, as standing for a variety of roles: actor, poet, thinker, adolescent. Hamlet is both the man exposed on the stage before the public and the hero of a personal occult tragedy of everlasting fascination because it is indecipherable. Mallarmé converted the hero whom Shakespeare called Hamlet into a ritualistic portrait of himself which, calling upon the prerogatives of the stage and ritual, appears in many metamorphoses.

Early among these is the child of the prose poem, *L'Orphelin*, written at Tournon in 1864 and first published in *La Revue des Lettres et des Arts* of November 24, 1867.[24] Later it was completely rewritten and given the title, *Réminiscence*, in the collected volume of *Divagations*. The orphan boy, dressed in black like some child Hamlet, is wandering about looking for a family. He is the prefiguration of the Poet. Almost as if he were the actor Hamlet looking for a stage and a playwright, he stops beside the tents and improvised platforms of a fair. He feels drawn toward the comedians and watches the children of the group as they wait for their turn at a performance. The note of sacredness is struck in referring to the performance as 'the holy hour of lamps'.[25] He sees a child wearing a Dantesque looking cap and eating bread and cheese. Another child comes up to the first—a young tumbler (*un petit saltimbanque*) who is naked in his tights, and who speaks to the timid orphan. The first question dramatically opens up the Hamlet-theme: 'Where are your parents?' When the orphan confesses he has no parents, the tumbler, all the while performing his exercises of stretching, explains the amusement of having a father and mother who are able to make people laugh.

The orphan-child, recognizably Hamlet in his search for a father, becomes, in the essay bearing the title, *Hamlet*,[26] the adolescent emerging and remaining from each one of us, whose principal struggle comes from that necessity demanded by life of appearing before people. The young tumbler, in the prose poem, had been trained to perform before a crowd, but the orphan child was already wearing the mourning costume of solitude. Contemporary with the prose poem is the first version (1864) of the clown sonnet, *Le Pitre Châtié*, where the clown escaping from his nightly public appearance is punished. In the final version of the sonnet the clown is called the 'bad Hamlet' (*le mauvais Hamlet*) because of this infidelity to the actor's vocation. The orphan drew near to a group of circus performers in his search for a father who would provide him with a role to learn and play. Hamlet has to play many parts in his tragedy: the jilted lover, the friend of the two courtiers, the king's nephew, the avenging son, the son of his mother. Only briefly in his soliloquies does he manifest the part he didn't invent: the grief-stricken son unable to execute the revenge and whose mind wavers under the tragic burden. To continue living he needs a theatre, a play in which to test himself and the world he knows. To live one's own part is not sufficient for Hamlet and for the poet. A scene has to be constructed by them in which their destiny may be re-enacted theatrically. In his ordinary life a man, in his lack of knowledge and imperfect vision, is unable to comprehend his own fatality. Only by projecting his life into an art form, a Shakespeare tragedy or a Mallarmé poem, is he able to discover some reasonableness in the mystery that is his. The tragedy of *Hamlet*, as Mallarmé saw it, is a supreme expression of a man and his ghost, of a man and the phantom he becomes in the glare of the footlights, of a man's will unable to realize his dream, of a man who acts out the torments of his spirit because he is unable to live with them, of a man who creates a spectacle of himself for others to see because he is no longer able to stand the reflection in his own mirror. Mallarmé sees in *Hamlet* the necessary condition for poetry, that void which is the lighted stage on which life will be performed and not lived.

As early in his career as 1862, when he was twenty, Mallarmé, in writing to Henri Cazalis, describes himself as a sulking individual who spends days on end with his head leaning against the marble of a mantelpiece, 'a ridiculous Hamlet who doesn't realize his collapse'.[27] And in the opening paragraph of the essay, *Hamlet*, of 1886, written when he was forty-four, Mallarmé describes nature as preparing its theatre in autumn for the Poet, whose solitude, at the approach of winter will permit him to penetrate the meaning of his destiny. The opening of the theatre season is the leaf-falling period when man considers a restlessness, *un malaise*, in himself and a desolate scene in nature. The earth wears a mourning comparable to Hamlet's, and both are related to a mysteriously recurring anguish. The play is a labyrinth of grievances, as the seasonal changes are circuits. *Hamlet* is the solitary drama of dream and fate, and of their antagonism. Shakespeare's hero has become such a steadfast role, so steadily the prototype of man's spirit, that the Renaissance original, dressed in Northern furs, may appear in contemporary Paris, in a costume of Goya-like nudity, and not shock anyone.

Hamlet himself is a kind of ghost, an emblematic hero, when compared to Laertes who plays vigorously down stage. But Laertes was made into a second Hamlet by Hamlet. Hamlet is the creator of a character, and is therefore a poet, who incites the rage of Laertes by slaying Polonius. The multiple parts which Hamlet plays, of mime, thinker, actor, reveal him as the daemon or the fey, the fated prince. Mallarmé calls him that: *le fatidique prince*. He creates a second Hamlet out of Laertes and then finally absorbs him by slaying him. The essence of the theatre consists of this double series of relationships: the actor's relationship to the role (the actor seen as mirroring himself in the age-old text) and the spectator's relationship to the actor. If Hamlet symbolizes the hero, the spectator following the play has to give himself over to the 'sacredness' implied in any symbol. The metamorphosis of actor to character is followed by that of spectator to character. The theatre offers a means of expression to our multiple personality.

Dramatic as well as lyric poetry are ceremonials which involve a double ritual. First, that of the poet who organizes and composes the art capable of recreating a world each time it is heard or read. Secondly, that of the spectator or reader who in his turn organizes and composes what he hears or reads. The writer is an invisible actor in his text. Mallarmé was concerned with this problem throughout his career. Three creations of his especially testify to it and to its evolution in his work: *Hérodiade* (begun in 1864), *Igitur* (1869), and *Un coup de dés* (1897). They represent the various phases of his dramaturgy, which is narrated in the orphan's search for his father (*L'Orphelin* and *Réminiscence*) and in the orphan's metamorphosis into actor (*l'histrion* and *le mauvais Hamlet* of *Le Pitre Châtié*).

Hérodiade is Mallarmé's female protagonist whose desire is self reflection and self perpetuation. She wants her hair to be as resistent as gold and hard metal. The mirror before which she stands is to contain the self which will continue for ever, the ghost of a living being:

> *Je m'apparus en toi comme une ombre lointaine*

In the later sonnet, *Le vierge, le vivace,* the same situation occurs when the swan is immobilized in the freezing lake. Hérodiade wills to become as unreal as her reflection in the mirror which she refers to as 'frozen water' (*Eau froide par l'ennui dans ton cadre gelée*).

Igitur is Mallarmé's male protagonist, his Hamlet-hero, whose desire is self-immolation, as opposed to Hérodiade's self-perpetuation. The demon of impotency had so tortured Mallarmé that he undertook the writing of the story, *Igitur*, to prove to himself that he could do something and therefore cure himself.[28] The writing of the work was a self-imposed psychiatric measure, and yet the subject matter was the dissolution of the hero, the Phoenix-act of Igitur's merging with the ashes of his ancestors in their tomb. At the end of the second scene, the stairway, Igitur hears the clock sound the hour for him to leave. At the same time, its purity returns to the mirror, as if the person standing before it had departed. But with his leaving, the light goes also and night plunges the pure mirror into total darkness.[29] The principal action of Igitur-Hamlet is the merging of the protagonist and sole character with the void. It is an emptying of himself. The image of the abandoned self (*le moi abandonné*) corresponds to the empty castle. The noise of the night and the ticking of a clock become identified with the beating of Igitur's heart. His mystery is that of being, of being in the world.

If *Hérodiade* describes the metamorphosis of a girl into a mirrored reflection, and *Igitur*, the dissolution of the last of a race, *Un coup de dés* transposes the universe: the ocean and the sky, into a vast theatre. The poem is a scene and finally becomes a totally empty scene over which a constellation rises. In all three works the subject becomes unreal and vain. The words of Mallarmé end always by celebrating an unreal world: a phantom princess in *Hérodiade*, a phantom prince in *Igitur*, and a phantom ship in *Un coup de dés*, which, when it is engulfed in the ocean, leaves no trace of its existence. As soon as the words have performed in the poem (as if they were actors on the stage) what they have re-enacted disappears. Language is an ambiguous domain and presents the same multiple effects that a theatrical presentation does before a large public. A poem is an alteration of life and the theatre is an alteration of all the arts. When dance becomes ballet, for example, Mallarmé sees in it a celebration in hieroglyphic form.

Death, for Mallarmé the ritualist, is the ultimate ceremonial, the ultimate transposition of man's existence into something that exceeds existence and that is infinite. In two firm statements at least, Mallarmé has defined his belief about the 'absolute' which man becomes at death: the phrase of *Igitur: moi projeté absolu*, and the opening line of the sonnet on Poe, *Tel qu'en lui-même enfin l'éternité le change.* Mallarmé is always thinking of the poet, and his doctrine on immortality is really that of impersonality or the absolute of the poem. The poet will be judged by his word. The bare sword (*un glaive nu*) with which the poet resurrects his age, in *Le Tombeau d'Edgar Poe*, is comparable to the poem which he is able to 'wield' only after he had disappeared as living poet. The etymology of *Edgar* and *glaive* is the same (*gladius*), as mysteriously co-ordinated as the *noir mélange* of the sonnet is with the alcoholism of Poe, and as the mixture of words in a poem is with witchcraft (*sortilège*). The universe of language presents perils analogous with those of existential life. The 'obscure disaster' referred to in the sonnet, *Calme bloc ici-bas chu d'un désastre obscur*, is both the birth and death of Poe. According to the striking stellar image, a poet is a fallen god, a daimon who has to suffer and die, in accordance with the myth of Dionysus, but whose work grows into itself in the future.

Baudelaire's poetry is that of death, but Mallarmé's although the theme of death is present in it, confounds death with the birth of the poem. The dead move and have their being in the words they leave. To live is to endure dangers, to move from one disaster to another. And poems, as they are being written, comply with this rule: they endure the dangers of over-statement and mis-statement. Only in their final reduced form, do they attain a life of their own, unalterable, beyond disaster. Because all poems wear a penitential garb and celebrate something that was once alive, they are implicitly concerned with the theme of death. This is the figure of speech called 'preterition', whereby Mallarmé, by not speaking of death in the usual sense, calls fuller and deeper attention to it.

One of his early poems, *Las de l'amer repos*,[30] illustrates how intricately the images of death and birth are related to art. Seven times, in keeping with the mystical number par excellence, the poet has sworn a pact to labour on his work. The nightly vigils are compared to the digging of a grave: the poet is gravedigger and the cemetery is his mind, infertile and bored with holes. What can be said of this labour when dawn comes:

> *Que dire à cette Aurore, ô Rêves?*

for the empty holes will appear joined and the roses pale in the new light. The gardens and flowers of Mallarmé always represent the hyperbole or the culminating result of poetic creation. They testify to a nostalgia of an Eden-like perfection and illustrate a favourite metaphor which is almost identical to a metamorphosis.

But the poet as gravedigger is an unrewarding and infecund role. Mallarmé, in his second stanza, speaks of wanting to renounce European art.

> *Je veux délaisser l'Art vorace d'un pays*
> *Cruel*

which is so involved with a personal kind of agony. He lists the familiar Mallarmean themes of friendship, past, genius, lamps. If he could only imitate an Oriental artist whose heart is clear and whose ecstasy consists in painting a flower on a porcelain cup! Not the flower of a garden which at night turns into a cemetery, but the simplified reproduction of a flower like one whose perfume he had smelled as a child. Death, then, would be like the end of art, the dream of the sage.

> *Et, la mort telle avec le seul rêve du sage . . .*

The word, 'death', mysteriously introduced in this line of the poem, is seemingly related to the serenity of the artist and the simplified landscape he is painting.[31] For Mallarmé the work of the poet is precisely a simplification of the world, an adding to it of the void and night.

A poem is composed of words and the silences around the words. Both death and the words of a poem, in the Mallarmean sense, represent a process of simplification. The full magic of a poem occurs when a word uttered is sufficiently strong to evoke the ideal reality of the object named. *Je dis une fleur!* Mallarmé writes in the *Avant-Dire* of René Ghil's *Traité du Verbe*, and a flower, exiled from all bouquets, rises up in his mind (*l'absente de tous bouquets*). Such a word is an incantation and foreign to ordinary language.[32]

If death and poetry are two processes of simplification and magical transformation, the poetry on death, in the work of Mallarmé, contains the most highly evocative and ritualistically conceived passages. Of all the 'tombs' composed by Mallarmé, the one dedicated to Verlaine illustrates the most subtly the ritual of death and poetry. It is not certain, but these verses may have been the very last written by Mallarmé. Verlaine died in January 1896, and the poem was written for the first anniversary of his death, in January 1897. The poet, whose life no scandal touched, takes leave of the poet whose life was continuous scandal. The rock of Verlaine's tomb is black and angered, a picture of human woe. The wind rolls it, for even in death Verlaine remains the agitated soul and perpetual vagabond. The pious hands of the mourners, in touching it, feel the anguish of a man's existence. In the cemetery, those who come feeling grief in their heart are also touched by the blaze of glory growing around the name of Verlaine. His very name is used in the tercets of the sonnets, as an incantation. 'Who is looking for Verlaine?' is the question asked. And the answer comes, 'He is hidden in the grass, Verlaine.' He is not even concealed in the ground because he has not drunk of the river of death. He breathes still in his poetry. Death is not the sinking into a deep and permanent grave, nor is it the drinking from the river of oblivion. That river is shallow and too often slandered.

In the long 'toast' to Gautier and in the three sonnet 'tombs' of Poe, Baudelaire and Verlaine, Mallarmé opposes the death of the poet with the life of the poem. Out of the darkness of physical death (*Le noir roc courroucé* of Verlaine; *Le temple enseveli* of Baudelaire; *Calme bloc ici-bas chu* of Poe) rises a strange luminosity which is going to grow and fill the future (cf. *un scintillement argentera la foule*, in the sonnet to Verlaine). The words of the poem will resurrect and re-enact the life of the poet, but utterly transformed. As in the original hero cults, where the body of Dionysus was slain and scattered and then resurrected, so the cult of the poem celebrates the agony and the transfiguration of the poet.

NOTES TO CHAPTER IX

1. 'Tout, au monde, existe pour aboutir à un livre.' *Le Livre, instrument spirituel,* ed. Pléiade, p. 378.

2. 'L'écrivain, de ses maux, dragons qu'il a choyés, ou d'une allégresse, doit s'instituer, au texte, le spirituel histrion.' *L'Action (or L'Action Restreinte),* appearing first in *La Revue Blanche* of February 1895.

3. *Enquête sur l'Evolution Littéraire, Echo de Paris,* March 3-5, 1891. cf. Pléiade edition, pp. 866-872.

4. 'Il doit y avoir toujours énigme en poésie, et c'est le but de la littérature— il n'y en a pas d'autres—*d'évoquer* les objets.' Pléiade edition, p. 869.

5. Published in *L'Artiste,* 15 Sept. 1862. Mme Noulet was the first critic to demonstrate the importance of this article. cf. *L'Oeuvre Poétique de Stéphane Mallarmé,* pp. 36-37.

6. This important letter is reproduced in part in Mondor, *Vie,* p. 105, and in the Pléiade edition, pp. 1428-29.

7. ibid., p. 1438.

8. ibid., pp. 1438-9.

9. To Aubanel: 'Je ne t'écris pas aujourd'hui, parce que toute distraction même la plus charmante, m'est odieuse, et j'ai besoin de la plus silencieuse solitude de l'âme, et d'un oubli inconnu, pour entendre chanter en moi certaines notes mystérieuses.'

10. This is explained in the article, *De Même,* first published in *The National Observer,* 7 May 1892, under the title, *Solennités,* and now printed in the Pléiade edition, pp. 395-397.

11. The poem has been set to music by Maurice Ravel. The song is an admirable adaptation of the unobtrusiveness and simplicity of the poetic tone. Published by Durand, Paris, 1907.

12. In a letter to Cazalis of December 5, 1865, Mallarmé states that the poem was written for Mme Brunet, wife of Jean Brunet of Avignon, one of the Félibrige poets. Mme Brunet became the godmother of Mallarmé's daughter Geneviève. According to the title on the original manuscript (collection of Henri Mondor), *Sainte Cécile jouant sur l'aile d'un chérubin,* the poem is about Saint Cecilia, patron saint of Mme Brunet, to whom the poem was sent for the feast day, 22 November. Quite literally an 'occasional poem' (*une pièce de circonstance*), *Sainte* was held back by Mallarmé for almost twenty years. In 1883, he gave it to Verlaine for *Les Poètes Maudits* where it was published in April 1884, after a previous appearance in Verlaine's same study, published in magazine form in *Lutèce* of November 24 and 30, 1883. See the Pléiade edition, p. 1463, for the text of the original manuscript containing variants in seven verses.

13. At the window hiding
The old sandalwood shedding its gold paint
Of her viola shining
Formerly with flute or mandoline,

Is the pale Saint, spreading out
The old book which unfolds
Of the shimmering Magnificat
Formerly in Vespers and Compline:

At this monstrance stained-glass window
Which a harp touches formed
By the Angel with her evening flight
For the delicate bone

Of her finger which, without the aged sandalwood
And the aged book, she balances
On the instrumental plumage,
A musician of silence.

14. Mallarmé's translation reads:
     La! dans cette niche splendide d'une croisée, c'est bien comme une statue
     que je te vois apparaître, la lampe d'agate en la main . . .

15. *Plaisir Sacré*, first published in *Le Journal*, Dec. 5, 1893. cf. Pléiade edition, pp·
     388-390.

16. 'Le moyen âge, à jamais, reste l'incubation ainsi que commencement de
     monde, moderne.' *Catholicisme*.

17. . . . 'des réminiscences liturgiques exclusivement notre bien propre ou
     originel . . . ' *Catholicisme*.

18. cf. Richard Wagner, *Rêverie d'un poète français*.

19. cf. the important sentence in *Solennité*: 'C'est bien le pur de nous-mêmes par
     nous porté, toujours prêt à jaillir à l'occasion qui, dans l'existence ou hors
     l'art, nous fait toujours défaut.'

20. 'Le miracle de la musique est cette pénétration, en réciprocité, du mythe et
     de la salle.' *Catholicisme*.

21. cf. the paragraph in *Le Genre ou des Modernes*, beginning with the words, 'Notre
     seule magnifique, la scène . . . '

22. A brilliant essay on this subject, *Mallarmé fondateur de religion*, has been pub-
     lished by Albert-Marie Schmidt, in *Les Lettres*, 1948, pp. 106-113.

23. 'A quelque amphithéâtre, comme une aile d'infinité humaine, bifurque la
     multitude, effarouchée devant le brusque abîme fait par le dieu, l'homme—
     ou Type.' *Catholicisme*, p. 393.

24. This original version is reproduced in the Pléiade edition, pp. 1552-3.

25. This phrase, *l'heure sainte des quinquets*, becomes in *Le Pitre Châtié*, *la suie ignoble
     des quinquets*, after first being *où fument les quinquets*.

26. Written in October 1886, in Paris, and published with very few changes in
     La Revue Indépendante, November 1, 1886, under the title, *Notes sur le Théâtre*.

27. 'Ridicule Hamlet qui ne peut se rendre compte de son affaissement.' The
     letter was written from Sens, May 5, 1862, and is in the Bibliothèque de Jean
     Lahor, Giraud-Badin et Cornuau, Paris, 1938, *Catalogue d'Autographes et
     d'Editions originales*.

28. 'C'est un conte, par lequel je veux terrasser le vieux monstre de l'Impuis-
     sance . . . S'il est fait, je suis guéri.' Letter to Cazalis, 14 Nov. 1869.

29. 'L'heure a sonné pour moi de partir, la pureté de la glace s'établira, sans ce
     personnage, vision de moi—mais il emportera la lumière!—nuit!'

30. First published in *Le Parnasse Contemporain* of May 12, 1866, and probably
     written in Tournon, in 1864.

31. cf. stanza VI of Wallace Stevens' *Le Monocle de mon Oncle*, which begins
     If men at forty will be painting lakes
     The ephemeral blues must merge for them in one,
     The basic slate, the universal hue.

32. 'Un mot total, neuf, étranger à la langue et comme incantatoire.' *Avant-Dire
     au Traité du Verbe* de René Ghil.

CHAPTER X

SYMBOLISM AND POST-SYMBOLISM

1   MALLARMÉ AND SYMBOLISM

(a) MALLARMÉ'S PLACE IN LITERARY HISTORY

It is paradoxical that the position of three of the major poets of modern France: Baudelaire, Mallarmé and Valéry, may be defined with some degree of accuracy in terms of their relationship with the American poet, Edgar Poe. All three acknowledged Poe as their master, and their work as derivative in some fashion from his. No American or English poet has felt such allegiance to Poe. In a recent essay[1] on this subject, Mr Eliot has pointed out that there are aspects of Poe which have not been seen by English and American critics, most of whom have been puzzled by the favour Poe has received in France and the importance granted by the French poets to his work.

Almost one hundred years extend between Baudelaire's translations of Poe and the final poems of Paul Valéry. Mallarmé occupies the central position in this period which was strangely and persistently concerned with the example and the work of Poe. For Baudelaire, the example of Poe's life, the image of the vituperated artist, counted as much and perhaps even more than the work itself. And yet Baudelaire was the first, in commenting on Poe's essay, *The Poetic Principle*, to define the purpose of poetry in words that became the basis of an aesthetic doctrine expounded and followed by all three French poets and those who consider themselves their disciples. The cogent phrase that 'the goal of poetry is its own principle and that it must have nothing else in view but itself'[2] contained the elements of the major modern belief about the nature of poetry.

Poe's other essay, *On Poetic Composition*, known to the French by Baudelaire's translation, *Sur la Genèse du Poème*, is an explication of his poem, *The Raven*. It contains the much quoted claim that beauty is poetry's province (*Or, je désigne la Beauté comme le domaine de la Poésie*) and the doctrine on the impossibility of a long poem. Mallarmé, more than Baudelaire and Valéry, studied the technique of

Poe's poetry, the incantatory element of his verse, the resources and strangeness of his art and its peculiar musical effect. Poe's obsession with night, inherited by Baudelaire, Nerval and Mallarmé, was probably not so important as his combined role of poet and critic who gave in its earliest form a poetic theory that was to become, especially with Valéry, the doctrine of 'pure poetry'.

Mallarmé continued and deepened principally one of the aspects of modern poetry founded in France by Poe and Baudelaire. It is concerned with the practice and the mastery of the means of poetry, with the belief that the subject of a poem is important only as a means of expression which should exist within the poem as an integral part of its texture. The unique power of poetry's language and hence the sacredness of the poet who speaks this language and finds himself almost subconsciously its source, are two lessons of Poe which Mallarmé made significantly his own. The other aspect of modern poetry initiated by Poe and Baudelaire, and not entirely developed by Mallarmé, was the will of such artists as Rimbaud, Lautréamont and the surrealists to recreate a primitive psychic state capable of revealing the powers of the subconscious. In these two aspects, the formal or classical, and the psychic or romantic, the poetry of the last one hundred years has shown its greatest powers of renewal and achievement.

The beautiful, by Baudelaire, was given its very modern definition of 'that which causes despair', of that which saddens.[3] The kind of despair, used in this definition, is that which disillusions man and enlightens him. We are yet far from fully understanding the particular kind of sadness which pervades modern poetry. The so-called *poètes maudits* gave to it its most histrionic form, and Mallarmé, although he never resembled them in dress or social behaviour, was grouped with the *poètes maudits*. Bohemianism and disaster were somehow commingled. Mallarmé was marked with the same spiritual sign as Baudelaire and Verlaine. From a few insignificant personal experiences each one created a poetry which went far beyond the literal experience into that special understanding which the genius brings to the banal and the trivial and the sordid.

If Mallarmé's poetry can be related to the immediate influence of the romanticism of Poe and Baudelaire, it also has affinities with the older modes of preciosity and baroque poetry. Scève and Gongora, and to some lesser degree, the court poets of the early 17th century, are literary ancestors of Mallarmé, even if he didn't read them. But it is curious that in this instance it is the modern poet Mallarmé who has led the way back to preciosity which owes more to Mallarmé than he does to it. After studying the sonnets of Mallarmé, we are better equipped to read the dizains of *La Délie*. With very few exceptions, among whom Maurice Scève is outstanding, French poets before Mallarmé were accessible in their ideas and sentiments. Mallarmé first set the mode in modern France for difficult poetry. His type of poetry exceeds the usual world of sentiments and ideas in its painstaking deliberate search for perfection of form. Even a text of Baudelaire teaches us something concerning the poet's state of mind, concerning the subject of the poem. But the great texts of Mallarmé are different. They are not there to teach us anything. It is difficult to paraphrase them and say what they are about. They exist by themselves, integrated and complete units. We think of them and not what they are about. They possess a life or a way of being of their own.

For a year or two, about 1941, it seemed that *la poésie engagée* had replaced the Mallarmean type of poetry. The oratorical, socially-minded eloquence of Hugo seemed to be inspiring the 'resistance' poets in their facile popular poetry. But that mode passed quickly. The best lines of Eluard and Emmanuel are unquestionably closer to the Mallarmé ideal.

More implicitly than did even Baudelaire, Mallarmé placed his highest confidence in the sole aesthetic value of a work of art. By this faith, he was the real literary model for such writers as Valéry, Proust and Gide. Of the necessary solitude of a poet he made almost a religion. No poet more steadfastly than Mallarmé, believed that the subject of all poems is poetry, that the reason for every poem to be written is to become engaged in the creation of poetic language. For almost thirty years Mallarmé considered the challenge of a Work to be made and the doctrine whereby that Work should be made. He saw language as a force capable of destroying the world in order to rebuild the world so that it might be apprehended differently. The title of hero he ascribed to Verlaine might be granted to him in his brave assumption of the state of poet. To be a poet, in Mallarmé's sense, is to engage in a perpetual warfare with oneself. It means the daily destruction of convention, the repudiation of dogma, the removal of all the various assurances which life offers. Being a poet forces a man to a constantly increasing degree of self-consciousness, self-awareness, to a wilful exploration of the unknown in himself. The poet is one of those men who each day learn more about their human impermanence without which nothing permanent can be created.

(b) DECADENCE

The history of the word 'decadence', as it appears in French letters between Baudelaire and the end of the century, is difficult to trace and make precise, because it was used variously as a cry of defiance and as a warning of self-criticism.

Théophile Gautier used the word in his preface to *Les Fleurs du Mal* of 1869. From that time on, it was used with pride by those artists who boldly called themselves 'decadent' and with scorn by journalists and critics who proffered it as accusation. The typical *décadent* came to designate the seeker of rare sensation, a combination of dandy and roué, a cultivated dilettante. The stronger word of *maudit* ('accursed') joined with it, when in 1883 *Lutèce* published Verlaine's three studies on Corbière, Rimbaud and Mallarmé[4]. Far from making apology for the *décadent* or the *maudit*, Verlaine aggressively praises the type who, exemplified in the three poets he chose, opposes the civilization in which he lives and is repulsed by his society. All three poets he considered as revolutionaries (*révoltés*). Corbière was characterized by his scorn and power of mockery.[5] Rimbaud's career as *fils de soleil* upset the society in which he lived, and the bold imagery of *Bateau Ivre* acted as a ferment on the poetry of his day. It is open to question whether Verlaine understood Mallarmé's poetry in any profound way, but he included as examples of his art such pieces as *Placet, Le Guignon, Apparition, Sainte, Don du Poème, Cette Nuit*[6] and *Le Tombeau de Poe*. The essay on Mallarmé was Verlaine's opportunity to cast opprobrium on those critics and readers who had considered him insane and ridiculous. Although Mallarmé's personal life would never place him with Poe, Baudelaire, Rimbaud and Verlaine himself, his fate as poet was that of revolutionary, one cursed by the existing society.

In the same year as the publication of *Les Poètes Maudits* (1884), Huysmans' novel, *A Rebours*, provided the French public with the fullest theory of 'decadence' it had yet the opportunity of reading. The hero des Esseintes was the prototype of all decadents who hold ordinary life in horror, who see nothing but stupidity (*bêtise*) in the world around him. The book reflects a Schopenhauerian pessimism about human destiny as well as a very extended treatise on the

refinements and practices of a supersensitive intellectual and dilettante. Des Esseintes, in keeping with Baudelaire's example, emphasized the olfactory sensation in his various sensory experiments.
He read the Latin writers of the decadent period: Petronius, Apulius,
Claudius; and such modern writers as Poe and Baudelaire. One of
his favourite books, especially bound in leather, was *Quelques vers de
Mallarmé*, whose art delighted him by its quintessential form. He saw
it as a striking illustration of literature in a state of over-refinement
and decline.

The cult for Wagner and the spread of 'Wagnerism' began at the
composer's death, in 1883. Edouard Dujardin founded *La Revue
Wagnérienne* in 1885 and chose as first collaborators: Schuré, Edouard
Rod, Villiers de l'Isle-Adam and Mallarmé.[7] Wagner is seen by
these men as much more than musician and composer. He is a poet
and philosopher as well. He is taken to be the great exemplar of
pessimism, whose *Parsifal* typifies modern man's renunciation of his
will to live. Paul Bourget was the first critic to analyse this particular
form of modern pessimism in his studies of Baudelaire, Leconte de
Lisle, Tourguéniev, Amiel. Even in his first volume of 1881, *Essais
de Psychologie Contemporaine,* his lucidity was remarkable for the time.
Four years later, in 1885, his *Nouveaux Essais de Psychologie Contemporaine* continue and deepen his observations on the moral atmosphere of the period.

An actual group of *Décadents* was formed in Paris, who took Verlaine as their leader and spokesman. Léon Vanier published Verlaine's two books, *Sagesse* and *Jadis et Naguère*, and the poet, with
surprise, found himself to be an important figure. Maurice Barrès
spoke of him in *Les Taches d'Encre*, and other critics, such as Bourget
and Léon Bloy, began paying serious attention to the Bohemian poet
who had been the most instrumental in creating the legend of the
decadents. It was a movement, or the beginning of a movement,
which lent itself easily to satire. The most witty to appear was *Les
Déliquescences, poèmes décadents*, by Adoré Floupette. The cover stated
that the book was published in Byzantium, by Lion Vanné.[8]

In this central year of 1885, began what critics[9] are calling a
literary revolution, when some of the young 'decadent' writers repudiated the word and insisted upon being called 'symbolists'. But
the idea of decadence had its own peculiar force, strong enough to be
caricatured. It corresponded to a real malady whose origin was in
Baudelaire and whose presence was first demonstrated by Gautier.

The word itself had been used by Verlaine and the type of man it represented had been described in des Esseintes of Huysmans' novel. Under his somewhat flagrant and histrionic exterior, the decadent concealed a suffering or an illness which Bourget, in his essays of 1881 and 1885, had defined as a moral illness which had reached by this latter year its most acute stage. By this time decadence seemed to signify a kind of moral solitude of an artist, coupled with an exasperated and perverse form of mysticism. In many ways it was the familiar moral and physical drama of the young of all periods, but the generation of 1885, even more than that of 1820 with which it had traits in common, felt depression and defeat more poignantly, more tragically than others. The fashion of decadence was their way of steeling themselves against bourgeoisism and triviality (*la vie quotidienne* of Laforgue), against industrialism and naturalism. It concealed their deepest aspirations, because in their feeling that reality was something other than the real world (*la vraie vie est absente*, Rimbaud had said), they touched on a new sense of mystery or mysticism of which Mallarmé was the most subtle and persuasive exponent. Baudelaire had been the first to point out this new mysticism in his theory of 'correspondences' and Bourget had called Baudelaire 'le théoricien de la décadence'. By becoming deeply and exaggeratedly oneself and individualistic, the artist had grown away from any possibility of adapting the strange and the artificial in his personal behaviour, and Mallarmé was emphasizing the same traits in his poetry.

If the most frequently used word in Baudelaire's poetry was *esprit* and its adjective, *spirituel*, the word which would seem to be the most centrally used in the poetry of the period of 1885 is *âme*. Not by Mallarmé, but by the lesser poets: Laforgue, Samain, Maeterlinck and especially Verlaine, who saw the soul as a landscape (*Votre âme est un paysage*), ever changing, an adequate symbol for modern man's sensitivity. The experiences of his soul which he provoked were exceptional and sensational. In his disgust for himself and his lassitude, strongly reminiscent of the romantic *ivory tower* attitude, he explored deeply in himself until he passed beyond an exterior suffering and a provincial boredom to a feeling of universal nostalgia.[10] The garden settings of Mallarmé, and, to a lesser degree, those of the other poets, have behind them an Eden-like serenity.

(c) THE FORMULA OF SYMBOLISM

More than one battle-cry was sounded during the year 1885-1886, but that of Jules Laforgue, *Aux armes, citoyens! Il n'y a plus de RAISON!*[11] was the most resonant. He was 26 at the time and was to die the following year, in 1887. Of all the symbolists he was perhaps the most intelligent and solitary. His Pierrot is the ironic and tender projection of his Hamlet-nature, of his *cœur hypertrophique*. Laforgue, with Moréas and Samain, belonged to the second generation of symbolists. The older men, *les aînés* or *les maîtres*, were all forty or more by 1885: Villiers de l'Isle-Adam (born in 1840), Mallarmé (born in 1842) and Verlaine (born in 1844). Jean Moréas, of Greek origin, had been one of the most vigorous in protesting against the word 'decadent' and urged the use of 'symbolist'. There was a still younger group of poets who were won over to Mallarmé and the cause of symbolism about 1885: Ephraïm Mikhaël, who was to die at the age of 24; the Belgians, Maurice Maeterlinck, whose first poetry was published in *La Pléiade,* in March 1886, and Albert Mockel, who was to write in 1899[12] a moving testimonial to Mallarmé; and the two Americans, Stuart Merrill and Vielé-Griffin.

The movement was heralded by the appearance of new magazines, each one of which had its particular group of editors and contributors. The first number of *Scapin* appeared in December 1885. *Le Décadent* seemed to be largely inspired by Verlaine. Dujardin directed *La Revue Wagnérienne*. René Ghil, Merrill, Mikhaël and Maeterlinck contributed to *La Pléiade*. Ghil's *Traité du Verbe*, of 1887, was considered a manifesto for the new school. It is a kind of hymn to the magic word of SYMBOL and the hieratic name of Mallarmé. Simultaneously with the revolutionary statements of the poets and their denunciation of positivism, Henri Bergson defended his thesis on *Les Données Immédiates de la Conscience*. Maurice Barrès, in his *Taches d'Encre* signalled out symbolism as the most curious movement of the times. The year 1886 also claims the publication of *Le Roman Russe* by Vogüé,[13] whose *Avant-Propos* supported the note of idealism and change which the poets were claiming.

This preface of Vogüé is as important as Bourget's essays in depicting and analysing the current mode of pessimism in France. He chooses Flaubert's *Bouvard et Pécuchet* as the leading example of a work which manifests the author's total scorn for mankind. Vogüé calls the book a grotesque epic of nihilism (*l'Iliade grotesque du nihilisme*) and the inevitable conclusion of a realism without faith and charity. Two forms of pessimism are apparent to Vogüé in France of 1885: a materialistic pessimism, the more nihilistic, and a pessimism of revolt which he believes conceals some element of hope under its denunciatory exterior. This latter form he compares favourably with the Russian realism of the novelists his book treats, and tries to point out that it may lead to a moral resurrection.[14]

The left-bank poets, headed by Verlaine, were noisy and boisterous in their cafés, and often affected the more lurid decadent trappings. The right bank poets had a more tranquil centre in their Tuesday evening meetings on the rue de Rome. Mallarmé was becoming more and more the focal point of all artistic currents of the day: Wagnerism, mysticism, idealism, pessimism. At the beginning of 1884, Verlaine's *Poètes Maudits*, and three months later, Huysmans' *A Rebours,* revealed Mallarmé to a wider public than he had known heretofore. By the end of 1884, he was unquestionably an important writer in the eyes of the literary public in Paris. Barrès had devoted a long study in his *Taches d'encre*[15] to Mallarmé's work, and attempted to define the poet's originality as an 'intellectual conception'.[16] The publication in January 1885 of *Prose pour des Esseintes*[17] was a literary event, which proved and accentuated Mallarmé's growing fame. The fervent admiration of the poets for the mysterious poem was offset by the strongly articulated jeers of the journalists and opponents. The poem helped to win over to Mallarmé many younger poets such as René Ghil and his friends known as 'le groupe de Condorcet'. This was the time when Mikhaël, Fontainas, Vielé-Griffin and Henri de Régnier began attending the Tuesday gatherings.

A literary movement was gradually taking form. The rallying force was unquestionably Mallarmé's conversations, not one of which has been recorded. For an accurate and full understanding of the genesis of symbolism, the most vital document is lacking. But around Mallarmé, and largely due to his influence, interviews and documents and manifestoes began appearing. An investigation on 'the definition of poetry' was made by Léo d'Orfer and published in *La Vogue* of April 18, 1886. Mallarmé gave to it his celebrated definition[18] which was later included in *Divagations*. Teodor de Wyzewa, in *La Revue Wagnérienne*, undertook to elucidate the aesthetic doctrine which would combine and harmonize the theories of Wagner and Mallarmé. Dujardin had taken Mallarmé to the Lamoureux concert on Good Friday of 1885, and from then on, Mallarmé never missed a Sunday concert. It is difficult to define exactly what the revelation of Wagner's music did for Mallarmé. It doubtless confirmed many of his beliefs and especially his belief concerning the state of abstraction toward which his poetry was moving. René Ghil published in a Brussels magazine, *La Basoche*, between June and October 1885, a series of articles on the contemporary movement in poetry which represented Mallarmé as an officiating high priest of the 'Symbol'. These articles, later recast in *Traité du Verbe*, were an attempt to unite music and the symbol and the force of suggestion which comes from their union[19].

These pages of criticism were much needed by all groups in Paris. The *décadents* became more vociferous in their cafés and those who attacked the new school became more resolute. Paul Bourde, for example, attacked Moréas who in his reply[20] suggested the use of the word 'symbolist' to designate the 'decadents'. By the end of 1885 there was no coherent or collective body of doctrine, but the Tuesday evenings, *La Revue Wagnérienne* and the articles of René Ghil were preparing a new consciousness which was to grow during the following year. Mallarmé was growing aware of the extent of his influence, but he remained persistently unwilling to head a group or school. This fact is perhaps the most important message in his *Autobiographie*, written for Verlaine on November 16, 1885. He remains the independent artist, bent upon devoting himself more and more exclusively to 'the Book'.

The year 1886 was initiated by the publication of the first group effort of the symbolists: the sonnets to Wagner in the January issue of *La Revue Wagnérienne*. The sonnets of Verlaine and Mallarmé especially created a scandal sufficiently widespread to incite both sides and precipitate the founding of several short-lived literary magazines, such as *La Pléiade*, created in March, and *Le Décadent*, in April, as well as *La Vogue* which, under the direction of Gustave Kahn and Léo d'Orfer, was to publish *Les Illuminations* of Rimbaud. Mallarmé's two page preface to Ghil's *Traité du Verbe* was a remarkable condensation of his thought about the primitive function of language and the role of dream and song in poetry. The treatise itself was widely read by those who wanted clarification concerning the meaning of symbolism. The document of Moréas, *Un Manifeste Littéraire*, published in the literary supplement of *Le Figaro*, on September 18, 1886, was a disappointing attempt at theory and justification.

By this time the general public were confusing 'decadents' and 'symbolists', despite the continued effort of those who still called themselves 'decadents'. *Le décadisme* was created by Baju in 1888 and became the new term for the magazine, *Le Décadent*, whose issues through 1888 failed to reveal any new doctrine. This was the moment when René Ghil began to move away from Mallarmé and set himself up as an independent theorist. His magazine, *Les Ecrits pour l'Art*, was directed by Gaston Dubedat and although still claiming Mallarmé as master, initiated the newer name, *Groupe Symbolique et Instrumentiste*. The first number appeared on January 7, 1887. In the same year, Ghil published a second edition of his *Traité* with additional notes (Alcan-Lévy, Paris). Stuart Merrill's volume, *Les Gammes*, appeared with the dedication, *A René Ghil, Maître de la musique du Verbe*. The poetry of Merrill, still fairly close to Verlaine's lyricism, was less personal and formed on broader rhythmical patterns. In a letter to Vielé-Griffin, Merrill wrote in English, 'I am not the only American who is trying to endow the French Alexandrine with a little of the enchanting music of the English verse.'[21]

Only six issues of *Les Ecrits pour l'Art* appeared. By 1888, Ghil had alienated most of his early Mallarmean friends. The third edition of his *Traité* (1888) more or less announced his break with symbolism. At the same time he stopped attending the meetings on the rue de Rome. *La Revue Indépendante*, in a second series, directed by Fénéon and Wyzewa, became the acknowledged official organ for symbolism. In it Mallarmé published his articles on the theatre, later to be grouped under the title, *Crayonné au théâtre*. Gustave Kahn replaced Ghil as a kind of spokesman for the Mallarmé group. His new poetry was among the first examples of *vers libre*, although he was far from being the sole writer to claim the creation of the new form. Mallarmé in a letter to Kahn[22] commented on the younger poet's metrical innovations and called them *une aventure inouïe* and *un délicieux affranchissement*. It is impossible and futile to name the real originator of free verse. Was it Kahn or Moréas? or the Montmartre poet, Marie Krysinska, who claimed to have published free verse poetry in *Le Chat Noir* as early as 1882? or Jules Laforgue? or Rimbaud in his poems, *Marine* and *Mouvement?* Vielé-Griffin became a firm defender of the form in his volume, *Les Cygnes*, of 1887, and Verhaeren developed and enlarged the possibilities of free verse. This formed one more group, *les vers-libristes*, whom the general public confused with *décadents* and *symbolistes*. The most striking demonstration of

1887, in favour of symbolism, occurred when Lamoureux tried to perform *Lohengrin* at the Eden-Théâtre. There was actual fighting in the street. Although the performance was forbidden by the police, the symbolist and Wagnerian sympathizers had declared themselves openly and forcibly.

(d) THE SUCCESS OF SYMBOLISM

A publication in 1888, by Papus, *Traité élémentaire de science occulte*, became favourite reading for the symbolists and helped them to substantiate and clarify their aesthetic doctrine. In the following year, Schuré published his *Grands Initiés* (Perrin), whose preface was concerned with the occult action of the great religious leaders. He pointed out how religion and science should not be eternally opposed, as they had been throughout the 19th century, but should be harmonized in their similar aspirations. Schuré, since he was both occultist and poet, was admirably placed to point out to the poets how Mallarmé's aesthetics were gradually joining the mystical spiritualism of the major religious traditions. The principal point of the preface was that the esoteric doctrine was not a science or a philosophy or a religion, but that it was *the* science, *the* philosophy, *the* religion of which all others are but preparations.

The young and enthusiastic literary critic, Charles Morice, undertook to integrate the general philosophical assumptions of esoterism and the literary doctrines of symbolism. His important book, *La Littérature de tout à l'heure*[23] is an attempt to unite the meaning of the poet's inspiration (and aspiration) with the meaning of his critical judgment and philosophy. The book became a guide for the younger poets who believed in their movement and wanted for it a critical and aesthetic justification. Although he disclaimed, in his preface, any right to represent a group, the symbolists considered it as a faithful transcription of their belief. For Morice, Mallarmé stood as the absolute.[24] The poet, as interpreter of beauty, makes a constant effort to renew and restore the great traditions. 'Art,' says Morice, 'not only reveals the Infinite, it provides the poet with the means to enter upon the Infinite, and there he goes farther than the philosopher.'[25] In the elaboration of this lesson, Morice rightfully calls upon the examples of Poe, Wagner, Baudelaire. By discovering the unity of the world and human experience (cf. *Les Correspondances* of Baudelaire), the poet recovers his earliest sacerdotal role. In his use of symbols, the modern poet has discovered for truth a new kind of radiation far different from the dryness of abstractions. In a masterful definition, Morice describes art as 'the recapture by the soul, of its own profundities'.[26] Although the book today appears vitiated by dogmatism and lacunae and vague generalities, it does state, with justice, that the leading characteristic of modern poetry is the consciousness it has developed about itself.

Many new literary magazines helped to usher in the central year (1890-91) of the symbolist movement. The directors of *La Plume* held Saturday gatherings in a café of the Place Saint-Michel. *L'Ermitage* was edited by Henri Mazel.[27] *Les Entretiens Politiques et Littéraires* united such names as Paul Adam, Henri de Régnier and Vielé-Griffin. The former *Pléiade* became *Le Mercure de France*,[28] and soon, under the expert direction of Alfred Vallette, grew into the official magazine of the school. More than ever, Mallarmé was the leading literary figure. No foreign writer or artist came to Paris without paying homage to him. In February 1890, Mallarmé left Paris for a lecture tour in Belgium where he spoke on 'Villiers de l'Isle-Adam' in Brussels, Antwerp, Ghent, Liége, Bruges. This was the period when Debussy began attending the Tuesday evenings, as well as the painters, Redon, Gauguin, Vuillard.

Painters and poets were joining forces in an effort to understand one another and the art they served. In 1890 Gauguin with some friends founded in Paris *le groupe symboliste ou synthétiste*. The main spokesman for this synthesis of ideas was the young critic, Albert Aurier, whose article on *Le Symbolisme en Peinture* was published by *Le Mercure de France*, in March 1891. Edmond Bailly, in his bookstore and publishing centre on the Chaussée d'Antin, *Librairie de l'Art Indépendant,* had founded a meeting place for poets and painters, especially those interested in the occult sciences.

Mallarmé presided over a banquet of poets, on February 2, 1891, which although nominally in honour of Jean Moréas, turned out to be a celebration of symbolism. Even Anatole France was toasted. Never had the opposition to the slander of the music-hall jokesters seemed so strong. Soon after this banquet, Jules Huret, for *L'Echo de Paris,* began his extensive interviewing of poets and writers which was eventually published as *Enquête sur l'évolution littéraire.* This important document on the status of symbolism around 1890, contains a wide variety of opinion, extending from the overt scorn of Zola, Leconte de Lisle and Coppée, to impassioned statements of belief and definition. Brunetière's article in *La Revue des Deux Mondes,* of

April 1891, marked a real triumph for symbolism when an eminent figure in the opposition finally acknowledged the seriousness of the new school.

Whether a real school of symbolism ever existed, remains a problem of speculation. The agitated years of symbolism were characterized by confusions and incoherences. Each poet developed and represented a single aspect of an aesthetic doctrine that was perhaps too vast for one historical group to incorporate. It is not difficult, however, to distinguish between the histrionics or the exterior trappings of the symbolists and the more concealed meaning of the histrionics. The decadent poets, for example, reflected an age-old conflict between man's reason and his heart. They believed in the rights of the inner life, of a sensitivity which would cultivate the subconscious and the intuitive aspects of a poet's life. A deeper belief in idealism presided over the aspirations of the symbolists. Their mediaeval settings, their attraction to Wagner, to Lohengrin's swan and Parsifal's grail, all denote a nostalgia for the past, for a sense of purity and a striving toward the absolute. Mallarmé's effort to attain to a pure expression of poetry and his belief that behind the appearance of things there is a hidden world of reality testify to a search for the absolute and a quasi-Platonic philosophical attitude. But more than on any other article of belief, the symbolists united with Mallarmé in his statements about poetic language. The theory of the suggestiveness of words comes from a belief that a primitive language, half-forgotten, half-living, exists in each man. It is language possessing extraordinary affinities with music and dreams. Poetry, in the putting to use of this exceptional language, is the establishment of relationships between things in the world and the sensitivity of the poet. This is a form of esoterism, a way toward a spiritual knowing of the universe when the symbol will be found to be ever real and ever suggestive.

2 . AFTER MALLARMÉ

The first meeting between Paul Valéry and Mallarmé, in the autumn of 1891, marked the beginning of one of the most significant friendships in the history of French letters. Of that precise meeting, Valéry remembered very little and nothing of what was actually said. He was struck by general things: the atmosphere of the apartment, the gentle politeness of Mallarmé, the musical quality of his voice.

The coming together of these two men had been long prepared. It can be safely said that no one of the countless visitors to the salon on the rue de Rome was more profoundly and spiritually prepared to listen to Mallarmé and profit from his veiled pedagogy than Valéry. He was young but excessively precocious. His intellectual and poetic gifts were already developed. The year before, in 1890, he had heard of Mallarmé by reading Huysmans' *A Rebours*. In July, at Montpellier, he met, by chance at a café, a Parisian dandy, Pierre Louis, who told him more about Mallarmé and sent him, later, from Paris, some of the rare fragments of *Hérodiade* and other poems. These first readings were a major revelation. They separated him from Hugo and Baudelaire. They provided him with the clearest example he had yet had of the power of poetic language. He believed that Mallarmé's art had culminated in a synthesis of incantation, in the discovery of a magic formula of language.[29] The first lines of *Hérodiade* which he read took possession of him in an almost unaccountable way.

He sent his first letter from Montpellier on October 21, 1890, in which he described himself as a young man hidden in the depths of his province who was imbued with the doctrines of the great Poe. He enclosed two poems, *Le Jeune Prêtre* and *La Suave Agonie*.[30] With his customary politeness, Mallarmé replied three days later, acknowledging Valéry's gift of subtle analogy and musicality and envying his provincial solitude.[31] The second letter, written, also from Montpellier, on April 18, 1891, touches more significantly on literary doctrine, on belief that the poet's kingdom is analogy, that his work is comparable to a symphony uniting the world around him with the world that haunts him. In France the poem which Valéry believes best realizes this lofty ideal is *L'Après-Midi d'un Faune*.[32] Mallarmé's reply, written on May 5, 1891, agrees on the whole with the young poet's theory of great art being a symphony, but adds that all art reflects consciously or subconsciously this goal without having perhaps ever achieved it.[33]

Although Valéry remembered no precise topics discussed with Mallarmé on the first meeting, in October 1891, he often spoke of Mallarmé's great powers of speech and conversation. They were words seemingly spoken far above a very secret thought which had been profoundly elaborated. By the time of this first meeting, the Tuesday evening gatherings had achieved their definitive form. Valéry became a faithful visitor, but he never became a servile imitator. He owed particularly to Mallarmé his general conception of art, his poetic technique, and his vocabulary. But nothing in Valéry's character would induce him to venerate another man. His affection and admiration for Mallarmé remained constant throughout his life, but he realized very soon after the first meeting the risk which such a marked influence as Mallarmé's would be. Between the older and the younger man was established an intellectual interchange. Valéry probably inherited from Mallarmé general attitudes toward poetry, and ways of suggesting truths rather than any specific set of truths. From Mallarmé's example he doubtless learned to prefer in his own work the infinite gradations and varieties of sensations rather than the monotonous exploitation and indiscretion of sentiments. In Mallarmé he found one more of those artists, dearest to him, who have been buffeted about and slandered by the world. To the image of Mallarmé, ridiculed by the most insignificant journalists, he could add that of Poe, who died in destitution; Baudelaire, pursued by his creditors; Wagner, hissed at the Opéra; Verlaine and Rimbaud, vagabonds under grave suspicion; Villiers de l'Isle-Adam, impoverished and ill in his attic room.[34]

In preference given to certain images of Valéry's early poetry (collected in the volume, *Album de Vers Anciens*), the influence of Mallarmé is fairly precise: swans, lilies, precious stones. These and a general atmosphere of distant lands and castles and fairy stories pervade almost all of the symbolist poetry of the time. In the poem, *Narcisse parle*, Valéry appropriated the figure of Narcissus and made it into one of his most significant themes. Valéry's Narcissus bears a relationship with Mallarmé's faun. In both poems the world is depicted as a mirror reflecting the poet's image. The detached and somewhat scornful attitude of Valéry's own temperament is in his *Narcisse*. At the age of 20, Valéry went through a revolt against poetry, as Gide did, and entered upon a long poetic silence of twenty years during which the image of Narcissus seemed to be completely effaced. The new example of Leonardo da Vinci drew Valéry's attention to the mystery of the creative process, to the study of the mind as a function of man. The savant took precedence over the poet in Valéry. He began his life-long study of the power of the mind and the ways by which man can make himself universal. But Mallarmé's lessons on analogy and metaphor were never completely forgotten. In Valéry's last great poems, *Fragments du Narcisse* and *La Jeune Parque*, and in most of the new poems of *Charmes* (1922), he is concerned mainly with attempts to explain what the act of poetry is.

Like Mallarmé, Valéry knew that poetry, as it is being composed, always tends to become prose, to fill itself with impurities. 'Pure poetry' was for Valéry the great discovery of symbolism. This was Mallarmé's ambition, to purge poetry of all intellectual, didactic elements and reach in it a pure music. Valéry is wary of the critic's use of symbol which is made to stand for whatever the critic wants. He has pointed out[35] how the teaching of Mallarmé was opposed to the doctrines of his contemporaries in being almost exclusively concerned with the general problem of poetic form. The very existence of Mallarmé represented for Valéry the highest form of literary ambition, a man who in the publication of a few poems had raised the question of the very purpose of literature.

Valéry never wrote solely of the poetics or the poetry of Mallarmé. The example of the man is inextricably associated with the art. When he first read the poetry of Mallarmé, the surprise and the enchantment were so intense that he broke with his former idols. Still today, Mallarmé continues to make similar decisive conquests. A first sympathetic reading of Mallarmé leaves one with the conviction that poetry previously read was naive and elementary. His particular accomplishment in poetry is a work representing the antithesis of naive literary intuition. By renouncing the world and the facileness of the world, Mallarmé put himself into a state of understanding it. To read Mallarmé, one has to learn all over again how to read, because the majority of readers tend to read only what they themselves might have written. Valéry saw immediately that the very articulation of Mallarmé's verse, the mystery of his syntax, placed him apart from all other poets. The elements of other kinds of writing which made them accessible were all lacking in Mallarmé: familiar rhetoric, narrative, philosophical maxims, human passions. Mallarmé's poetry had nothing of this. It was poetry that had become synthesis of incantation[36] wherein one felt solely the strength of words.

Valéry has always opposed Mallarmé to the writers of his age and to those who followed him, in calling him the martyr of the idea of perfection. Other writers would be characterized by their adherence to the provisional, the temporary, the facile. Mallarmé alone was disciplined by his belief in poetic purity and perfection. His lifework represented one of the noblest efforts man ever made to convert disorder into order and chance into power.[37] Mallarmé's life testified to himself as a unique and remarkably original poet, but in addition to that, it helped a younger poet like Valéry to understand that the gift of poetry accompanies an ancient nobility and involves an Orpheus-like way of feeling the universe and reacting to it. For his closest friends and disciples, Mallarmé did become a demi-god, half real, half legendary. For those who read him as passionately as Valéry did, Mallarmé renewed a vital way of considering poetry as a compromise between two major effects of language: the transmission of a fact and the creation of an emotion. Both Mallarmé and Valéry would acknowledge that their work is only an approximation to their ideals. Mallarmé believed in pure poetry but realized there was no such thing as a pure poem. Valéry often stated that an accurate transmission of one's thought is impossible.[38]

At the death of Mallarmé, Valéry wrote that he would never be able to discuss with anyone else certain subjects which he had reserved for their conversations. Throughout his subsequent work in prose, Valéry has made a number of critical observations on symbolism and poetry which are at least reminiscent of Mallarmé if not directly inspired by him. First in importance among these is the already famous definition of the modern poetic movement, which Valéry sees as a will to isolate poetry from any other essence save its own. Poe is named by Valéry the precursor of this movement and Baudelaire the first to be profoundly preoccupied by it.[39] In the same article Valéry defines symbolism as that intention of several groups of poets (not always friendly to one another) to recover from music the heritage that was due to them.[40] In accord with Mallarmé's own definition of poetry,[41] Valéry describes the young poets, contemporary with himself, as founding in their particular cult of art, a discipline, a truth perhaps, even a species of religion.[42] To speak today of philosophical poetry, Valéry continues, is to fail to understand the goal of the modern poet which is that of producing in us a state (*un état*), an exceptional state of enjoyment.[43] This might well be juxtaposed with one of Mallarmé's earliest theories of his poetry: *peindre non la chose, mais l'effet qu'elle produit.*[44]

In Valéry's many passages on the 'accident' in poetry, the gratuitous line given to the poet without his having searched for it, he adumbrates and analyses one of Mallarmé's central beliefs. A pure work, Mallarmé has written, gives over the initiative to the words themselves. The deliberate rhetoric of the poet disappears in them.[45] The poet's system, for both Valéry and Mallarmé, must leave a place for the unpredictable accident of language. There are two kinds of verses, according to Valéry: those that are 'given' and those that are 'calculated'.[46] Even in prose a writer is often forced to put down what he doesn't wish to or plan for. The tragic conclusion of their symbolism—is that it is impossible to construct a poem containing only poetry.[47] By the very idea of constructing or composing, a poem is destined to contain some impurity. The concept of 'pure poetry' is a long sought-for goal, a peril, an impossibility. In an explicit image, Valéry calls it an idea of perfection which we traverse in the same way as a hand puts out a flame. But the flame itself is uninhabitable.[48] The poetic despair of a Mallarmé and a Valéry, comes from such conviction as this.

(b) GIDE

A principal source of André Gide's fervent attachment to literature is unquestionably his early friendship for Mallarmé. In many places throughout his work, he has testified to the 'example' that Mallarmé was to him and his generation, to the exceptional quality of the master's temperament, to his disinterestedness which, more than all his other traits, impressed the young neophyte.

Gide was introduced to Mallarmé by his friend, Pierre Louis (eventually to become Pierre Louÿs), in 1891. Of the two visitors, both in their early twenties, Gide was certainly the more reserved, the more ill-at-ease. In a letter accompanying the gift of one of his books,[49] Gide excused himself for his prose written before he had met

Mallarmé and before he had read Mallarmé's poems which he called the verses he had dreamed of composing.[50] Gide became an habitué of the Tuesday evening gatherings which he has described in some detail in his autobiographical *Si le grain ne meurt*.[51] In those pages he speaks more of the visitors than of Mallarmé himself. But in other works (*Prétextes*, 1903; *Journal*, 1939; *Interviews Imaginaires*, 1943) he has traced his portrait of Mallarmé, the man for whom literature was the goal and the end of life, who sacrificed everything to it, by believing exclusively in it, by developing about literature the deepest conviction that has perhaps ever been held. In an article published on the occasion of the death of Mallarmé,[52] Gide evoked the silence that pervaded the salon just before the poet began speaking. Then when he said his first words, uttered in a voice that was gentle and unforgettable, those present felt they were touching 'the reality of thought'. What they were looking for and desiring existed in the man standing before them as a being totally dedicated to art.[53]

Gide's admiration was so total that when, on the publication of Mallarmé's sonnet to Verlaine,[54] the poet was seriously attacked and ridiculed, especially by Adolphe Retté, the disciple wrote a letter of defence which he published in *Le Mercure de France* for which he secured the signatures of Valéry, Verhaeren, Schwob and Vielé-Griffin. In the same year, Gide wrote a fervent letter to Mallarmé about *Un coup de dés*, in which he compared the emotion he felt on reading the last page of the work to the emotion created by a Beethoven symphony[55].

In 1943, during the Second World War, when Gide wrote about Mallarmé, he acknowledged that the poet's life, his behaviour and his temperament, as much as his poetry, influenced his young disciples during the last years of the century.[56] The example of Mallarmé's 'disinterestedness' and his unique absorption in the problems of art kept Gide for years away from subjects that seemed transitory, such as politics and history. In a *Journal* entry of 1935, Gide almost blames Mallarmé's influence in this regard and says that he didn't realize at the time of the Tuesday meetings that it is important to distrust what is flattering, that we are best educated by those forces and masters who oppose us.[57]

If Gide's first work, *Les Cahiers d'André Walter*, was written before he knew Mallarmé, his second work, *Le Traité du Narcisse*,[58] was a short document directly inspired by Mallarmé and his doctrinal conversations of the rue de Rome. The subtitle of the work, *Théorie du Symbole,* as well as the title, indicates the slightly pedantic tone, the neophyte's desire to write a manifesto. The myth of Narcissus is a kind of explanation of a basic impulse in symbolism: man's search for his own image. By recasting the myth, Gide exposed at the same time poetic doctrines central to the thought of Mallarmé.

The introductory four pages are explanation of the power of the myth in general and of literature which is a subsequent amplification of myths. The story of Narcissus is reviewed. But that is not the subject of the treatise, Gide says. He describes Narcissus as alone and questioning himself. He has a desire to see himself, to understand his soul, and he departs in order to discover a mirror for self-reflection. He comes to a river and decides to follow it as a road. As he looks in it, he sees the trees and sky and banks, and begins to dream of Paradise. The first part of the treatise begins here: 'Le Paradis n'était pas grand; parfaite, chaque forme ne s'y épanouissait qu'une fois; un jardin les contenait toutes.'[59] This first picture is the Mallarmean garden of ideas, reminiscent of *Prose pour des Esseintes: Chaste Eden! Jardin des Idées!* Everything has the perfection of numbers. At the foot of the tree, Ygdrasil, is the book of magic (*le livre du Mystère*) or Mallarmé's *grimoire.* Adam, the one being, as yet a-sexual, looks at the spectacle around him. He breaks off a branch of the tree and the spell is broken. The tree cracks, the leaves of the Book are scattered, Adam desires the woman who has suddenly arisen. The second part is the beginning of the doctrinal message, one that is closely related to Mallarmé. *Le Paradis est toujours à refaire.* The perfect beauty which Adam had once seen in Eden always remains to be recreated. It is always just below the appearance of things. Everything in nature is striving to recover its lost form (*Tout s'efforce vers sa forme perdue*). 'Truths are symbols remaining behind the forms', Gide tells us in an important note to this section of the treatise, written at the same time as the main text, in 1890. The artist must not prefer himself to the truth he wants to make manifest. 'Every phenomenon is the symbol of a truth', Gide says in the same note. The poet himself is the subject of the third and last part of the work. He is the man who looks—and sees Paradise. (*Le Poète est celui qui regarde. Et que voit-il?—Le Paradis.*) Paradise is everywhere. Only the appearance of things is imperfect. The poet, like the scholar, recomposes an ideally simple world. A symbol is 'everything that appears' (*tout ce qui paraît,* Gide emphasizes in a note) and each thing reveals its archtype. A contemplation of symbols is a descent into the heart of things, at the end of which the poet is able to give an eternal Form to the object, *sa Forme véritable enfin, et fatale—paradisiaque et cristalline*. As Narcissus bends down to the water to kiss the vision, it disappears. A kiss is impossible. All he can do is to contemplate the world.

Gide soon separated himself from symbolism. His revolt from aestheticism and his early deep interest in Mallarmé's work was marked by his departure for Tunisia in 1895 with Paul-Albert Laurens and by the writing of *Les Nourritures Terrestres*.[60] Narcissus seemed quite forgotten in the new fervour and Nietzschean affirmation of life. There are, however, many passages in *Les Nourritures Terrestres* which resemble symbolist poems, those especially in which things seen and not seen are simultaneously described, as in the passage beginning, *Nathanaël, je te parlerai des attentes*. Gide had learned his first manner of writing at the school of symbolism. Under the influence of Mallarmé he developed a poetic awareness of the world, a taste in matters of art, and, above all, a sense of the artist's duty and vocation. Even if Gide cut himself off from a Mallarmean use of the symbol, all of his work possesses a poetic quality that can be traced back to the earliest literary influence he underwent.[61]

(c) CLAUDEL

Both the surface and the depths of the two works of Mallarmé and Claudel would seem to separate them widely and allocate them to opposing poles. Claudel, the Catholic poet of contemporary France; Mallarmé, the poet of the 80's and 90's whose life was untroubled by religious problems and whose art is essentially non-religious even if it may be characterized as ritualistic in a general sense.

Claudel's faith is inseparable from his work. The religious experience he underwent at the age of 18 changed the world for him. It was a revelation whereby he saw the world as the work of God and worthy of the song and praise of the poet. This was the genesis of his great theme of joy, the one reality for Claudel, the one requirement for the making of an artistic work. Without it, man has nothing to say. This would be for Claudel the explanation of what he calls the tragic attitude of Mallarmé, or of any 'pure artist'.[62] It was stated twelve years after he wrote his first letter of warm admiration to Mallarmé, and from then on throughout his career, his attack on Mallarmé's principles and sensitivity grew increasingly strong.

The fullest statement of his divergence from the older poet was written on the occasion of the first printing of *Igitur,* in 1925. His article, *La Catastrophe d'Igitur,* is at once a severe criticism of Mallarmé and one of the most penetrating studies on his work. Claudel associates Mallarmé with Baudelaire and Poe in their being 'poets of the night', but he sees in Baudelaire and Poe poets more 'lucidly despairing' than Mallarmé. Igitur he takes as the epitome of the 19th century man, obsessed with the material world, who tries to escape from it by some mental game of abstraction. The world for Claudel, with his faith of a mediaeval artisan, is a text-book which can be read and must be read. It speaks to us of two things: first, of its own limitations, of its own 'absence' as Mallarmé would say, and secondly, of the presence of its Creator.[63] Claudel contrasts the sorcerer's book (*le grimoire*) of the symbolist poet with the Word (the *Logos*) in which everything has been uttered. In a subsequent writing of 1938 (*Salut à Francis Jammes*), Mallarmé is placed by Claudel in a list of poet-theorists and pedagogues, a position which would have been humiliating to him: Horace, Boileau, Gautier. The goal of Mallarmé's poetics would seem to be the destruction of all that has been created in order to reach its pure essence. The flower becomes the one absent from all bouquets (*Cette fleur—l'absente de tous bouquets*). But things, in the system of Claudel, are really a part of what they are named.[64] There is a definiteness and a definedness in the world of Claudel, whereas everything concrete, in Mallarmé's system, vanishes in order to become its own sign, its own symbol. 'Nothingness is truth', Mallarmé would say (*le Rien, qui est la vérité*). 'I am here with God', Claudel would say, 'I believe in all things visible and invisible'. (*Je suis ici avec Dieu. O credo entier des choses visibles et invisibles.*)

The poet's mind, in Mallarmé, is constantly reducing its perceptions, condensing and purifying its thought. The poet is one being in him seeking the unity and quintessence of experience. Claudel's mind explores in another direction, toward the embracing of fullness and plenitude. He is many poets and many voices singing of a richness that is inexhaustible. Mallarmé is impersonal as a poet. He divests himself of personal traits as he diminishes any given object to its minimized and abstracted reality. But Claudel names himself and speaks of himself in his work as a man having a face that can be recognized and a temperament that can be defined. He is a person, with the fullest dignity, whom God addresses. Poetry, for Mallarmé, is an activity and an experience, which replaced all others, even the experience of love and religion. For Claudel, poetry is one means of expressing and celebrating such experiences as love and religion.

Such, then, would be the divergences between Mallarmé and Claudel, separations on the grounds of philosophical belief and temperament. But Mallarmé was among the first masters of Claudel. As early as 1895, Claudel wrote to him from Villeneuve-sur-Fère (Aisne) on the occasion of the publication of *La Musique et les Lettres* (Perrin). The letter is a glowing statement on Mallarmé's high position in letters, of his revindication of 'intelligence' in the domain of poetry, where he performs the role of leader.[65] Claudel continues in this letter to say that for him the primal element in Mallarmé's sentence is the syntax or the design created by the words. He claims that the so-called obscurity of Mallarmé is not due to vagueness, but to a mind accustomed to extreme precisions and elegances. In a letter to Mallarmé, written from China, July 26, 1897, Claudel speaks of the fervour with which he read *Divagations*. In this letter he also acknowledges his supreme debt to Rimbaud,[66] a passage which should be joined with his celebrated letter[67] to Jacques Rivière (*Rimbaud a été l'influence capitale de ma vie*).

Claudel was not, in any profound sense, the disciple of the symbolists, and yet his work represents the accomplishment and the culmination of many themes of symbolism, especially those whose purpose was the understanding and the demonstration of the poetic act. By temperament, Claudel belongs to the race of revolutionaries and conquerors, poets such as D'Aubigné and Rimbaud, but he is also close to Mallarmé in his will to define poetry in its essence. A comparison between Claudel's *Connaissance de l'Est* (his 'book of exercises', as he called it) and Mallarmé's *Divagations*,[68] would reveal that both the diplomat-poet and the professor-poet were trying to decipher the universe as if it were a text. The questioning was the same even if Mallarmé believed that a void existed behind the material world whereas Claudel believed that the Source existed behind it.

From Mallarmé, Claudel learned especially his lesson on the metaphor, the essential element of his poetics. He learned that a metaphor is a relationship between two objects. (It may even be a relationship between God and the world.) The poet's role is to apprehend, to seize the metaphors which exist in the world. This means naming each object and restoring it to its rightful place in a new ordering of the universe, in a new lexicon of the world. Each of the many times that Claudel states that with each new breath of a man, the world should appear new to him, as fresh and virginal as it appeared to the first man with his first breath, he is reiterating Mallarmé's belief about the metaphor, about the endless metaphorical richness of the world. Both Mallarmé and Claudel are cosmological poets in a deeply religious sense. By naming an object, the poet gives it its meaning, as God had originally done when he created the world by naming it. The total word, or the total poem, is therefore the universe. Each poet bears in himself a picture of the universe, a subjective maze of images which have relationships with one another. Mallarmé follows an instinctive quest in naming various objects and seeking to understand their metaphorical meaning. Claudel goes farther in willing this quest as if it were a religious obligation. Symbolism, under the initial guidance of Mallarmé, was a spiritual way of understanding and celebrating the universe. It became later, in the art of Paul Claudel, a more frankly religious way of discovering in the midst of endless variety a secret unity.

The theocentric foundation of Claudel's doctrine is not without support in Mallarmé's belief. Claudel affirms a more universal symbolism than the older poet. *Tout est symbole ou parabole* (*Introduction au Livre de Ruth*), is a fuller statement of all that Mallarmé lived by. Both believed that all poets in the world participate in some vast liturgy of which they can be only partially aware. Both thought a great deal about all the metaphors which lay beyond those they used and were familiar with. Any use of symbolism implies a painful ambivalence on the poet's heart. Mallarmé felt that in the symbol he achieved his goal, but Claudel felt that it was a flight from Reality and only a preparation for a subsequent return to It. In his *Art Poétique*, of 1903, Claudel states that the metaphor is the logic of the new poetry, comparable to the syllogism of the older logic.[69] Things in the world are not only objects to be known, they are means by which man is being constantly reborn. He had not altered this basic belief when, in 1925, he commented on *Igitur* and called the world, not a sorcerer's handbook (Mallarmé's *grimoire*), but the Word engendering all things.

(d) OTHER POETS

The work of Valéry, Gide and Claudel shows, in varying degrees, an influence of Mallarmé, as well as a reaction against Mallarmé, which is, of course, another kind of influence. There are few important French writers today who owe him nothing. Among the poets, one especially, by some of the themes and certain aspects of his style, belongs to the Mallarmé tradition. A willed mysteriousness presides over the life and the writings of Alexis Léger, who uses the pseudonym, St.-John Perse. In his career of public service and diplomacy, he has maintained a strict aloofness from literary activity in the usual sense. He belongs to no group or *cénacle*.

His important poem, *Exil*, was written in America during the war.[70] By fulfilling his condition of exile and wanderer, the poet moves into the greater vocation of possessor of the world who follows the natural cycle of the seasons. The story is not of a place, but of a soul who begins his poem from nothing. There is a Mallarmean insistence on the void (*un grand poème né de rien*) and a Gidean fervour of discovery (*toute chose au monde m'est nouvelle*).

Today in France the vogue of 'engaged poetry' is over, and the position of Perse is gradually assuming the importance it deserves. He owes a great deal to Mallarmé for his belief about poetry, although he is wary of literary criticism ('scientific cooking', as he calls it). Any direct influence of Mallarmé on Perse would be difficult to establish, but he appears as one of many poets who would not have accomplished their poetic destiny in the way they did without the example of Mallarmé: Apollinaire, Valéry, Reverdy, Jouve, Eluard. Mallarmé taught these poets the sacred character of the poet, the ancient role of the priest. Perse has much of the ritualist in him, the man who creates a poem out of nothing by having recourse to the primitive power of words.

In many instances in Perse's poetry, one is reminded of Rimbaud's violent and vigorous diction. But again, no specific influence can be tracked down. One senses a similar freshness of language and metaphor, the same effort to recreate through the medium of poetry a primitive psychic state. The actual form of the single line, the long versicle, measured by the breathing necessary to recite the unit, recalls the form of Claudel's poetry. The two diplomat-poets have much in common: an elegance of sustained poetic diction, an epic tone in the quasi-narrative poems, a precision and technicality of vocabulary which is almost a new poetry and a new language. Perse and Claudel are poetic linguists, students of the accurate and unusual word, of the pristine meaning of words, and they perpetuate one of Mallarmé's principal preoccupations. Some of their pages (especially Perse's) are lengthy enumerations, almost incantations, which accumulate fervour from a mere exposing of knowledge. After Mallarmé, Perse and Claudel are the two major poets of France who are the most difficult to read. *Anabase* of Perse is one of the most 'hermetic' of French poems, and *Cinq Grandes Odes* of Claudel is one of the most profound.

St.-John Perse avoids all literariness in his writings, but he is a lettré in the highest sense of the word. Often the actual content of his poetry makes him a revolutionary and a conqueror, characteristics most closely associated with Rimbaud and Claudel, but persistently throughout all his poems runs the theme of the experience with language, the effort to create the poem, the semanticist's revolt, the conquest of the philologist. Here, Perse continues the work of Mallarmé whose poems are on the subject of poetry, for whom the world exists in order to end in a poem. If, on one level, Perse's poetry tries to expound the totality of man's knowledge, to destroy superstition and exorcise the monsters of man's dreams, on another level, of greater import, it implies the belief that the secret of poetry, if found, might reveal the secret of the universe and of man.

The study of St.-John Perse responds better than most contemporary poetry to our constant need of redefining the meaning of poetry, of rediscovering its value. The reading of such a work as *Exil* demonstrates how to logical thought poetry opposes analogical thought. In the creation of his metaphors, the poet draws from himself and from his familiar world analogies and 'correspondences'. The symbol is a synthesis of his experience, and the word, in becoming a symbol, reveals its full power and force. St.-John Perse proves once again that poetry is the metaphorical expression of the universe. Even when there is no palpable symbol in his verse, his lyricism seems to be urging him toward its discovery, prophesying the presence of the symbol about to be uttered.

Marcel Proust has been called the 'novelist of symbolism' and his name, more than that of any other prose writer, has been linked with Mallarmé's. This has always been done in an exaggerated and unspecific way. Mallarmé's influence on Proust is of the most tenuous kind. Proust is the one of the four major French writers, born about 1870 (Valéry, Gide and Claudel are the others) who was the least responsive to Mallarmé. He met Mallarmé only two or three times, thanks to his friend, Reynaldo Hahn, a new friend of Méry Laurent. At the beginning of his career, Proust published an article, *Contre* l'*Obscurité*, which was a more or less veiled attack against the 'obscurity' of Mallarmé, or rather against the desire of certain writers to protect their work from the masses.[71] What is common to these four writers is their marked concentration on self-analysis, their power of relentless introspection. In this respect, Mallarmé was unquestionably for all four, one of their leading models. If Proust cannot be called the 'novelist of symbolism', he may well be called a 'representative' of symbolism in Valéry-Larbaud's phrase.[72] Proust went much father than the symbolists in his analysis of the hidden dramas of the ego, but he went less far in his use and understanding of the symbol. His brilliant use of analogy is quite different from Mallarmé's, in that it is almost always the analogy between a sensation being experienced in the present and the memory of the same sensation at some past moment.[73]

Outside of France the three countries where Mallarmé's influence has been the most directly felt are Germany, England and America. In Germany, Stefan George, who had met Mallarmé in Paris, in March 1889, wrote ecstatically of him and translated some of the poems for his magazine, *Blätter für die Kunst*. With Verlaine and Baudelaire, Mallarmé is the French poet the most carefully studied by the school of poets which formed around George and his review. The Germans were the first to recognize the sacerdotal quality of Mallarmé's poetry and character, and exaggerated it far beyond the degree which Mallarmé himself would have approved.[74] The importance of the musical element in the new German poetry has reference not only to Verlaine and Mallarmé, but to earlier German prophets: Novalis, Hölderlin, Jean-Paul. Mallarmé's sense of humour and infinite delicacy are lacking in George's poetry which reveals other influences at work, especially that of Nietzsche and the worship of the superman, the *Übermensch*.[75]

The influence of Mallarmé on English poetry should be the object of a long study. Today his influence is still very apparent, especially in the writings of those poets who are close to Joyce and Eliot. The problems of language and linguistic innovation are more discussed in England and America today than in France. Swinburne, only five years older than Mallarmé, carried on a correspondence with the French poet. His belief about poetry, close to that of Shelley, accented, in accord with Baudelaire, the importance of subjective experience and the musicality of poetry. Arthur Symons and George Moore both attended the Tuesday evening gatherings and took back to England the new theories of French symbolism. Symons became one of the first exponents of Mallarmé's aesthetics.[76] Yeats, writing in 1897, defines the symbolist movement in terms of the achievements of Wagner in Germany, of the Pre-Raphelites in England, and of Villiers de l'Isle-Adam and Mallarmé in France. He calls it a theory of life which renders mystery familiar. For the young English symbolists of the *Rhymers'* Club, who wrote for *The Yellow Book* and *The Savoy*, Huysmans and Verlaine appeared more important than Mallarmé. The influence of *A Rebours*, for example, is very strong on Wilde's *Portrait of Dorian Gray* and his *Salomé*.

In a brief essay, Cecily Mackworth has pointed out that the real symbolist poet of England, in the Mallarmé tradition, was Gerard Manley Hopkins rather than Swinburne.[77] The Jesuit priest knew nothing of Mallarmé or symbolism, but he worked according to a poetic method similar to Mallarmé's analysing and studying the structure of language, of phonetics and poetic rhythm. Hopkins, with Mallarmé only two years younger, and Joyce, have done the most in renovating the French and English languages. Hopkins and Mallarmé are, philosophically, very far apart but as poets they both tried to surpass the subject of the poem, to abolish it by integrating words with an intellectual excitement about the subject and the poetic method to be employed.

A few dates of books and articles would be sufficient to prove an early American interest in Mallarmé. During his travels in the United States in 1893, Paul Bourget noted the intelligence with which Verlaine and Mallarmé were being read.[78] The earliest translations appeared in 1890[79] and the earliest article on Mallarmé appeared in *The Bookman*, in April 1896.[80] Six years before his book, *The Symbolist Movement in Literature* (1899), Arthur Symons published in *Harper's Monthly*, of November 1893, an article on *The Decadent Movement in Literature*. Even earlier than Peck's article, Alin Gorren, in 1893, made some intelligent remarks about Mallarmé in his article, *The French Symbolists*.[81]

The poet, Richard Hovey, an admirer of Mallarmé, translated *Hérodiade* in blank verse and published it in *The Chap Book* of January 1, 1895.[82] Amy Lowell and John Gould Fletcher are called 'American Symbolists' by the French critic, René Taupin,[83] but their work seems to be more a repetition of familiar symbolist patterns than a continuation of the movement. Eliot, Pound and Stevens have all (and especially Eliot) shown an understanding of Mallarmé and a sympathy for his work. Centring about *The Little Review*, from 1917 on, the American poets reflect a precise and knowledgeable interest in French poetry. There is great need for critical studies continuing the pioneer work of René Taupin.

1. T. S. Eliot, *Edgar Poe et la France, La Table Ronde,* 1949, pp. 1973-1992. Translated by Henri Fluchère.

2. 'Il croyait que le but de la poésie est de même nature que son principe, et qu'elle ne doit pas avoir en vue autre chose qu'elle-même.'

3. 'Quelque chose d'ardent et de triste . . . le mystère, le regret sont aussi des caractères du Beau.' *Journaux Intimes.*

4. The volume appeared in April, 1884, *Les Poètes Maudits.* The second edition, of 1888, contained additional studies of Marcelline Desbordes-Valmore, Villiers de l'Isle-Adam and Verlaine.

5. 'Le Dédaigneux et le Railleur de tout et de tous.'

6. The first title of the sonnet, *Quand l'ombre menaça.*

7. The first number was sold before the doors of the Concert Lamoureux, on the 8th of February 1885.

8. The publisher's name, strongly reminiscent of Léon Vanier, employs one of Verlaine's and Laforgue's favourite words: *vanné* (winnowed).

9. cf. especially Guy Michaud, *Message Poétique du Symbolisme,* Nizet, Paris, 1947. This three volume work is the first important history of symbolism. I have drawn on it constantly for this final chapter of synthesis.

10. Amiel, 'Cette souffrance, c'est la nostalgie universelle.'

11. in *Simple Agonie,* published in *La Vogue* of October 18, 1886, and in the volume, *Poésies,* t.II: *Derniers Vers.*

12. Mockel, *Stéphane Mallarmé, Un Héros,* 70 pages, Mercure de France, 1899.

13. Vte. E. M. De Vogüé, *Le Roman Russe,* Paris, Plon, 1886. Avant-Propos, VII-LV, mai, 1996.

14. French translations of Russian works had already begun appearing: in 1884, *Crime et Châtiment* of Dostoievsky and *Guerre et Paix* of Tolstoi. In 1885, *Anna Karénine* of Tolstoi and *Les Ames Mortes* of Gogol.

15. Quoted by Mondor, *Vie,* p. 445, and by Michaud, *Message Poétique,* p. 318.

16. 'Art toujours voulu, médité, et développant quelque conception intellectuelle.'

17. in *La Revue Indépendante.*

18. 'La poésie est l'expression, par le langage humain ramené à son rythme essentiel, du sens mystérieux des aspects de l'existence: elle doue ainsi d'authenticité notre séjour et constitue la seule tâche spirituelle.' The phrase 'des aspects' is removed from the *Divagations* text.

19. Ghil, *Les Dates et les Oeuvres.*

20. *Le XIXe Siècle,* 11 août 1885. 'La critique, puisque sa manie d'étiquetage est incurable, pourrait les appeler plus justement des symbolistes.'

21. This letter is quoted by Marjorie Louise Henry in her excellent study: *Stuart Merrill, La Contribution d'un Américain au Symbolisme Français,* p. 58.

22. Letter of June 8, 1887. Quoted in Mondor, *Vie,* p. 513, and Michaud, *Message Poétique,* p. 360.

23. Perrin, 1889.

24. 'là comme symbolique figure du Poète, qui cherche à le plus possible s'approcher de l'Absolu.' *La Littérature de tout à l'heure,* p. 190.

25. 'L'Art n'est pas que le révélateur de l'Infini, il est au poème un moyen même d'y pénétrer. Il y va plus profond qu'aucune philosophie.' ibid., p. 35.

26. 'L'Art est une reprise, par l'âme, de ses propres profondeurs.' ibid., p. 367.

27. Mazel has written a history of the heyday of symbolism: *Aux beaux temps du Symbolisme.*

28. The first number of *Le Mercure de France* appeared in January 1890.

29. cf. Valéry, *Je disais quelquefois à Stéphane Mallarmé, Variété III.*

30. This letter is in the collection of Mme E. Bonniot. It is quoted by Mondor, p. 582.

31. 'Le don de subtile analogie, avec la musique adéquate, vous possédez cela, certainement, qui est tout.' 24 Oct. 1890. Letter shown to Mondor by Valéry and published in Mondor, p. 583.

32. In collection of Mme E. Bonniot. Mondor pp. 606-7.

33. Letter shown to Mondor by Valéry. Mondor, p. 609.

34. Valéry, *Le Symbolisme n'est pas une école, Figaro Littéraire*, 18 juillet 1936.

35. cf. *Variété II, Dernière visite*, pp. 204-5.

36. cf. *Variété III*, pp. 9-32.

37. 'Le plus bel effort des humains est de changer leur désordre en ordre et la chance en pouvoir.' ibid., p. 23.

38. 'la transmission parfaite des pensées est une chimère.' ibid., p. 18.

39. 'On voit enfin, vers le milieu du 19e siècle, se prononcer dans notre littérature une volonté remarquable d'isoler définitivement la Poésie de toute autre essence qu'elle-même. Une telle préparation de la poésie à l'état pur avait été prédite et recommandée avec la plus grande précision par Edgar Poe. Il n'est donc pas étonnant de voir commencer dans Baudelaire cet essai d'une perfection qui ne se préoccupe plus que d'elle-même.' *Avant-Propos à la Connaissance de la Déesse* (1926). Reprinted in *Variété*, p. 32.

40. 'Ce qui fut baptisé le Symbolisme, se résume très simplement dans l'intention commune à plusieurs familles de poètes (d'ailleurs ennemies entre elles) de reprendre à la Musique leur bien.' ibid., p. 95.

41. cf. note 18.

42. 'elle (une jeunesse) croyait trouver dans le culte profond et minutieux de l'ensemble des arts une discipline, et peut-être une vérité, sans équivoque. Il s'en est fallu de très peu qu'une espèce de religion fût établie.' *Variété*, pp. 97-99.

43. 'le poète moderne essaye de produire en nous un *état*, et de porter cet état exceptionnel au point d'une jouissance parfaite.' *Variété*, pp. 97-99.

44. Letter to Cazalis, of 1864. Pléiade edition, p. 1438.

45. 'L'œuvre pure implique la disparition élocutoire du poète, qui cède l'initiative aux mots.' *Crise du Vers*, 1892.

46. 'Deux sortes de vers: les vers *donnés* et les vers calculés.' *Littérature*, p. 35 (1930).

47. 'Construire un poème qui ne contienne que poésie est impossible.' ibid., p. 40.

48. 'Nous traversons seulement l'idée de la perfection comme la main impunément tranche la flamme; mais la flamme est inhabitable.' *Avant-Propos, Variété*, p. 100.

49. Probably *Les Cahiers d'André Walter* which had appeared anonymously at La Librairie Didier-Perrin, 1891.

50. 'Vous m'avez appris la honte de mon livre et l'ennui de la Poésie, car vous avez chanté tous les vers que j'aurais rêvé d'écrire.' Letter of 5 Feb. 1891, collection of Mondor.

51. 1920 (Bruges, Imprimerie Sainte Catherine). cf. Gallimard edition, pp. 263-282.

52. Gide, *Mallarmé, L'Ermitage*, Oct. 1898.

53. 'Et pour la première fois, près de moi, on sentait, on touchait, la réalité de la pensée; ce que nous cherchions, ce que nous voulions, ce que nous adorions, dans la vie existait; un homme, ici, avait tout sacrifié à cela.' ibid.

54. On the anniversary of Verlaine's death, 15 Jan. 1897, Mallarmé's sonnet, *Tombeau*, appeared in *La Revue Blanche*. The manifesto-letter of Gide was pubshield in *Le Mercure* of February.

55. 'La dernière page m'a glacé d'une émotion très semblable à celle que donne telle symphonie de Beethoven.' Letter of 9 May 1897, in collection of Mondor. cf. also Gide, *Oeuvres Complètes*, t. 7, p. 426.

56. *Interviews Imaginaires*, 1943.

57. *Journal*, p. 1237.

58. First published in *Les Entretiens politiques et littéraires*, Jan. 1891, and immediately afterwards in *La Librairie de l'Art Indépendant*.

59. Paradise was not large; perfect, each form was manifested there only once; a garden contained them all.

60. 1897, Mercure de France.

61. cf. Jean Hytier, *André Gide*, p. 68.

62. 'Là est l'explication de l'attitude tragique de Stéphane Mallarmé, ou de l'artiste pur, s'apercevant qu'il n'a vraiment rien à dire.' Letter to Rivière, 1907.

63. 'le monde est un texte qui nous parle de sa propre absence, mais aussi de la présence éternelle de quelqu'un d'autre, à savoir son Créateur.'

64. 'les choses sont *réellement* une partie de ce qu'elles signifient.' *Intro. à un poème sur Dante*, 1921.

65. 'Nul esprit plus que vous n'était fondé à revendiquer ce haut droit des Lettres dans lesquelles vous exercez la magistrature: l'intelligence.' Letter dated 25 March 1895, in collection of Mondor.

66. 'Je puis dire que je dois à Rimbaud tout ce que je suis intellectuellement et moralement.' Collection of Mondor.

67. *Correspondance*, p. 142.

68. '*Connaissance de l'Est* est mon œuvre la plus mallarméenne.' Interview de F. Lefèvre, *Sources de Paul Claudel*, p. 141. Quoted by Ernest Friche, *Etudes Claudeliennes*, 1943, p. 144.

69. 'Un nouvel Art Poétique de l'Univers, une nouvelle Logique . . . L'ancienne avait le syllogisme pour organe, celle-ci a la métaphore, le mot nouveau, l'opération qui résulte de la seule existence conjointe et simultanée de deux choses différentes.'

70. First published in French in *Poetry* (Chicago), March 1942. The text and its English translation by Denis Devlin was published by Pantheon Books, N.Y. in 1949.

71. Published in *La Revue Blanche*, juin-juillet 1896. Appeared subsequently in volume, *Chroniques*.

72. cf. preface of Valéry-Larbaud to *L'Esthétique de Marcel Proust* by E. Fiser. The actual phrase is: 'le représentant le plus authentique du mouvement symboliste,' which also seems exaggerated.

73. There is no adequate study as yet on Mallarmé and Proust. Michaud has made very pertinent remarks about the subject in his *Message Poétique du Symbolisme*, p. 583.

74. cf. *Mallarmé et l'Allemagne* by Frederic Hagen, *Les Lettres*, 1948, pp. 225-229.

75. ibid., p. 228.

76. *The Symbolist Movement in Literature*, London, Heinemann, 1899.

77. *Mallarmé en Angleterre, Les Lettres*, 1948, pp. 217-224.

78. *Outremer*, p. 96.

79. *Pastels in Prose*, translations from the French by Stuart Merrill, N.Y. Harper's, (passages of Villiers, Huysmans, Baudelaire, Mallarmé, Mikhaël Régnier).

80. by Henry Thurston Peck. cf. his article, *Stéphane Mallarmé*, Bookman, Nov. 1898, the first serious essay by an American.

81. *Scribner's*, Jan.-June 1893.

82. *The Chap Book* was founded on May 15, 1894, by two Harvard students, Stone and Kimball, with the intention of making it the official organ of the American symbolist poets. By 1896, it had ceased showing any interest in French writers.

83. *L'Influence du Symbolisme Français sur la Poésie Américaine* (1910-1920), Paris, Champion, 1929. This is the best study on the subject. It is to be hoped that a continuation will be made.

3. CONCLUSION

MALLARME WAS deeply a poet of his age, allied with the aesthetic aspirations of the poets around him. Moreover, the tradition of poetry he believed in has its antecedents throughout the history of French literature: in the *grands rhétoriqueurs* of the 15th century, in the Lyonnaise school of the 16th, in preciosity of the 17th, and in his immediate masters of the 19th, Poe and Baudelaire. And yet, in reading certain of the brief secretive poems of Mallarmé, one hears a completely original voice. One has the impression that these poems consummate a break with tradition, or at least that they indicate a marked deviation from the permanent form of French verse. This, of course, is not true of those poems retaining a rhetoric reminiscent of Baudelaire: *Angoisse, L'Azur, Quand l'ombre menaça;* nor of the poems which like those of Parnassian ideal have specific subject matter: *Hérodiade* and *L'Après-Midi d'un Faune.* I have in mind many of the late sonnets which are unique and incomparable. They all have great precision of form and compactness and completeness. Like some still-life painting, before which one forgets the literalness of the objects depicted, to follow the intricate harmonies of colour and composition, each one of these sonnets is a world cut off from all the rest, untranslatable, whose subject has been deftly immobilized and mysteriously sunken into the words and the rhythms.

One ends by believing that the poem must have been made from nothing, or from the fascination of some simple word that grew of its own will. No sonnet illustrates better than *Petit Air II* what I am trying to say. It is poetry from which the subject seems to have been emptied to make way for the expression of the poem, the musical connotation of the subject. It is one of Mallarmé's rare poems of a seven syllable line, beginning in the manner of the 'sun suicide' sonnet, with a long adverb.

> *Indomptablement a dû*
> *Comme mon espoir s'y lance*
> *Eclater là-haut perdu*
> *Avec furie et silence,*

Voix étrangère au bosquet
Ou par nul écho suivie,
L'oiseau qu'on n'ouït jamais
Une autre fois en la vie.

Le hagard musicien
Cela dans le doute expire
Si de mon sein pas du sien
A jailli le sanglot pire

Déchiré va-t-il entier
Rester sur quelque sentier!

(Indomitably had to
As my hope hurls itself
Burst up there lost
With fury and silence,

Voice foreign to the grove
Or followed by no echo,
The bird one never heard
A second time in life.

Will the wild musician,
That ends in doubt
Whether from my breast not his
The greatest sob gushed forth

Torn completely
Remain on some path!)

The bird of the poem, the wild musician, has sung high in the air notes that will never be heard again. The sound, briefly sung with passion (*furie*), was followed by silence so complete that no real memory of it remains. Was it a bird's song or the pure idea of a poem? The poet speaks in the symbol of the bird (cf. *Tombeau de Baudelaire*). One of his thoughts reached such height that it was silenced. A moment of ecstasy (*sanglot*), almost caught in some audible form, in some words or phrases, and then the collapse, the mangled remains on the path.

This sonnet is a pure example of Mallarmé's art, distinguishable from that of every other French poet. The bird is no usual metaphor, but a symbol in which the thing symbolized has become so obscured that there is no need for its being revived and named. The poem has moved to the point farthest from its original subject, beyond which it would cease being a poem. The metaphor has become metamorphosis. In this final change for the artist, the world opens up before him and he beholds it in a new light. Metamorphosis for the artist is what ecstasy is for the mystic: the total vanishing of the world.

With the great persuasion that gentleness is, Mallarmé recalled to his age the meaning of poetry. His purest poems seem to us impeccable, and his spirit, in its communion with his fellow poets and painters, seems irreproachable. He was a magician, who used no discernible tricks of magic, and the master who had shed all pedantic pretention. But he revealed to the principal writers of the 20th century certain domains of art that are best characterized by the word 'sacred'. As a man he lived in almost a sublime way by refusing to recognize the usual material sufferings and privations. First as a man he made himself different from other men. And then as a poet he celebrated language, the sanctity of language, as a new Orpheus. After living a long time with some ordinary object: a console table, an empty vase, a mirror, until it had become the familiar figure of his dream and meditation, it changed into an idea. The final step of his process was the change of the idea to a symbol, the mutation of the idea to the word. At the end of this long process only the most vital and the most reduced word would be communicated. The anecdote of Vielé-Griffin, related by Rolland de Renéville in *L'Expérience Poétique* (pp. 43-44), illustrates Mallarmé's extraordinary veneration and fear of the word. Many of the visitors had been puzzled by the number of slips of paper (*fiches*) Mallarmé kept on his desk and which were to be burned after his death. One day Vielé-Griffin entered the study and found Mallarmé looking at one of the slips and murmuring, 'I musn't even write that—it would reveal too much.' Before Mallarmé put away the paper, Vielé-Griffin was able to see the single word written on it: *Quel*.

In the example of his poetry and in his conversations, which were far from being pedantically conceived and uttered, Mallarmé in-structed those who listened and read, especially on what poetry, in its purest form, was not. It was not philosophical, as Vigny had made it. It was not prophetic, as Hugo had made it. It was neither the sentimental confidings of Lamartine nor the garrulous distress of Musset. What poetry was for Mallarmé is far more difficult to define than what it was not. It was art turning back on itself, art of self-reflection. Art of intense sobering silence. It was poetry of *absence* in which the clear outline of objects and their physical appearance were blurred and dimmed and decomposed so that the idea or mean-ing or symbolism of the object should assume the life of the poem. In being poetry of *silence*, it was not deathlike, but life-capturing, life-deepening silence. The silence of dreams, perhaps. When Mallarmé called himself a man accustomed to dreaming and one speaking of another man who is dead, he presented his truest self-portrait. It is the opening sentence of the lecture on Villiers de l'Isle-Adam. *Un homme au rêve habitué, vient ici parler d'un autre, qui est mort.*

Symbolism belongs to all periods of art. Mallarmé, more sensi-tively than other men of his age, with the ardour of a man convinced, rediscovered the power of the word-symbol. The slowness and the faith with which he worked allowed him a poet's passivity within his symbol. He learned how to obey it and encourage it to flower within him. He learned, prior to the surrealists of the 20th century, how to give over all initiative to the words themselves.

Mallarmé's thought is not easy to transcribe: it is only a bit less difficult than his verse. But he seems to us to be saying that the ways of poetry are not rational but mystical. Poetry is a sacerdotal calling. Poets are the composers of sacred celebrations. And yet, if the pur-pose of poetry is its own creation, its own beauty, it is not mystical in the final sense. The way of poetry is mystical, but poetry is not. The poet's duty is to see divinely (*L'homme chargé de voir divinement*, Pléiade edition, p. 375) so that each poem is a résumé of his life, whether it be on Hérodiade's cold winter, or a faun's summer day. No sleep is permitted him because he is the man of vigils and lamps and dream hallucinations.

Mallarmé suffered because of the essential paradox of poetry and all art. The paradox of man's seeking in it some approach to the absolute, some way of knowing himself and knowing the absolute, and the very nature of the absolute which has no limitation. For poetry has its limitation of form. At best, it can only announce the absolute and reveal a sublime human restlessness in its creation. Every poetic word is first an idea. Rimbaud, as well as Mallarmé, pronounced this truth: *Toute parole étant idée* (*Lettre du Voyant*). But when the poet meditates and composes, he mobilizes such cosmic forces that his achieved word, when sung, has the power of enchanting the beasts and all nature.

SELECTED BIBLIOGRAPHY

1. Editions of Mallarmé's works (selected list, arranged chronologically).

L'Après-Midi d'un Faune, Paris, Derenne, 1876. 195 copies. The illustration (not signed) is by Manet.

Les Poésies de Stéphane Mallarmé, La Revue Indépendante, 1887. 40 copies.

L'Après-Midi d'un Faune, Paris, Revue Indépendante, 1887. 500 (?) copies.

Les Poésies d'Edgar Poe, traduction de Mallarmé, avec portrait et fleuron par Manet. Bruxelles, Deman, 1888. (850 copies).

Vers et Prose, avec portrait par James M. N. Whistler, Paris, Perrin et Cie, 1893.

Divagations, Paris, Fasquelle, 1897.

Poésies, Bruxelles, Deman, 1899.

Poésies, N.R.F., 1913 (édition complète).

Un coup de dés, N.R.F., 1914.

Vers de Circonstance, N.R.F., 1920.

Autobiographie, Messein, 1924. (publication en fac-similé).

Igitur, Gallimard, 1925.

Poems by Mallarmé, translated by Roger Fry, commentaries by Charles Mauron, London, Chatto & Windus, 1936.

Oeuvres Complètes, édition par Henri Mondor et Jean-Aubry. Bibliothèque de la Pléiade, Gallimard, 1945.

Poésies de Stéphane Mallarmé, Gloses de Pierre Beausire, Mermod, Lausanne, 1945.

Propos sur la poésie, choisis par Henri Mondor, Editions du Rocher, Monaco, 1946.

2. Books on Mallarmé.

Aish, Deborah A. K., *La Métaphore dans l'oeuvre de S. Mallarmé*, Paris, Droz, 1938.

Aubry, G. Jean-, *Une Amitié Exemplaire: Villiers de l'Isle-Adam et Mallarmé*, Mercure de France, 1942.

Beausire, Pierre, *Essai sur la poésie et la poétique de Mallarmé*, Lausanne, Roth, 1942.

Bonniot, Edmond, *Les mardis de Mallarmé*, Les Marges, 1936.

Chassé, Charles, *Lueurs sur Mallarmé*, Nouvelle Revue Critique, 1947.

Chisholm, A. R., *Towards Hérodiade: A Literary Genealogy*, Melbourne University Press (and Oxford), 1934.

Cohn, Robert Green, *Mallarmé's 'Un Coup de Dés'*, Yale French Studies, New Haven, 1949.

Cooperman, Hayse, *The Aesthetics of Mallarmé*, The Koffern Press, New York, 1933.

Davies, Gardner, *Stéphane Mallarmé. Fifty Years of Research*, French Studies, Jan. 1947, Oxford, Blackwell.

Davies, Gardner, *Les 'Tombeaux' de Mallarmé*, Paris, Corti, 1950.

Delfal, Guy, *L'Esthétique de Stéphane, Mallarmé*, Paris, Flammarion, 1951.

Dujardin, Edouard, *Mallarmé par un des siens*, Paris, Messein, 1936.

Fabureau, Hubert, *Stéphane Mallarmé. Son Oeuvre*, Nouvelle Revue Critique, 1933.

Fauré, Gabriel, *Mallarmé à Tournon*, Horizons de France, 1946.

Mallarmé. *Documents Iconographiques*, Genève, Pierre Cailler, 1947.

Mallarmé. *Essais et Témoignages*, Neuchatel, La Baconnière, 1942. (études de Matthey, Eigeldinger, Zimmermann, Jouve, Haldas, Raymond, Courthion, Guyot).

Mauclair, Camille, *Mallarmé chez lui*, Paris, Grasset, 1935.

Mauron, Charles, *Introduction à la Psychanalyse de Mallarmé*, Neuchatel, A la Baconnière, 1950.

Mauron, Charles, *Mallarmé l'obscur*, Paris, Denoël, 1941.

Mockel, Albert, *Stéphane Mallarmé. Un héros*, Mercure de France, 1899.

Mondor, Henri, *L'Amitié de Verlaine et de Mallarmé*, Gallimard, 1940.

Mondor, Henri, *Vie de Mallarmé*, Gallimard, 1941-42.

Mondor, Henri, *Mallarmé plus intime*, Gallimard, 1944.

Mondor, Henri, *Histoire d'un Faune*, Gallimard, 1948.

Noulet, Emilie, *L'Oeuvre poétique de Mallarmé*, Paris, Droz, 1940.

Noulet, Emilie, *Dix Poèmes de S. Mallarmé*, Genève, Droz, 1948.

Orliac, Antoine, *Mallarmé tel qu'en lui-même*, Mercure de France, 1948.

Roulet, Claude, *Elucidation du poème de S. Mallarmé: Un coup de dés jamais n'abolira le hasard*, Neuchatel, Aux Ides et Calendes, 1943.

Roulet, Claude, *Eléments de poétique mallarméenne*, Neuchatel, Editions du Griffon, 1948.

Royère, Jean, *Mallarmé*, Paris, Messein, 1931.

Schérer, Jacques, *L'expression littéraire dans l'œuvre de Mallarmé*, Paris, Droz, 1947.

Soula, Camille, *La poésie et la pensée de S. Mallarmé*, Paris, Champion, 1926.

Soula, Camille, *Gloses sur Mallarmé*, Paris, Editions Diderot, 1946. (préface de Jean Cassou).

Thibaudet, Albert, *La Poésie de Mallarmé*, Paris, N.R.F., 1912 (8e édition, Gallimard, 1930).

Wais, Kurt, *Mallarmé*, München, C. H. Beck'sche Verlagsbuchhandlung, 1938.

Woolley, Grange, *S. Mallarmé. Commemorative Presentation*, Madison, N.J., Drew University, 1942.

3. Articles on Mallarmé and books containing articles.

Blanchot, Maurice, *Faux-Pas*, Gallimard, 1943.

Blanchot, Maurice, *Mallarmé et le langage*, L'Arche, mars-avril, 1946.

Bonniot, Edmond, *La genèse poétique de Mallarmé d'après ses corrections*, Revue de France, 15 avril, 1929.

Bonniot, Edmond, *Mallarmé et la Vie*, Revue de France, 1er janvier 1930.

Bonniot-Mallarmé, Geneviève, *Mallarmé par sa fille*, N.R.F., 1er nov. 1926.

Borgese, G. A., *Studi di letterature moderne*, Milan, Treves, 1915.

Bos, Charles Du, *Pages de Journal*, Revue de Paris, oct. 1946.

Cahiers du Nord, No. 2-3, 1948, Charleroi, Belgique. Stèle pour S. Mallarmé: Mondor, Bellivier, Lavaud, Marcou, Faré, Dujardin, Fontainas, Noulet, Royère, Charpentier, Orliac, Mauron, etc.

Charpentier, Henry, *De Stéphane Mallarmé*, N.R.F. CLVIII, 1926.

Chassé, Charles, *Mallarmé Universitaire*, Mercure de France, oct. 1912.

Claudel, *Positions et Propositions*, Gallimard, 1928. (*La Catastrophe d'Igitur*, pp. 197-207).

Dujardin, Edouard, *De S. Mallarmé au prophète Ezéchiel*, Mercure de France, 1919.

Eliot, T. S., *Mallarmé et Poe*, N.R.F., juillet 1926.

Eliot, T. S., *Edgar Poe et la France*, La Table Ronde, 1949, pp. 1973-1992.

Fiser, Emeric, *Le Symbole Littéraire*, Corti, 1943.

Fontainas, André, *De Mallarmé à Valéry*, Revue de France, 15 sept. 1927.

Fontainas, André, *Mallarmé et Victor Hugo*, Mercure de France, 15 août 1932.

Fowlie, Wallace, *La Pureté dans l'Art*, Montréal, L'Arbre, 1941.

Fowlie, Wallace, *The theme of night in four sonnets of Mallarmé*, Modern Philology, May 1947.

Fowlie, Wallace, *Myth in Mallarmé's Hérodiade*, Yale Poetry Review, No. 8, 1948.

Fowlie, Wallace, *Three Masks of Mallarmé*, Zero, No. 1, Paris, 1949.

Fowlie, Wallace, *Mallarmé's Afternoon of a Faun*, The *Tiger's Eye*, No. 7, 1949.

Fowlie, Wallace, *Mallarmé as Hamlet*, The Outcast Chapbooks, No. 16, Yonkers, N.Y., 1949.

Frétet, Jean, *L'Aliénation poétique*, Janin, 1946.

Ghéon, Henri, *Note sur Mallarmé*, N.R.F. IX, 1913, pp. 290-296.

Gide, *Oeuvres Complètes*, t. VII, p. 411-443. Gallimard.

Gourmont, Rémy de, *Promenades Littéraires* II, Mercure de France, 1920, pp. 33-48.

Gourmont, Rémy de, *Promenades Littéraires* IV, Mercure de France, 1920, pp. 1-18.

Lemonnier, Léon, *Baudelaire et Mallarmé*, La Grande Revue, juillet-octobre, 1923.

Lemonnier, Léon, *L'Influence de Poe sur Mallarmé*, Revue Mondiale, 15 fév. 1929.

Lemonnier, Léon, *Poe et les poètes français*, Paris, 1932.

Les Lettres (Stéphane Mallarmé), Nos. 9, 10, 11, 1948, Paris. articles par Béguin, Bousquet, Charpentier, Davies, Mackworth, Magny, Noulet, Schmidt, etc.

Mauclair, Camille, *L'Art en Silence*, Paris, Ollendorff, 1901. (*L'Esthétique de S. Mallarmé*, pp. 72-116).

Mauclair, Camille, *Princes de l'Esprit*, Ollendorff, 1920.

Moore, George, *Première Rencontre avec Mallarmé*, Le Figaro, 14 oct. 1923.

Natanson, Thadée, *A Valvins, auprès de Mallarmé*, La Nef, fév. 1949.

Noulet, Emilie, *Etudes Littéraires*, Mexique, 1944.

Le Point, Lanzac, Lot, fév.-avril 1944. Textes de Valéry, Mondor, Bachelard, Fontainas, Rouveyre, Charpentier. Bibliographie Mallarmé et la peinture.

Régnier, Henri de, *Hamlet et Mallarmé*, Mercure de France, mars, 1896.

Régnier, Henri de, *Figures et Caractères*, Mercure de France, 1901. (*Mallarmé*, pp. 115-143).

Saurat, Denis, *Perspectives*, Paris, Stock, 1938. (*Don du Poème*, pp. 113-116).

Simons, Hi, *Wallace Stevens and Mallarmé*, Modern Philology, May, 1946.

Souffrin, Eileen, *Un sonnet inédit de S. Mallarmé*, Fontaine, nov. 1946.

Thibaudet, Albert, *Mallarmé et Rimbaud*, N.R.F. fév. 1922.

Valéry, Paul, *Variété* II, Gallimard, 1930.

Valéry, Paul, *Variété* III, Gallimard, 1936.

Verlaine, *Les Poètes Maudits*, Vanier, 1884. (*Mallarmé*, pp. 41-54).

Wyzewa, Teodor de, *Sonnets de Mallarmé*, La Revue Indépendante, janvier 1887.

4. Books relative to the study of Mallarmé's poetry and period.

Apollinaire, Guillaume, *La Poésie Symboliste*, Paris, L'Edition, 1909.

Baudelaire, Charles, *Edgar Poe. Sa vie et ses oeuvres*, préface de la traduction des *Histoires Extraordinaires*.

Béguin, Albert, *L'Ame Romantique et le Rêve*, 2 vol., Cahiers du Sud, Marseille.

Benda, Julien, *La France Byzantine*, Gallimard, 1945.

Bourget, *Essais de psychologie contemporaine*, 2 séries, 1883-85.

Cassou, Jean, *Pour la Poésie*, Corréa, Paris, 1935.

Coléno, Alice, *Les Portes d'Ivoire*, Plon, 1947.

Cornell, Kenneth, *The Symbolist Movement*, New Haven, Yale University Press, 1950.

Friche, Ernest *Etudes Claudéliennes*, Editions des Portes de France, Porrentruy, 1943.

Ghil, René, *Les Dates et les Oeuvres*, Crès, Paris, 1923.

Gide, *Le Traité du Narcisse*, 1891.

Henry, Marjorie Louise, *Stuart Merrill*, Paris, Champion, 1927.

Huret, Jules, *Enquête sur l'Evolution Littéraire*, Paris, Fasquelle, 1901.

Huysmans, Joris Karl, *A Rebours*, Paris, Charpentier, 1884.

Johansen, Svend, *Le Symbolisme. Etude sur le style des symbolistes français*. Copenhague, Munksgaard, 1945.

Kahn, Gustave, *Les Origines du Symbolisme*, Messein, 1936.

Mauclair, Camille, *Le Soleil des Morts*, Paris, Ollendorff, 1898.

Michaud, Guy, *Message Poétique du Symbolisme*, 3 vol., Paris, Nizet, 1947.

Morice, Charles, *La Littérature de tout à l'heure*, Perrin, 1889.

Proust, Marcel, *Contre l'obscurité*, 1896, in volume, *Chroniques*.

Raymond, Marcel, *De Baudelaire au Surréalisme*, Corréa, 1933.

Raynaud, Ernest, *La Mêlée Symboliste*, 3 vol., Paris, Renaissance du Livre, 1918-22.

Renéville, Rolland de, *L'Expérience Poétique*, Gallimard, 1938.

Renéville, Rolland de, *Univers de la Parole*, Gallimard, 1944.

Stahl, E. L., *The Genesis of Symbolist Theories in Germany*, Modern Language Review, June, 1946.

Symons, Arthur, *The Symbolist Movement in Literature*, London, Heinemann, 1899.

Taupin, René, *L'Influence du Symbolisme Français sur la Poésie Américaine* (1910-20), Paris, Champion, 1929.

Viatte, Auguste, *Sources Occultes du Romantisme*, Paris, Champion, 1928.

Villiers de l'Isle-Adam, *Axel*, 1890.

Vogüé, E. M. De, *Le Roman Russe*, Paris, Plon, 1886.

Woolley, Grange, *Richard Wagner et le symbolisme français*, Paris, Presses Universitaires, 1931.

Yeats, *Essays*, Macmillan. (*The Symbolism of Poetry*, p. 191).

INDEX OF POEMS

INDEX

PHOENIX BOOKS

PHOENIX BOOKS

PHOENIX BOOKS

PHOENIX SCIENCE SERIES